DEDICATION

Zach:

My first live NHL game was Islanders-Rangers, February 13, 1993. Perhaps that's how hockey became my favorite sport. They say you only get one chance at a first impression, and what is more impressive than the Battle of New York?

I was eight and had no idea where I was going. All I knew was that the Rangers were playing. When we rolled into the Nassau Coliseum parking lot, I thought, Wow, that was quick. Who are these Islanders people, and how come they play so close to our house?

One of the most enchanting qualities of the old "barn" was the smell—a combination of hot pretzels, stale popcorn, wet cigarette, some Bacitracin, and steamed vinegar, if that's a thing, which on second thought, I don't believe it is. The pre-renovation Garden had a smell, too—boiled hot dogs and Budweiser.

I was captivated by the bigness of the event and by hockey culture—how the people screamed and cursed at one another and couldn't agree on anything until intermission, when an Islanders fan proposed to his girlfriend on the ice, and the whole crowd pleaded, "Say No!"

I also picked up on hockey sweater demographics. Every woman had a Pierre Turgeon jersey. But young men, particularly long-haired grunge-types (it was 1993, remember), wore the tough guys' jerseys—Mick Vukota, or Rich Pilon, or Tie Domi, or Ken Baumgartner. I found that hysterical. "Don't mess with me. My favorite player can beat you up."

Turgeon drew an empty-net breakaway to cap the night. The moment he touched the puck, the entire place jumped up at once and homemade confetti fluttered everywhere. I climbed my chair to catch a glimpse as he glided toward the goal without a drop of ostentation in his blood, gently laid the puck in flat along the ice, curled into the left-wing corner, head down, and skated away. It was so elegant and, in my opinion, taught nothing more about empty-net goals than it did about life: keep your eyes on the prize, do what you have to, be grateful, even prideful, but don't ever show off, even for your biggest rivals.

This book is not dedicated to Pierre Turgeon, though he will be well reviewed down the pages. It is dedicated to my father, David Weinstock, and his buddy Alan Peyser, who drove me 15 short miles to Nassau Coliseum, which in turn drove me to the wonderful insanity known as hockey fandom.

Stan:

One of the most interesting "rivalries" that I know involves my younger son, Simon, and his son Ariel as well as older daughter Odel, who live in the Golan Heights area of Israel. All three are avid hockey fans. Simon and Odel are Islanders-rooters, and you would think that Ariel would follow suit. But such are the vagaries of NHL support. It turns out that my grandson is a Rangers fan. And thus, another intrafamily rivalry. What I like most about it is that when the teams are not playing each other, Simon and Odel root for the Rangers, and Ariel roots for the Islanders to do well—and that's nice.

Continents away, my older son Ben and his sons, Ezra and Niko, take a more distant view of the ice wars but appreciate our intensity nonetheless. From my end of the rink, this book is dedicated to the families of Simon and Ben and their continued support and understanding of my hockey-mania.

TABLE OF CONTENTS

ON RECORDS, POINTS, AND GAMES IN HAND

You might notice that National Hockey League standings are presented throughout this history book in a manner to which you may not be accustomed.

It will read like a baseball pennant race, with "games" and "half-games" as opposed to "points" and "games in hand."

Do not be alarmed. Everything is fine.

Instead of points, we use a team's record. Now, ready for the big secret?

Points and record are directly correlated.

They are the same thing, only record is accurately adjusted for discrepancies in the all-important—but constantly overlooked—"games played" column.

Whenever games played are equal, the team with the better record always has more points, at a rate of exactly one point per game over or under the .500 mark. We promise.

Try the math for yourself. We'll wait . . .

. . .

Pretty cool, right?

So at the end of the season, when every team has played the same amount of games, NHL standings will always go in order of record. And what else could we possibly care about?

In fact, go check. Any year, any division . . .

. . .

Told you.

THE CHANTS

Islanders fans and Rangers fans like to get on each other's nerves.

Broadway backers refer to their chief rival as the "Ice-landers," and its late suburban arena as the "Nassau Mausoleum."

Isles fans call the Rangers the "Strangers" and the "Rags." In print, they add a dollar sign, as in "Rag$."

Then there are the chants and the songs, sung over the years in both arenas at every game against every NHL team.

For those unfamiliar, a beginner's guide:

Potvin Sucks
TUNE OF: "Let's Go Band," traditional.
LYRICS: Pot! Vin! Sucks!
WHEN APPLIED: As the closing three notes of the traditional marching band tune, "Let's Go Band," after anyone in the audience whistles the first four bars. Usually during a lull in play, such as line changes.
OR: Any time two or more Rangers fans are in the same place.

1940
TUNE OF: Chant.
LYRICS: Nine! Teen! For! Ty! Clap, clap—clap-clap-clap!
WHEN APPLIED: Every Rangers visit to Nassau Coliseum between 1981 and 1994.
OR: Any time an Islanders fan saw a Rangers fan anywhere during those years.

1940 was the one chant that spread outside New York. By the '90s, the Rangers were hearing it in buildings all over the league.

The Chicken Dance
TUNE OF: "The Chicken Dance," by Werner Thomas.
LYRICS: The Rangers Suck.
WHEN APPLIED: To close every verse of "The Chicken Dance," when played by Coliseum organist Paul Cartier at games between November 8, 2001, and the 2010–11 season.

The Right Stuff
TUNE OF: "You Got It (The Right Stuff)," by New Kids on the Block.
LYRICS: Rangers Suck.
WHEN APPLIED: At Islanders home games in the late '80s and early '90s, when the Coliseum public address system would play the chorus of the New Kids on the Block hit, which in real life culminates with the boys chanting, "The Right Stuff."

Heave-Ho! Rangers Blow!
TUNE OF: No tune.
LYRICS: Heave-ho, Rangers blow.
WHEN APPLIED: In the '70s and '80s, by Islanders fans. No one knows why.

—k the Rangers!
TUNE OF: Chant.
LYRICS: —the Rangers!
WHEN APPLIED: During the national anthem at Islanders games from the mid-late '90s through the early 2000s, between "And the rockets' red glare . . ." and "The bombs bursting in air."

If You Hate the Rangers, Stand Up!
TUNE OF: No tune.
LYRICS: If you hate the Rangers, stand up . . .
WHEN APPLIED: At random times during random Islanders games, usually between whistles, over a frenetic, dub-step beat of speed-clapping, as the entire crowd stands up.

If You Know the Rangers Suck, Clap Your Hands

TUNE OF: "If You're Happy and You Know It," by Isaak Dunayevsky.

LYRICS: If you know the Rangers suck, clap your hands;

Clap. Clap.

If you know the Rangers suck, clap your hands;

Clap. Clap.

If you know the Rangers suck, and they never win the Cup

If you know the Rangers suck, clap your hands;

Clap. Clap.

WHEN APPLIED: Whenever Islanders fans congregate.

We Want Fishsticks!

TUNE OF: Chant.

LYRICS: We want fishsticks!

WHEN APPLIED: From 1995–1998, after the Islanders changed their classic Nassau County uniforms to some sort of toothpaste-looking, maritime-themed concoction with a logo featuring an older gentleman who bore resemblance to the mascot of the Gorton's frozen seafood company.

We Want Hextall!

TUNE OF: Chant.

LYRICS: We want Hextall!

WHEN APPLIED: In the mid-'90s, by Rangers fans, after Islanders goalie Ron Hextall allowed the Blueshirts 16 goals in three games during the 1994 playoffs, mostly through his legs, and was ergo jettisoned off Long Island.

Oo, la-la, Sasson

TUNE OF: "Oo, la-la, Sasson," Sasson Jeans commercial.

LYRICS: Oo la-la! Sasson.

WHEN APPLIED: In the early-'80s, by Islanders fans, making fun of a flamboyant ad campaign featuring several Rangers players.

Beat Your Wife, Potvin

TUNE: Here We Go

LYRICS: Beat your wife, Potvin, Beat your wife.

WHEN APPLIED: In the late '70s and early '80s, by Rangers fans, after Islanders captain Denis Potvin's ex-wife accused him of domestic violence. The claims were found to be false.

Crackhead Theo!
TUNE OF: Chant.
LYRICS: Crack-head-Thee-o!
WHEN APPLIED: Any time Theo Fleury played at Nassau Coliseum after the star Rangers forward entered the NHL's substance abuse program in 2001.

You Can't Beat Us!
TUNE OF: Chant.
LYRICS: You can't beat us.
WHEN APPLIED: During the 2003–04 season, by Rangers fans, as their 13th-place squad blew the playoff-bound Isles out in all six meetings.

And finally, this one has nothing to do with the Rangers, but it's too good:

Honk, honk. Honk-honk-honk
TUNE OF: Chant.
LYRICS: Honk, honk. Honk-honk-honk!
WHEN APPLIED: When an Islanders fan gets in a car. If 16,000-plus voices of varying degrees of inebriation make the ideal instrument for a "Let's Go Islanders" chant, then a parking lot full of car horns is surely a close second. R.I.P. Nassau Coliseum.

INTRODUCTION

What's the best rivalry in major American pro sports?

"The best?" Why, that's a matter of opinion, of course.

But is it *really*?

. . . Yes sillies, that's what "best" means.

Fair enough.

But let's at least admit this—in sports, certain things are quantifiable, for instance the Who, the What, the When and, most important, the *Where*.

Add it up, and what seemed like a subjective question yields one objective answer. There *is* a "best" rivalry in American pro sports, and it's Islanders-Rangers.

Because, as they say in real estate, "Location, location, location."

The Rangers and Islanders compete in the same market and in the same National Hockey League division. Sorry, pro baseball and football fanatics, but that setup simply does not exist in your sports.

Hockey has three other examples—Rangers-Devils, Isles-Devils, and Kings-Ducks—but none with the storied history of Islanders-Rangers.

In fact, Islanders-Rangers would be a first-class NHL rivalry even if the teams did not share a town. They fought eight playoff battles in a 20-year span, including four springs in a row and six within a decade. Three of those "Expressway Series" matchups—1975, 1979, and 1984—are certified-platinum NHL classics, while another—1990—is considered among the most bitter, brutal ice affairs of all time.

And that's just the teams themselves. But enough about them.

Rivalries are for the fans, not the players. Today's St. Louis Cardinal could be tomorrow's Chicago Cub. But the fans? They aren't going anywhere.

So if one fan base hardly ever butts heads with the other, well then, what kind of "rivalry" is that?

Islanders fans and Rangers fans mix regularly—*too* regularly, if you were to ask most of them. They split arenas when their beloved teams face off and split communities, workplaces, worship-places, and even families in between.

Which is why, unlike every other supposed rivalry in America, this one has not waned, and will not ever, and has proven as such many times.

There have been ample opportunities for subpar Islanders teams or subpar Rangers teams to drag the rivalry with them to irrelevancy. But instead, the passion in those eras burned just as white-hot as when both teams were good, if not hotter.

For example, you'll notice that this history, while describing Islanders-Rangers games from over the years, rarely mentions attendance figures. It is because we don't need to: they are all sellouts.

Now, who hasn't heard the story of the fabled Yankees-Red Sox rivalry in baseball? But try selling those tickets the next time either team is out of the pennant race. And if, God forbid, one of those teams were bad *two* years in a row?

And how about Red Wings-Avalanche? It was the best rivalry in hockey, until nine years later, when it wasn't one at all.

When it comes to rivalries, they each come and go. They each ebb and flow. *Or*, it's Islanders-Rangers.

The strongest attestation to detestation is the notice each team gets in the other's home arena, while not even present. Rangers fans at Madison Square Garden still whistle and shout, "Potvin Sucks" at every game, against every opponent—an ode to the longtime Islanders captain Denis Potvin.

Meanwhile, Islanders fans have more "Rangers Suck"-themed tunes than Elton John has "Candle in the Wind" remakes. There were years when the loudest cheer you heard at any Isles home game was when the Rangers score was flashed on the scoreboard, and they were behind. Think fans in Detroit still monitor Avalanche scores?

This is a tale of two franchises that really dislike each other, in hockey and in business, ever and always.

Actually, make it *three* franchises.

Chapter 1

THE ORIGINAL BROOKLYN-MANHATTAN HOCKEY RIVALRY

From a historical perspective, the most unusual aspect of Islanders-Rangers is that it is rooted in a previous rivalry between the Rangers and the long-forgotten New York Americans. One could say that the Americans were the earlier Islanders, but with a different name. A glance at that New York-New York rivalry will explain why.

It all goes back to the NHL's desire to bring major US cities into the circuit.

The first two American clubs to be admitted were the Boston Bruins and Pittsburgh Pirates in 1924–25, but both were considered inadequate because they played in small arenas.

As NHL luck would have it, a palatial building was being constructed in Manhattan—Madison Square Garden III—on Eighth Avenue between 49th and 50th Streets.

It was built to boast more than 15,000 seats for a hockey game; that is, if only the Big Apple had a hockey team.

That team was eventually found in, of all places, Hamilton, Ontario.

A Canadian-born New York sportswriter named William McBeth believed that if hockey could be properly staged in the new Garden, it would be an instant hit. But the MSG backers, led by promoter Tex Rickard, were dubious about hockey's potential. McBeth had to go elsewhere for money. His choice was "Big Bill" Dwyer, a character among characters in that era of wonderful nonsense.

A native New Yorker, the pot-bellied Dwyer grew up in the area around the new Garden, living the life of a quasi-Dead-End kid. He did a short stretch at Sing Sing Penitentiary and bounced around the West Side of Manhattan until Prohibition arrived. Dwyer's big moment came precisely then.

While others warily wondered whether to plunge into the gold mine of rum-running and other "industries" created by the new law, Big Bill made his move fast, and the money rolled in even faster. By the mid-twenties Dwyer's empire comprised a couple of night clubs, racetracks, a fleet of ships and trucks, as well as warehouses and a full-fledged gang appropriately stocked with the Jimmy Cagneys and Edward G. Robinsons of the day.

As far as McBeth was concerned, Dwyer was the perfect choice to back his team because Big Bill liked sports and wanted very much to improve his image by owning a hockey club. A little prestige never hurt any bootlegger, and owning the Americans promised a lot of it, possibly even the Stanley Cup, as well.

The next step was finding a team. This, too, was accomplished in a typically bizarre manner. During the 1924–25 NHL season the Hamilton Tigers went out on strike for more money, marking one of the few times in sports history that a team ever marched on a picket line.

The Hamilton players remained firm in their strike, and early in April 1925, league governors got wind of Dwyer's desire to own a hockey team. They reasoned that the Hamilton problem could be simply resolved by selling the franchise to the Manhattan bootlegger, and on April 17, 1925, it was agreed at an NHL meeting that the Hamilton club would be transplanted to New York at the start of the 1925–26 season.

Dwyer obtained both the franchise and the suspended players (quite appropriately he bought them, even though their suspension had never been lifted) for $75,000. Thomas Patrick "Tommy" Gorman, one of

Canada's more ebullient personalities, was chosen as manager. The new team promptly was named the Americans and just as quickly nicknamed the Amerks by space-conscious headline writers.

The dream of bringing major league hockey to New York City was realized on December 15, 1925, when the Montreal Canadiens faced the Americans in the opening NHL game at Madison Square Garden.

Although the new Garden had already been open for business, the hockey premiere was greeted with the same respect and heraldry as the opening of the Metropolitan Opera House. Dignitaries from both countries decorated the arena, most wearing white ties and tails. Marching bands paraded impeccably across the ice, and then the Canadiens defeated the stars-and-stripes uniform-wearing Americans 3–1, a fact immediately forgotten in the waves of champagne poured by Big Bill Dwyer during his postgame party.

The Amerks played competitive if not championship hockey. Billy Burch scored 22 goals and finished seventh in the league; and the Green brothers (Shorty and Red), defensemen Leo Reise, Sr. and Alex McKinnon, and the peripatetic "Bullet" Joe Simpson gave New Yorkers plenty to cheer about.

The abundant distractions for the now adored Canadian boys kept them equally busy off-ice. Just a block away from the Garden sat the glittering White Way of Times Square with its wine, women, and song.

The New York Americans were usually drunk. As a pro hockey team, it was one of their biggest weaknesses.

Dwyer's bootleg hooch would find its way into the Amerks' dressing room, with amusing results. One time, Bullet Joe Simpson made a wrong turn in one of the hallways and walked straight into a room full of elephants and lions belonging to the Ringling Bros. and Barnum & Bailey Circus, which was to take place at the Garden later that week. Simpson wheeled in his tracks, fled back to the locker room, and grabbed the team trainer by the collar.

"Where in hell did that bad hooch come from?" Joe demanded. "Christ! I could swear I saw a herd of wild elephants out there!"

Though there were plenty of laughs, the Americans had also managed to become a serious business proposition. In their first year they proved hockey could be a money-maker in Manhattan and underscored this with enough big crowds to inspire the Madison Square Garden Corporation to get into the act with a team of its own. This was easy to do because the Garden already was collecting a healthy rental from the Amerks (it also shared in their gate receipts), and the emergence of another New York team would create a stimulating rivalry, matching the Giants and Dodgers in baseball.

When Dwyer first decided to bring the team to New York, he had been assured that the Garden would never install a club of its own. But Dwyer did not have a lawyer read the fine print of his contract. Conspicuously absent from the agreement was a non-compete clause, so Tex Rickard and MSG president Colonel John Hammond were free to obtain a second franchise for their beautiful new sports palace.

It stood to reason that it could be even more profitable for MSG to have its own team.

Moreover, the new team—as yet unnamed—needed not worry about any of the negative baggage the bootlegger-owned club brought to the rink. With that in mind, Colonel Hammond obtained the second Gotham NHL franchise, and the new team became known in the press as "Tex's Rangers" after Tex Rickard. The team then simply dropped the "Tex," and that was that—the New York Rangers were born. They even mimicked the Amerks' colors—some red, some white, and a great deal of blue.

With the demand for illegal booze at an all-time high and an income too big to even count, Big Bill was not overly concerned with his team's newfound competition.

But on the ice, a bitter Americans-Rangers rivalry was cultivated without need of even one spirited game or fight. The awkward business relationship between the teams provided more than enough animosity.

What made this rivalry so keen was the fact that the Madison Square Garden crew, under the direction of manager Conn Smythe and Coach Lester Patrick, proved artistically superior to the Americans from the very start. In 1928, while the Amerks were floundering near the bottom of the league, Patrick's Rangers won the Stanley Cup. This infuriated Amerks manager Tommy Gorman, who was determined to produce a winner.

Prior to the 1928–29 season, he began negotiating for Roy "Shrimp" Worters, a superb little goalie, and finally obtained him early in the season, thus giving the Americans the goalkeeping they needed. Gorman's team finished second in the league's Canadian Division—precisely where the Rangers finished in the American Division. That meant the intra-Garden enemies would meet in the first round of the playoffs, which was to be a two-game, total-goals series. The opener ended in a 0–0 tie, and the second match was 0–0 at the end of regulation time. True to form, the Rangers finally won when Butch Keeling beat Worters at 29:50 of overtime.

The Americans-Rangers rivalry took some peculiar turns. Once, Col. John Hammond, the Rangers' president, summoned Gorman to his office to complain about the Amerks' after-hours roistering. The Colonel went a step further and said at that very moment the Americans were cavorting around the corner at a big party.

Gorman wouldn't put anything past his skaters, but something told him that the Colonel was, at the very least, in error. The Americans' manager got hold of two Garden detectives and headed straight for the notorious address. "When we got there," Gorman said, "we found a terrific party—drinking, singing, the works—and a helluva lot of hockey players. But they were all Rangers."

Because of Dwyer's associations with the underworld, it was not uncommon for the Americans' rooting section to be graced with submachine guns, blackjacks, and cowbells. "There were dark accusations by rival coaches," noted New York sportswriter Frank Graham, "that referees and goaltenders and goal judges were intimidated by gangsters who had bet on the Americans and wished to insure their bets."

One night the Americans lost because of an especially poor call by the referee, who was then chased down 50th Street by a horde of Amerks fans threatening his life. Fortunately, he had better stamina than the irate rooters and sprinted away unharmed.

The fans had plenty to beef about in 1929–30. After the glorious playoff year, the Amerks sank back to the cellar and Gorman went to work, again hoping to mold a winner. He traded Lionel Conacher to the Montreal Maroons for Hap Emms and Mervyn "Red" Dutton in a deal that was to have enormous import for the New Yorkers in years to come.

Dutton, the tough son of a wealthy Canadian, had a red mane and the temper to go with it. That he was playing big-league hockey was

The face that haunted Rangers history for half a century. Mervyn "Red" Dutton was the legend of all Americans legends, as defenseman, coach, and manager. He was traded to the Amerks by the Montreal Maroons in 1930 and concluded his playing career in 1936, before taking over as boss. After a heated dispute in 1945, Dutton "hexed" the Blueshirts, promising they would not win the Stanley Cup again in his lifetime. Though seemingly unfathomable, his prediction ultimately came true. He passed away in 1987. *(Steve Cohen, Brooklyn Historical Society, and Marcia Ely.)*

tribute enough to his courage, since during World War I, he had served overseas with the Princess Pats and nearly lost both legs when an artillery shell exploded a few feet away from him. At first, doctors were prepared to amputate but decided against such a measure, and Dutton returned to Canada to recover and go on to star as a defenseman for Calgary and then Montreal before coming to New York. Right from the start, camaraderie developed between Dwyer and Dutton, at least partly inspired by Red's love of a good time.

"We knew what Bill was," said Dutton, who eventually became NHL president and later a millionaire building contractor, "but we loved him. Dwyer's policy was that nothing was too good for his players. Every time we won a game he'd throw us a big party. Worters used to say, 'Join the Americans and laugh yourself to death.'"

Big Bill didn't know it at the time—or maybe he did and wasn't letting on—but the laughter was about to be over for him. The end of Prohibition loomed and friends began deserting him. He was convicted as a bootlegger and sentenced to two years in Atlanta, leaving the Amerks with many bills to pay.

Help was in sight when Dutton agreed to divert some of his family fortune to the Amerks. He, in turn, became playing coach of the club and continued helping Dwyer with grants-in-aid.

"Once I had to lend Bill $20,000 when he was down in Miami Beach," Dutton recalled. "He blew it all in one night in a crap game."

The other New York team, meanwhile, was a model of stability, with both their finances and their hockey sticks. Led by a line of Frank Boucher with Bill and Bun Cook—three Hall-of-Famers—the Rangers won the Stanley Cup in 1932–33 and returned to the Finals in 1936–37.

At this point, prohibition was just a memory, and Big Bill Dwyer was a poor man, unable to support a team. The NHL took over the Americans, naming Dutton overseer while the endless debts were paid.

Despite his problems, Dutton still managed to ice a competitive team. During the 1937–38 season, his Americans finished second in the Canadian Division and once again faced the Rangers in the playoffs—this time, in a best-of-three series.

Dutton's sextet won the opener, 2–1, on Johnny Sorrell's overtime goal. The Rangers rebounded, winning the second match, 4–3, and setting the stage for the climactic finale on March 27, 1938, at—where else—the Garden, home of both clubs.

The largest crowd of the season, 16,340 fans, jammed the arena and saw a pulsating contest. Paced by Alex Shibicky and Bryan Hextall, the Rangers jumped into a 2–0 lead, but Lorne Carr and Nels Stewart tied the game for the Amerks, sending it into overtime. Neither team could break the tie for three sudden-death periods before Carr finally scored the winner for Dutton and Company.

"That," Dutton stated, "was the greatest thrill I ever got in hockey. The Rangers had a high-priced team then and beating them was like winning the Stanley Cup to us."

Unfortunately, the Americans were knocked out of the playoffs by Chicago, two games to one, in the next round and were never able to achieve such lofty heights again, although their fans continued to root them on, just as Brooklyn's "Faithful" supported the Dodgers. "We had fans mostly from Brooklyn," said Dutton, "while the Rangers had the hotsy-totsy ones from New York."

A year later, the Americans made the playoffs, only to be eliminated in the first round, two games to none, by Toronto. They slipped out of playoff contention in 1939–40, while the Rangers gave their fans Stanley Cup championship number three.

World War II broke out, and many Canadian-born players quit hockey to join the Armed Forces. By 1940–41 Dutton had lost 14 of 16 players to the Canadian Army and other branches of the services. The Amerks finished dead last.

When the 1941–42 season started, Dutton changed the club's name to the Brooklyn Americans. This gesture was rooted in a long-simmering idea harbored by Dutton, who closely followed the Big Apple baseball scene, particularly the bitter battles between the New York Giants of Manhattan's Polo Grounds, and the Brooklyn Dodgers of Ebbets Field in Flatbush.

Fed up with the second-class treatment accorded his team at the Garden, Dutton had decided as early as 1939 to build a new arena in Brooklyn that would not only compete with the Garden in the greater entertainment space, but would become home to his Brooklyn Americans.

The Amerks were re-christened the Brooklyn Americans for their final season, 1941–42—though the club continued to play in Madison Square Garden—because Red Dutton hoped to build a new arena housing the club in downtown Brooklyn. World War II intervened, and the arena was never built. *(Steve Cohen, Brooklyn Historical Society, and Marcia Ely.)*

In the meantime, Dutton moved his team's practices to the ancient Brooklyn Ice Palace on Atlantic Avenue between Nostrand and Bedford Avenues in the Bedford-Stuyvesant community of Kings County.

Dutton and his wife, Phyllis, as well as several of his players, moved to Flatbush, and even the traditional star-spangled uniform gave way to new colors and a sweater with the letters B-R-O-O-K-L-Y-N running from right to left diagonally down the jersey.

But as war spread across Europe, it took the free world's steel supply with it. With resources unavailable, the idea for a new arena in Brooklyn was put on hold. All Brooklyn Amerks home games were still played at the Garden in Manhattan, and Dutton's war-ravaged group finished last again.

At the start of the 1942–43 season, Dutton was forced to fold the club just when he was starting to pull out from under the debris of the

Dwyer days. "We had begun to pay off a lot of Bill's debts," said Dutton, "and it looked as though we were going to come out all right. A couple more years and we would have run the Rangers right out of the rink."

Though the Amerks were indefinitely shelved, Dutton secured a promise from NHL owners in Montreal, Chicago, and Detroit that he could revive the franchise after the war and move it into his blueprinted Brooklyn Arena.

The promise seemed even more solid after Dutton agreed to step in as hockey's chief executive after the death of NHL president Frank Calder in 1943. Likable as a player, coach, and manager, Red was just as beloved in the president's chair, although the war years were not kind to him. His two oldest sons, Joe and Alex, were killed over Germany, flying for the Royal Canadian Air Force.

Dutton served as president through the war's end in 1945, then resigned to make time for his businesses back in Calgary, as well as his beloved Brooklyn Americans franchise, which had been promised to him. Red had even secured a site for the new arena at the intersection of Atlantic and Flatbush Avenues.

At the annual NHL governors' meeting at New York's Commodore Hotel in 1946, Dutton handed the league presidency over to Lieutenant Colonel Clarence Campbell. The men applauded. Then Dutton raised another issue, "the franchise in Brooklyn."

Silence. And that was the moment he knew.

As Red scanned the faces across the NHL table, he could tell that something wasn't *kosher*. Yes, he once had the promises of Montreal, Chicago, and Detroit for his Brooklyn re-entry, but what about Toronto and Boston and, most of all, the New York Rangers, represented at the meeting by Madison Square Garden president, General John Reed Kilpatrick?

His answer was written all over Kilpatrick's stony face.

Garden brass wanted New York hockey to itself. In fact, they were even considering the prospect of maybe fielding a second team of their own down the line.

"But I've talked to the people in Brooklyn," Dutton snapped. "They've got a site and they're ready to put up a $7 million building as soon as I get the word from here."

More silence. A minute . . . now they couldn't even look Red Dutton in the eye.

"Gentlemen," Red finally spoke up. "You can stick your franchise up your ass."

Then he declared that as long as he was alive, the Rangers would never win a Stanley Cup.

And so it was.

Dutton returned to Calgary to grow his construction business. Kilpatrick and the Rangers largely forgot about him—at first—but with every passing year, the legend of Red's "Curse of the Cup" grew in credence, as an unprecedented string of bad luck seeped into the franchise.

In 1950, the Ringling Brothers Circus booted Frank Boucher's Blueshirts out of the Garden, forcing the team to play all seven games of the Stanley Cup Finals on the road.

The Rangers would miss the playoffs in 12 of the following 16 seasons—even as part of a league where four out of six teams qualified.

And whenever they *did* make it, Dutton and his kin would watch confidently from back home in Canada, never sweating the inevitable result.

"Any time the Rangers made the playoffs," recalled a member of the Dutton family in a 2015 interview, "our parents would say, 'They are going to lose, don't you know? Uncle Merv put a curse on them.'"

And sure enough, they lost—every year, through Dutton's death in 1987.

In the late 1960s, the Rangers had a rebirth under Coach Emile "The Cat" Francis but could not get it done in the postseason. They were 42–11–10 late in 1971–72 when leading scorer Jean Ratelle broke his ankle. The Boston Bruins skated off the Madison Square Garden ice with the Cup.

The one thing the Manhattan-men had going for them was that, with the author of "the Curse" living in Calgary, there was nobody in New York to rub their noses in it.

But bad luck was coming on that front, too.

Unbeknownst to most Rangers fans at that time, the NHL owners were huddling on ways to counteract a potential rival major league called the World Hockey Association, especially since the WHA threatened to put a franchise into the spanking-new Nassau Veterans Memorial Coliseum in Uniondale, New York.

The lords of the NHL decided that the best way to detour the WHA from the New York Metropolitan area was to place their own expansion franchise in the Long Island arena.

On February 15, 1972, the New York Islanders were born. Were they *good*? Well, that was a different story.

Chapter 2

BIRTH OF THE RIVALRY

"People never heard of our team my first season here. I had to tell them that we play the Rangers; then they'd say, oh yeah, they heard of us."

—Islanders forward Billy Harris

"A lot of them are from small towns and they were afraid of coming to New York, you know, after all the bad things that they read about. But we showed them that this was the suburbs. They never thought New York had suburbs."

—Islanders Coach Al Arbour

"They're New Yorkers. Islander fans are passionate. Ranger fans are as passionate. And whoever was winning had the bragging rights."

—Rangers, Islanders forward/Islanders General Manager/Rangers Executive Don Maloney

The hapless Islanders.

In the early 1970s, general manager Bill Torrey heard and read the description "Hapless Islanders" so many times, he said he thought it was the official name of his team.

He was joking, of course.

But for Long Island's brand-new National Hockey League franchise, earning a fan base worthy of the title "New York" proved less simple than just sewing the letters N and Y on its logo.

Hockey-wise, from 1941 to 1972, the New York Rangers owned the New York metropolitan area to themselves. The Blueshirts were the only major league club in town. They represented Big Apple hockey royalty—as much Long Island's team as New York City's—fresh off an exciting trip to the 1972 Stanley Cup Final.

The Rangers were loaded with brand names such as goalie Eddie Giacomin, the wonderful Goal-A-Game line of Vic Hadfield, Jean Ratelle, and Rod Gilbert, plus defenseman Brad Park (Norris Trophy runner-up the previous three seasons), to mention only a few.

Add head coach Emile "The Cat" Francis to the list of future Hall-of-Fame Rangers from that era.

The beloved Blueshirts practiced in Long Beach Arena on Long Island. Most of their players lived there. A sign at the city limits read "Welcome To Long Beach, The Home Of The New York Rangers." Long Beach is a mere twelve miles south of Nassau Coliseum in Uniondale, New York, which would become the home of the Islanders.

So early on, one couldn't blame the Isles for feeling like the team that nobody, except for a precious few, wanted in the first place.

Their customers were mostly Rangers fans. Their first two head coaches—Phil Goyette and Earl Ingarfield—were former Rangers.

Even the club's conception was less about competing with the mighty Rangers than it was about competing with the upstart World Hockey Association. In 1971, the WHA granted a franchise to Long Island attorney Neil T. Shayne, so the NHL hastily leased the Coliseum to block him from using it, then conceived its own Long Island expansion team and charged that team's owner, local businessman Roy Boe, a $4.8 million indemnification fee for invading the Rangers' territory. The Isles would not otherwise exist.

They were like orphans. And they played like it.

The expansion Islanders of 1972–73 set NHL records for most losses (60), fewest victories (12), and most goals allowed (an appalling 347). The home crowd grew fond of chanting, "We're Number Eight," a nod to the team's familiar position in the NHL's eight-team East Division.

The performance against Big Brother was especially fruitless.

The "visiting" Rangers scored a 6–4 pre-season victory on September 27, 1972, before a crowd of 11,053—mostly Broadway backers—in the first hockey game at Nassau Coliseum and then swept their new neighbors in the inaugural regular season series.

Goals in the six-game set were 25–5 for the incumbents, with little pushback from the challengers.

BENCHMARK GAME

THE FIRST
October 21, 1972
Nassau Coliseum

Rangers 2 Islanders 1
(4–3–0) (1–4–0)

A standing-room crowd of more than 16,000 crammed themselves into the 14,665-seat Nassau Coliseum for the first regular season Islanders-Rangers game, the first hockey sellout in the arena's history.

Another rarity: a Hall-of-Fame playmaker and a Hall-of-Fame goaltender tried to sock each other.

Less than a minute into the second period, Billy Smith and Rod Gilbert dropped their gloves. Unfortunately for Gilbert, gloves were all that Smith was interested in dropping. His face protector remained in place.

"How can I hit him in the mask?" begrudged the Blueshirts' right winger after the game. "That's all I need is to break my hand on his mask."

Looking for a fair fight, fans yelled at "Battling Billy" to unmask, but he could not be convinced. Later in the locker room, he employed the smug, dry sense of humor that would become his calling card.

"They don't understand that if I stopped to take off my mask," he calmly smirked, "the other guy could hit me."

Smith was also involved in crease-side tussles with Rangers forwards Glen Sather and Pete Stemkowski.

In the following morning's *New York Times*, Gerald Eskenazi called the mixed-allegiance atmosphere in the building "Theater of the Absurd."

Indeed, this opening chapter of the Isles-Rangers anthology was a fitting prelude to the decades of mayhem ahead.

"It won't be called a subway series [the Long Island Railroad one-way fare to Madison Square Garden is $1.85]," Eskenazi predicted. "But future games between the clubs, based on tonight's performance, probably will turn into grudging, belting affairs."

CHANGE IS GOOD (FOR SOME)

In fact, before one match at Madison Square Garden in February 1973, Isles defenseman Arnie Brown—himself a prior seven-year Rangers vet—told reporters, "I don't see a lot to get excited about. The Rangers will probably beat us."

They did, by a score of 6–0. After the match, Rangers defenseman Dale Rolfe spoke openly about it being tough for his side to "get up for games against these teams."

That annoyed Coach Ingarfield big-time!

"Where would Rolfe be if not for expansion?" he replied. "Still in Springfield! Expansion gave him a chance. . . . Now it's our turn. Everyone has got to give us a chance."

Three nights later Rolfe's team spanked the Isles at the sold-out Coliseum, 6–0, yet again. So much for that.

"6–0, 6–0," cracked Rangers goalie Gilles Villemure. "Sounds like a tennis match."

"The league is laughing at us," summarized Brown. "The fans are laughing at us. But they created us, and they're laughing at themselves."

The Islanders' first draft choice ever, Billy Harris, left, flanked by general manager Bill [Bowtie] Torrey. 1972. *(Fischler Collection)*

One man who was not laughing was Bill Torrey. The perpetually bow-tied Islanders boss set out to improve not only the talent level on Long Island, but the attitude, as well.

Enter Al Arbour, the first head coach in franchise history who had not been a longtime Ranger.

Also enter Denis Potvin, the first pick in the 1973 Amateur Draft. Potvin joined his older brother Jean Potvin, acquired in a March 1973 trade with the Philadelphia Flyers.

Add hardworking winger Bobby Nystrom, a late 1973 call-up; gritty defenseman Bert Marshall, unprotected by the Rangers in the 1973 intraleague draft; big Clark Gillies, the fourth overall pick in the 1974 amateur draft; and playmakers J.P. Parise and Jude Drouin, the spoils of two January 1975 trades with the Minnesota North Stars.

The new Islanders were hungry. They had nerve, swagger, and plenty of *chutzpah*. It caught the Rangers' attention.

The forty-year-old Arbour, nicknamed "Radar" for the thick glasses he wore in his playing days, was a tough "defenseman's defenseman" during his 14-year NHL career, and he coached that way, too. Radar immediately stoked the crosstown fire, telling reporters that for months he had refused to accept the Islanders coaching job until he visited Long Island and realized it was nothing like Manhattan. "I thought it would be like living on Seventh Avenue," he disclosed. "Overcrowded and dirty."

Others were not as critical of New York City but had plenty to say about its Blueshirts.

"Nothing would give me greater satisfaction than to beat the s—t out of those guys," Marshall told the *New York Times* in March 1975. "Nothing."

"After Denis drops his man," Jean told *Newsday* before the teams' first pre-season meeting in October 1973, "I'm going to skate up to the poor guy and say 'You mean you let a nineteen-year-old kick the s—t out of you? Tsk, tsk.'"

"I know what you're going to ask me," snapped Brad Park after the game, a 6–6 tie at the Coliseum in which rookie Denis scored two goals.

Park, cranky with a black eye from fighting Bobby Nystrom, pulled out the evening's program and showed reporters a note that said, "What do you think of Potvin?"

"See?" he said. "I wrote this before the game."

"Okay," answered Hugh Delano of the *New York Post* respectfully. ". . . So . . . what do you think of Potvin?"

Meanwhile, just one exhibition game into his coaching career, Al Arbour was already agitated with all things New York Rangers.

"I come behind our bench—it was our bench in our building—and the row behind me all have Rangers sweaters on. Am I in our building or are we in the Ranger building?

"And during the course of the game they kept hitting me in the back of the head. I said, 'I guess I know what I'm in for now.'"

"The Rangers scored the first goal," Clark Gillies later recalled, "and the place erupted . . . I said, 'What the hell is this? We're playing at the Coliseum.' The place went crazy . . . 13,000 Ranger fans. And at that point I said, 'That's got to change.'"

But any change would have to come gradually. The Islanders were better in 1973–74, though still quite poor, with a record of 19–41–18— good for last place yet again—and 19 whole games behind the third-place Rangers, who went back to the semifinals, bowing out in seven games to the eventual Cup champion Flyers.

The following year, Arbour's boys once again struggled to climb out of the cellar of the brand new four-team Patrick Division. It seemed like the same old story.

The city slickers moved to 12–1–1 all-time against the Nassau-men in regular season play, scoring 55 goals while surrendering but a measly 17 in the 14 games.

The Isles hated the Rangers, but with numbers like these, it was hard for the streaking Rangers and their fans to hate them back.

At least until the Islanders began a run of their own.

Between January 23, 1975, and their next meeting at the Garden on March 12, the Rangers won just 8 of 23 contests, while the Islanders— sparked by the new additions of Parise and Drouin—dropped only 6 of 22.

The Rangers were second in the Patrick Division, the Isles were now third, and the deficit was only 2 games!

"The 'comedy' has turned into serious drama," wrote Parton Keese of the *New York Times* before the March 12 showdown. For the first time ever, the New York Rangers and New York Islanders were to battle in a game with major playoff implications for both teams.

And nothing changed.

Gilles Marotte, Nick Beverly, and Jean Ratelle beat Islanders goalie Billy Smith from 55, 45, and 35 feet out, respectively, before the contest was seven minutes old. Smith was quickly lifted in favor of backup Glenn "Chico" Resch, but it was too late. The final score was 5–3 as the Rangers moved to 13–1–1 against the Islanders.

But the Islanders stuck with it, going 3–0–3 over the next two weeks, and trailed the men from Midtown by only half a game heading into a Saturday matinee at the Coliseum on March 29, 1975.

"Animosity," wrote Robin Herman of the *New York Times*, "not simple, professional competitiveness, describes the feelings held by the New York Islanders for the New York Rangers. The Islanders may talk big, but their hatred has not yet brought them a victory this season over their city neighbors."

Predictably, the game was a sellout. Less predictably, most of the backers came for the home squad, something new for an Islanders-Rangers game.

Among the many homemade signs and banners:

"BEAT THE MANHATTAN MISFITS."

"WE'VE GOT THE CAT BY HIS TAIL."

"RANGERS CHOKE WILL NEVER DRINK FROM CUP."

"CHICO IS THE MAN."

And perhaps most tellingly, "LONG BEACH LOVES THE ISLANDERS."

This time Chico Resch started and made 23 saves. It helped when the visitors formed a first-period conga line to the penalty box—Pete Stemkowski at 8:13, Park at 8:23, and Nick Beverley at 8:56, all minors. Clark Gillies punished the chippy Rangers with a pair of power play goals at 10:11 and 10:21, and the homesters moved out to a 5–1 second-period lead before holding on for the 6–4 win.

Instead of "We're Number Eight!" cries of "We're Number Two!" echoed through the crowd as the Islanders leapfrogged the Rangers in the Patrick Division standings.

"This meant a lot to us," said Potvin. "We wanted our fans to drown the Ranger fans in our building. Now this is a hell of a boost to us. To hear them yelling 'Good-bye Rangers,' we knew finally the majority of fans were on our side."

Ironically, when the Islanders clinched the first playoff berth of their young history on Friday, April 4, 1975, the New York team that was skating off the ice victorious was the Rangers, who defeated and eliminated the Flames in Atlanta, assuring their upstart neighbors a chance to finally play for the Cup. The following night the Isles returned the favor with a 4–1 home loss to the Flyers, assuring the Rangers second in the Patrick while locking themselves into third.

With the regular season finale between the Islanders and Rangers at Madison Square Garden less than 24 hours away, the teams had to decide how hard to push.

The Islanders franchise had still never won in Madison Square Garden. A breakthrough in the last game of the 1974–75 regular season would guarantee a first-round matchup with the Rangers—the team named "the bane of the Islanders' short existence" by that morning's *New York Times*. A Blueshirt win, however, would send the clubs their separate ways.

What to do?

"There's a certain amount of pride involved," said veteran Isles defenseman Gerry Hart. "We've got to show the Rangers that we can go out in the Garden and give them a good game."

"You can't go in there and waste 60 minutes," begged Coach Arbour. "You can't turn it on and turn it off. We gotta go out strong, and we will."

Behind 33 saves from Resch and a game-winning tally by Gillies— the 25th goal of his rookie campaign—the Isles finally claimed that elusive Garden victory, 6–4, to set up the first all-New York playoff series since the Rangers and the New York Americans lit up the city in 1938.

New York had full-blown hockey fever. The storybook rise of the Islanders put pucks back in the headlines, dominating the newspapers, radio, and TV. Both teams finished with 88 points, but the Rangers held the tiebreaker and would open the best-of-three series at home on Tuesday, April 8. The *New York Times* dubbed it the "Expressway series." *Newsday* preferred "Change-at-Jamaica series."

"When the bell rings Tuesday, the money will be on the line," warned Rod Gilbert. "Then we'll see who's better."

"We know we're better than the Rangers," countered Denis Potvin. "We're younger, stronger, and better. For some reason, though, we have too much respect for them. We treat them like gods. I guess we really have a bit of an inferiority complex, probably because we believe too much of what we hear and read about them."

But much of what was said and written was plain fact. One team had been there and done that, and the other had not. The Rangers had 16 players with NHL playoff experience—668 games and 354 points worth—whereas the Islanders lineup featured only five—Westfall, Parise, Marshall, Drouin, and Billy MacMillan.

A capacity crowd of 17,500 roared when the home team took the ice for Game One. Unlike in Nassau Coliseum, support at Madison Square Garden would not be bipartisan.

The first period was high-hitting and low-scoring.

BOOM! Down went Jean Ratelle, at the hands of a grinning Denis Potvin.

BLAM! Down went Denis, courtesy of husky Gilles Marotte. The fans erupted!

Then at 10:48 of the first, Ted Irvine of the Rangers and Garry Howatt of the Isles dropped their gloves. The series was off to a rollicking start.

If the young Islanders were nervous, they showed it on their first power play, failing to register a shot. Rangers players mocked the effort heartily right there on the ice.

Brad Park broke the scoreless tie at 8:11 of the second, banking a shot from the right circle off Denis Potvin's skate and past Chico Resch. Then with just 35 seconds remaining in the frame, Pete Stemkowski pounced on a funky carom off the backboards and cashed in for a 2–0 lead.

In the visiting room, Arbour did his best to relax some nerves. "Loosen up and take it to them," he told his boys. "The real pressure is on those other guys down the hall . . . They're fat cats out there. They're looking to be taken."

The third period did not begin the way Arbour or anyone in blue and orange had hoped. Gerry Hart went to the box 99 seconds in. But the Islanders killed the penalty, and momentum began to shift.

At 4:20 Marotte was sent off, giving the previously maligned Islanders power play a chance to redeem itself. Billy Harris skated through Walt Tkaczuk and Ron Harris to cap a nice passing play with Parise and Drouin. 2–1 Rangers.

Seven minutes later, Jean Potvin beat Giacomin to a loose puck in the right wing corner and curled behind the net for an uncontested wraparound. 2–2.

The Garden was so quiet, you could hear the SLAP of Giacomin's stick as he spanked the ice in disgust.

The game had turned, and the Islanders weren't about to let up. Some 99 seconds after Potvin's goal, Clark Gillies completed the comeback. He took a pass from Westfall at the blue line, split defensemen Marotte and Ron Greschner, and scored on a wrist shot.

With three goals in exactly eight and a half minutes, the Islanders led, 3–2.

Back came the Rangers, throwing anything and everything at Chico's net.

Vickers cruised in on a breakaway with under five minutes to play and labeled one for the top corner, but Resch nicked it—barely—with his shoulder.

At 16:55, the Blueshirts went to the power play. Nothing doing.

In the game's final minute they kept coming and coming and coming, but Resch held on, with help from his diving, sliding teammates.

"One more! One more!" screamed the elated visitors as they danced off the ice. Meanwhile, their hosts were good and mad. Greschner promised a thorough Game Two beatdown of the Isles.

"They're all going to be emotional games now," Bert Marshall predicted. "With two New York teams, it's got to be that way."

"Emotional," it turns out, was an understatement. Game Two on Long Island was nothing but a record-setting circus.

The Rangers were met with a vile procession of obscenities from the standing-room-only crowd. A banner above their end read "The GAG Line Chokes." In fact, there were "CHOKE" signs all over the building. Not that the Rangers weren't already in a bad mood anyway.

Francis went to Gilles Villemure over Giacomin, Arbour stayed with Resch, and the first playoff hockey game at Nassau Coliseum proceeded as a regular ho-hum affair.

For two and a half minutes.

Then referee Ron Wicks took out his whistle and started tooting.

Ratelle scored on a power play. Billy Fairbairn scored on a power play—and then again shorthanded. Parise answered on a power play, then Ron Harris made it 4–1 Rangers with the game's first even-strength goal. All in the first 11 minutes!

The calls were tight. The home fans seethed. But Wicks continued his symphony, frustrating the players, ratcheting the tension up and up until finally he had a line brawl on his hands.

Twenty-two penalties—yes, 22 penalties—were called in the first period alone! The Rangers were given eight minors, three majors, and a ten-minute misconduct. The Isles took seven minors and three majors. The frame took a full hour to complete.

Chico Resch's night was over midway through the second after even-strength goals by Vickers and Butler. He was replaced with Smith, who stick-jabbed Vickers in the face, launching yet another fracas. Marshall connected for the Isles. Tkaczuk got it back for the Blueshirts. The score was 7–2 after two periods.

With the score out of reach and a winner-take-all Game Three on the horizon, the final period was a predictable cesspool of testosterone.

Another 20 penalties were handed out. The Islanders were slapped with six minors, two majors, two ten-minute misconducts, and a game misconduct. The Rangers—well behaved in comparison—took only six minors, two majors, and one ten-minute misconduct.

In total, the teams combined for 50 penalties worth 170 minutes in the game—27 and 101 for the Isles, both NHL playoff records at the time.

"They lost their cool," said Gilbert. "It's going to be awfully tough for them to come back now."

"They wanted to fight us, so we obliged them," added Park.

As for Ron Wicks, his opus earned mixed reviews.

"He's a disgrace to the refereeing profession," screamed Arbour. "An ass."

"Wicks did a hell of a job," answered Rangers center Derek Sanderson.

THE MAVEN REMEMBERS: 1975 PLAYOFFS, GAME TWO

This was the first Islanders home playoff game ever televised, and I was doing the color along with play-by-play man Spencer Ross. After the opening win at the Garden, we were filled with anticipation that the Islanders could make it two in a row, thereby sweeping the series. My wife Shirley came along, and we were no doubt over-excited about the possibilities.

If ever there was a buildup to a letdown, this was it. The Rangers not only played to their potential, demolishing the Nassau-men with ease, but also did a more than adequate job winning the innumerable fights, which were sprinkled through the 8–3 Rangers victory.

Based on what we saw, Shirley and I can only conclude that the decisive third game at Madison Square Garden would result in a Rangers romp.

There would be no time for further debate. Game Two went late, and Game Three was the very following evening, April 11, 1975. Battered and bloodied, the teams packed up and went back to Manhattan for the biggest New York hockey game in 37 years.

Both coaches raised eyebrows with their choices in net: Smith vs. Villemure.

Smitty had been pulled after just seven minutes in MSG on March 12, and Villemure had bruised his left knee in Game Two.

But it was less Gilly's knee and more Giacomin's absence that took Blueshirts loyalists aback. Fan favorite "Ed-die! Ed-die!" was one of the era's top clutch goalies.

Unlike the night before, the first period of Game Three was all about hockey. Gilles Marotte threw the first hit of the game, a clean hard check that landed Islanders forward Billy Harris in the last place he would want to be, the Rangers bench.

Shots were 15–8 homeboys in the frame, but Battling Billy kept a clean sheet, while at 16:00, Clark Gillies finished a beautiful rush and pass by his center, Bob Bourne, beating Villemure on left wing from 25 feet for a 1–0 Islanders lead. Both teams were 0–1 on the power play.

The Rangers kept the pressure up early in the second, but again Smith stood tall, and with Greschner in the box for tripping at 6:30, the brothers Potvin connected—Denis from Jean and Bobby Nystrom. 8:26. Power play goal. 2–0 Islanders.

The fans were on edge. Soon they'd be falling apart.

1:12 into a Rangers power play, the teams got back to brawling, this time in front of the Islanders net. Jerry Butler and Isles defenseman Dave

Lewis did most of the punching. Seven seconds later, Denis buried a shorthanded goal off a two-on-one rush with center Lorne Henning. It was 3–0 Islanders.

Done was Villemure. In came Giacomin. The Rangers headed back to the power play at 14:20, and the Islanders killed it. Everything was coming up Nassau.

It was then that Giacomin decided, as he'd later tell the *New York Times*, that he needed to "stir up" his team. So with two and a half minutes to play in the second, he tripped Nystrom in the crease and got away with it. Then he cross-checked Garry Howatt. When the feisty winger turned to confront his attacker, Giacomin speared him in the stomach, leaped on him, and started wailing—all the way out to the top of the left circle—like a furious wife beating her confused husband with a pocketbook. Hoping to avoid penalty time, Howatt raised his hands like he was under arrest, refusing to punch back.

"ED—DIE! ED—DIE!" screamed the crowd.

Howatt earned two minutes at 17:34, Giacomin four, and Pete Stemkowski was ejected for being the third man in the fight, even though Howatt had never really engaged as the second man in the fight.

"To tell the truth, Howatt didn't do anything to me," Eddie admitted after the game. "I started it. I was cold and needed something to get me in the game."

Shots in the second were 12–11 Isles. Twenty more solid minutes and they'd be through.

But the Rangers had heart yet.

Billy Fairbairn broke the ice with a terrific individual rush and backhander at 4:44. It was 3–1 Islanders.

Then at 12:47, Gerry Hart took his second penalty of the night, and this time his club paid. Fairbairn's second goal of the game—and fourth of the series—from Vickers and Park on a power play brought the Rangers within 3–2.

Fourteen seconds later, Vickers banged home a perfect feed from Ratelle, sending the place into a frenzy.

The puffed-up Rangers had found their three goals—with 6:19 to spare—and started zeroing in on the fourth!

On the opposite bench, the untried Islanders were confused, caught in an active avalanche, with little clue how to escape. The Madison Square Garden roof was collapsing on their heads.

That's precisely when Smith began writing what would become one of the greatest big-game résumés of all time.

Over and over, the Blueshirts swarmed the Islanders' net for the winner, but Billy stood tall, turning back 11 shots in the period, mostly from right out in front.

Park with the backhander, Smith with the blocker! Tkaczuk on the doorstep, Smith with the pad!

The final horn was a godsend for the visitors. Smitty hung his head on the top of the cage and draped his weary body over the net. "Tired and disappointed," he later explained.

Sudden death. One goal would take the series, and with it, bragging rights over the metropolis.

The Islanders took the intermission to regroup. The Rangers could not wait to get back out.

The teams took the ice and the fans stood and cheered. LET'S GO RANGERS!

Giacomin was in goal, with Park and Nick Beverley on defense and Ratelle between Vickers and Gilbert.

Clap, clap. Clap-clap-clap. LET'S GO RANGERS!

Smith was in goal, with Marshall and Lewis on defense, and Westfall between Drouin and Parise.

Clap, clap. Clap-clap-clap. LET'S GO RANGERS!

Westfall won the puck back. Lewis threw it in the Rangers' right corner.

Clap, clap. Clap-clap-clap.

Vickers retrieved. Blind pass up the corner boards. Intercepted by Drouin.

LET'S GO RANGERS!

Parise snuck back door, right behind Brad Park.

Clap, clap. Clap-clap-clap.

Drouin slapped it through the goalmouth.

LET'S GO RA—

It was over.

With Park hooking him for dear life, J.P. Parise deflected Jude Drouin's centering feed past the helpless Giacomin at 00:11. The Islanders officially mattered.

The victors leaped over the boards, knocking over the bench, which landed on Al Arbour's toe, nearly breaking it. The bitter Garden faithful assumed Arbour was hot-dogging as he hopped around on one foot screaming at the top of his lungs. "Everyone thought I was yelling because I was all excited," he later explained. "What it really was, was that I was in pain."

Meanwhile, a mob of royal blue piled on Parise at the left post. The Rangers and their fans waited silently for the handshake line. They were stunned.

"You can hear a pin drop in the Garden," Arbour later recalled. "That's unusual in a hockey game. Everything was suspended for a period of time. It was just like being in church, it was so quiet."

Down in the Islanders' dressing room, Roy Boe, the Brooklyn-born beverage company owner who had paid the Rangers $4.8 million just to compete, hugged everyone in sight. So did Bill Torrey. P.R. Director Hawley Chester wept uncontrollably. The players laughed and screamed.

"I thought we had won the Stanley Cup," recalled Denis Potvin. "That series made us feel like we had accomplished the same level of victory by beating the New York Rangers."

Arbour went to an adjacent room to enjoy a cigarette alone. When reporters finally found him, his eyes started to mist.

Down the hall, devastation owned the night.

Vickers called it "the most embarrassing defeat I've ever suffered, losing to the Islanders.

"I won't recover until the Stanley Cup is over," added Stemkowski. "What hurts is walking into the outside world and facing all those fans, friends, and family who believed in us and stuck by us."

"It will be a long summer," Vickers predicted. "Having people keep asking about that."

Said Giacomin, "The most frustrating thing was when we went into the Coliseum and saw all those 'Choke' signs the Islanders fans had put up. And now this. I have some fans on the Island—or I *used* to. They might be Islander fans from now on."

"The Atlanta Flames are better than the Islanders," snapped Derek Sanderson, after playing hooky on the handshake line. "The Islanders won't win another playoff game."

For the second time that evening, Parise had the perfect response.

"I don't know about us," he said. "But I guarantee the Rangers won't win another playoff game this season."

BENCHMARK GAME

11 SECONDS
April 11, 1975
Madison Square Garden

Islanders 4 Rangers 3
(2–1) (1–2)

The origin of everything. The one that started it all. But it was almost just a footnote in another Rangers playoff run.

So it certainly seemed after a third period that left Billy Smith so exhausted, he basically took a nap on his goal-cage.

But before the Garden faithful had a chance to settle in for sudden-death overtime, Jude Drouin and J.P. Parise sent them home.

Here's what was written in the aftermath, in a *New York Times* piece entitled "For the Rangers, a Humiliating Finish" (April 12, 1975):

"The circle was completed last night at Madison Square Garden. Joining the New York Mets, who rose to outshine the Yankees in baseball; the New York Jets, who outclassed the venerable Giants in football; and the New York Nets, who upstaged the Knicks in basketball, the New York Islanders became No. 1 in the New York hockey scene, displacing the stunned Rangers.

"The embarrassing elimination for one of the National Hockey League's original six teams will probably be labeled the most humiliating event in the Rangers' 49-year history.

"That was one of the problems: The Rangers never really took the Islanders seriously—until it was too late . . ."

Chapter 3
ROLE REVERSAL

"Now I see the rivalry. It seems to me half the people were for the Rangers. It doesn't feel that much like a road game."

—Rangers defenseman Carol Vadnais

"I've never seen a player go to the Rangers and bloom."

—Islanders defenseman Denis Potvin

"Every time I picked up a paper, I read where some Islander was saying he'd rather beat the Rangers than Montreal. We were playing for the pride of the city."

—Rangers forward Don Murdoch

"It's always just a little sweeter when we beat the Rangers."

—Islanders goalie Chico Resch

Things only got worse for Rangers fans after the defeat of April 11, 1975.

They had to watch as their upstart captors, the neophyte Islanders, kept hockey in the New York news for another five weeks.

Though early on, that wasn't easy.

The Nassau-men nearly made a prophet of their biggest critic, Derek Sanderson, as they lost the first three games of their best-of-seven second-round matchup to the Pittsburgh Penguins but instead made NHL history, becoming the first team since the 1941–42 Toronto Maple Leafs to come all the way back from 0–3 down to win a playoff series.

The Isles almost repeated the feat in the semifinals against the Philadelphia Flyers, winning Games Four, Five, and Six after dropping the first three, before finally fading out in Game Seven. Along the way, every clutch Chico Resch save and Denis Potvin goal had Blueshirts-backers thinking, *"Gosh, we had this team buried weeks ago!"*

At the request of Rangers president Bill Jennings, General Manager Emile Francis fired Coach Emile Francis and replaced himself with forty-three-year-old Calgary native Ron Stewart, a veteran right wing of nearly 1500 NHL games.

Stewart happens to be one of only two players ever to be traded between the Rangers and Islanders. He was sent eastward on November 14, 1972, in exchange for cash. Thirty-seven years later, a defensive prospect named Jyri Niemi was moved from suburb to city for a sixth-round pick. You've just read the Islanders-Rangers trading history in its entirety.

The only other significant alteration to the Broadway lineup heading into 1975–76 was the acquisition of twenty-two-year-old rookie goal-tender John Davidson from the St. Louis Blues. The mustachioed 6-foot-3 Ottawa boy had been the fifth overall pick in the 1973 draft.

Out on Long Island, Al Arbour and Bill Torrey had a rookie of their own—a baby-faced center taken 22nd overall in 1974—by the name of Bryan Trottier.

THE MAVEN REMEMBERS: RANGERS KILLER, BRYAN TROTTIER

When Bryan Trottier arrived at the Islanders' camp in the fall of 1975 he was an afterthought to the afterthought.

How little we all knew.

Once I began to watch him play in the exhibition games, I realized that the nineteen-year-old was reminiscent of Henri Richard, who showed up at the Montreal Canadiens camp in the fall of 1955 and was dismissed out of hand as too young and too small.

P.S. the Pocket Rocket not only made the Habs, but went on to win 11 Cups, a league record, with Montreal.

Like Richard, Trottier simply turned into one of the best players on the ice, practice after practice and exhibition game after exhibition game.

You guessed it—he made the varsity and never had to look back.

One could say he was an instant Hall of Famer.

"Trots" immediately blasted off, taking his team with him. Runaway winner of the Calder Trophy, the 5-foot-11 dynamo potted 95 points as a freshman in 1975–76, while his teammate, Denis Potvin, claimed his first Norris Trophy as the NHL's top defenseman. These bona fide superstars filled Nassau Coliseum with bona fide Islanders fans. The Isles finished second in the Patrick Division and fifth overall with a record of 42–21–17. They were the toast of the hockey town.

Especially since, in Manhattan, things were beginning to unravel.

During a 7–1 Islanders drubbing of the Blueshirts on October 25, 1975, fans in Uniondale sang, "Hang it up, Ran-gers, hang it up." Based on the rest of the season, it may have been solid advice.

Come Halloween, Emile "The Cat" Francis made a move he should have known Rangers fans would view as trick rather than treat, waiving beloved goaltender Eddie Giacomin, who was immediately claimed by the Detroit Red Wings. It was sacrilege, and worst of all, Eddie and Detroit visited the Garden just two nights later, November 2, 1975.

Not only did Giacomin defeat his former club, but the sellout Rangers crowd rooted for his Red Wings the entire evening. Chants of "Edd-ie! Edd-ie!" rained onto the ice all game, embarrassing Francis mightily.

Feeling the heat, Francis reached for something drastic—even more drastic than waiving Giacomin. Jean Ratelle, Brad Park, and defenseman

Joe Zanussi were traded to the Boston Bruins for All-Star defenseman Carol Vadnais and legendary center Phil Esposito on November 7, 1975.

The last-ditch move did not work, at least in the short term. "Espo," the Boston loyalist, moped, his new team sagged, and on January 6, 1976, the Cat finally ran out of lives. Former scrappy Montreal Canadiens winger John Ferguson took over for Francis as general manager and for Ron Stewart as coach. The Rangers finished last in the Patrick Division, at 29–42–9.

In such a climate, it felt almost ho-hum when Long Island took the crosstown series for the first time ever—4–2–0—doubling up their downtrodden neighbors 28–14 in goals.

The torch was officially passed on April 3, 1976, with a 10–2 abasement of the Blueshirts in Nassau. Denis Potvin scored a goal and three assists, giving him 14 points—six red lights and eight helpers—in the six-game set against the Rangers.

The crowd taunted and teased the last-place visitors from the moment they arrived until the final horn, hoisting signs reminding the Manhattan-men of their agony.

Arbour's army distinguished itself in the postseason again, sweeping the Vancouver Canucks in the opening round and upsetting the Buffalo Sabres in six before dropping a tough semifinal series to the Canadiens.

Die-hard Blueshirters rooted hard against the suburbanites, but more casual hockey fans in the area were slowly converting to Arbour-dom, as the Islanders looked poised to become the next big thing in the NHL.

PJs for the Blueshirts, Playoffs for the Isles

Over in midtown, John Ferguson was scheming up ways to alter his new club's fortune. The thirty-seven-year-old ex-lacrosse coach cut payroll, removed team doctors, brought in new players—young goaltender Gilles Gratton, scoring whiz and sixth overall pick Don Murdoch, and tough Staten Island native Nick Fotiu—and even decided to change the uniforms.

In September, 1976, "Fergy" announced that he was doing away with the team's classic shirt—displaying the diagonal "R-A-N-G-E-R-S" from right shoulder to left hip—in favor of a simpler jersey with the Rangers logo centered on the chest. Ferguson actually helped design the new uniform himself.

The change was about as popular as the losing that had inspired it. Garden fans referred to the new outfits as the "pajama jerseys," which was fitting, because the 1976–77 Rangers so often looked asleep.

The Blueshirts finished last in the Patrick Division again with a record of 29–37–14 and missed the playoffs for the second consecutive year. They went 1–4–1 against the Isles in a season series best remembered for sparking a wild, bench-clearing brawl on April 3, 1977, at the Garden. Even the goalies, Bill Smith and John Davidson, danced in that one.

The Islanders cruised to a 106-point season and, for the third spring in a row, drove three rounds deep, sweeping the Chicago Blackhawks and the Sabres before bowing to the heavily favored Canadiens again in six.

Arbour's men were clearly not yet in Montreal's class but were just as clearly getting closer by the minute. Long Island, it appeared, was on the cusp.

1977–78: Show 'Em Who's Boss

Meanwhile, all the Rangers had to look forward to was the 1977 draft and their duo of first-round picks—numbers eight and 13.

Ferguson was in the market for offense and was keen on one particular right wing from Montreal, Mike Bossy, who had scored 309 goals in 263 career games with Laval National of the Quebec Major Junior Hockey League.

Rangers scout Tommy Savage caught a few of those games and sent a scathing report back to New York, describing how he watched the lanky sniper sit alone on the pine during a bench-clearing brawl.

"So what?" Fergy replied. "Coaches have been calling me every day telling me how good he is."

"He's too skinny," maintained Savage. "Won't fight. They'll chase him out of the league."

Despite his scout's protests, Ferguson remained interested in Bossy up until the day of the draft, June 14, 1977. But when the time came to call in the eighth overall pick, Fergy deferred to Tommy Savage. The Rangers did take a right winger from the QMJHL—200-pound Lucien DeBlois.

Bossy stayed on the board until the 13th pick, which to Ferguson only proved that other scouts around the league shared Savage's concerns about his toughness. So after much consideration, the Rangers opted for another forward—Ron Duguay of Sudbury, Ontario.

The 14th pick belonged to Buffalo. They selected a high-scoring right winger . . .

Ric Seiling.

The 15th pick belonged to Bill Torrey and the Islanders. They selected a high-scoring right winger . . .

Michael Dean Bossy.

Uh-oh.

It should be mentioned in Ferguson's defense—as well as Torrey's acclaim—that in the World Hockey Association's 1977 draft, comprised of the same amateur pool, Bossy was not taken until pick number 44, whereas Duguay went third overall and DeBlois went ninth.

But despite all the pass-overs, Bossy, it turned out, lacked nothing in the confidence department. During contract negotiations, Torrey asked the young "Boss" what he thought he could do for the team.

"I'm going to score 50 goals for you," he said without blinking. Torrey chuckled and signed the kid for $50,000.

Bossy-regret soon hit Ferguson and the Rangers big-time, especially come January 28, 1978, when the quick-shooting Quebecois recorded 12 shots on goal in a game against the Rangers at home, including 2 that went in for his 32nd and 33rd goals of the season.

Al Arbour's first line of Bossy, Bryan Trottier, and Clark Gillies combined for 26 shots on goal and eight points in the Isles' 6–2 win. No wonder it had taken only a matter of weeks for the threesome to earn the nickname, "Trio Grande."

For Blueshirts Nation, it was more like, *"Muy Frustrado."*

"We're in a state of chaos right now," admitted forward Steve Vickers. "We've got to play the same way the Islanders do, but we don't."

In a nationally televised Saturday matinee at the Coliseum on April 8, 1978, the Isles clinched another series victory over the Rangers—4–2–0 this time—as well as, more important, their first Patrick Division and Campbell Conference titles in franchise history.

And, as had become the trend, they did not waste any time shutting the door on the Rangers in the season finale. It was 5–0 suburbanites by the end of the first period and 7–0 early in the second.

Making the sting burn worse, Bossy scored his 53rd and final goal of the regular season, setting a rookie record that would last until Winnipeg Jets speedster Teemu Selanne came along 15 years later.

"WE'RE-NUM-BER-ONE!" chanted the crowd throughout their team's 7–2 triumph. Al Arbour was so excited, he ran out onto the ice the moment the game ended.

The Coliseum overflowed with high spirits and high expectations, but in the end it was a disappointing postseason for both New York squads as the Rangers were bounced by Buffalo in the preliminary round, and then the Isles fell in seven games to ordinary ol' Toronto.

New Faces at the Top

But as spring blossomed into summer, a rift was developing in Big Apple hockey that made all the on-ice collisions and stick-swinging anarchy look like child's play. Because after all, hockey is hockey. But business is business.

Islanders owner and president Roy Boe was two years overdue on his expansion fee to the NHL and his territorial fee to the New York Rangers. The former beverage baron from Brooklyn owed over $6.1 million around the league and over $3.2 million to the Blueshirts, as well as $19.5 million outside the NHL. The league ordered the Isles to reorganize and come up with the cash by any means possible.

So Mr. Boe showed up to the annual league meetings in June with an idea. He would offer the league and his cross-river rivals a lump sum of $3.5 million, and see what happens.

No sale.

"That's equivalent to paying 30 cents on the dollar," complained one anonymous adversary. "And that's ridiculous."

Back and forth this went all summer, until finally, the New York State Supreme Court removed Boe from control of the Islanders and appointed John O. Pickett, an investment counselor from Long Island, as managing general partner. In August, the league and the Rangers approved a plan to have the Isles pay them back contingent upon future income.

So in a way, the Rangers now owned the Islanders. Even if on the ice, it certainly seemed the other way around.

With or without the Islanders' money, the Blueshirts were entering a new era. On June 1, 1978, the new president of Madison Square Garden, David "Sonny" Werblin, poached two-time Stanley Cup-winning Flyers bench boss Freddy Shero away from Philadelphia, and was docked a first-round pick and cash for the trouble. It was a gutsy move.

The bespectacled fifty-two-year-old Winnipegger—nicknamed "The Fog" for his absentmindedness—signed a five-year deal to become coach and general manager on Broadway, ending the Ferguson era after only two full seasons.

The newcomers, Werblin and Shero, quickly rebranded the organization, tossing John Ferguson's "pajama" uniforms in the trash, along with the idea of practicing in Long Beach, Long Island, or "Islanders Country," as Rangers officials called it.

Instead, the Garden-men would return to their vintage blue shirts and would practice up in Westchester County. The idea was not only to move a bit closer to the city, but to also step out of the large and ever-growing shadow cast by the Islanders in Nassau County.

"I've got nothing against Long Beach," said Sonny Werblin. "But I want my players out of there."

He may have been on to something.

The Rangers went from seven games under .500 in 1977–78 to 11 games over .500 in 1978–79—an 18 point improvement—thanks to Shero's mastery and two enormous contributions from the man (or scapegoat?) he replaced, John Ferguson.

Back in 1978, Ferguson signed a pair of twenty-seven-year-old forwards from the WHA's Winnipeg Jets for the upcoming season, Anders Hedberg and Ulf Nilsson. The beneficiaries of Fergy's work turned out to be Werblin, Shero, and the fans, who watched with delight as the Swedish superstars soared to the top of the team scoring list in 1978–79.

"The Rangers have talent now," cautioned Islanders defenseman Bert Marshall. "It's going to be a long season."

"We're on different paths," echoed Chico Resch, "but we're converging."

One evening the Rangers wished they hadn't converged was Saturday night, December 23, 1978, at Nassau Coliseum—one of Trio Grande's greatest *tours de force*.

How does 17 points sound?

Bryan Trottier netted five goals and three assists, Mike Bossy scored twice and added three assists, Clark Gillies recorded four assists, and there you have it—17 combined points for the top line in the Islanders' 9–4 win.

Needless to say, the franchise record book needed a full "re-Trotting" after Bryan's brilliant breakthrough. Five goals? Islanders record. Eight points? Islanders record. Six points in the second period alone? Obviously, an Islanders record.

BENCHMARK GAME

EIGHT POINTS
December 23, 1978
Nassau Coliseum

Rangers 4 Islanders 9
(18–11–4) (21–4–7)

Two Nights Before Christmas; **inspired by "The Night Before Christmas," and Bryan Trottier.**

'Twas two nights before Christmas, when all through the Rangers,
The defense was invaded by a mustachioed stranger;

And word then soon spread, from Nassau Coliseum,
'Twas a creature named Trottier, you just gotta see him;

He bobbed and he weaved and he brought down the joint,
Because when he was done he had tallied eight points;

It was goalie Wayne Thomas whose bubble Trots burst,
With a rebound at 13:40 of the first;

And a beautiful end-to-end rush in the second,
Minutes later, from the crowd, flying hats did he beckon;

Goal four they first gave to Stefan Persson's credit,
But on review, Trots last touched it, official scorers did edit;

For the third period, the Rangers gave Thomas a breather,
And Trots said, "John Davidson, you cannot stop me either";

A power play strike, with the flick of his wrist,
But that was just his five goals! What about his assists;

On Bossy, on Howatt, on Bossy again,
Two points shy of Daryl Sittler's league record ten;

But for points in one period, the record is six,
Thanks to this second stanza, and one Islander's tricks;

Not Crosby, not Mario, not even the Gretz,
That record is Bryan's, to the Rangers' regret;

A performance that gave all the Blueshirts the willies,
"He's the best player in the league," gushed his linemate, Clark
Gillies;

The holiday crowd concurred, and they hollered with glee,
Happy Christmas to all, and to Trots, M-V-P!

What the "statement victory" demonstrated was that even in this renaissance season on Broadway, the Islanders were still a huge pain. They went on to take the season series from the City boys for the fourth consecutive year, 5–3–0.

Birth of "The Chant"

It was one of the three games the Rangers won that ended up hurting the most.

Because on February 25, 1979, in Madison Square Garden, Ulf Nilsson and Denis Potvin ventured into the Rangers' left-wing corner at 18:40 of the first period. Nilsson came out with a fractured ankle, and Potvin came out the enduring icon of vitriol in arguably the most vitriolic rivalry in American pro sports.

The drama came nine seconds after Rangers rookie Don Maloney had tied the contest at two. Nilsson won the ensuing faceoff and tipped the puck past Potvin, spurring a two-on-one that was broken up by Denis's linemate, Stefan Persson.

As Nilsson collected the loose puck along the boards, Potvin came over and smashed him. It seemed like an innocent play—which was how referee Bruce Hood saw it—but poor Ulfie's right ankle snapped like a cheap old guitar string.

The biggest shame of it, from a Broadway perspective, was how well Nilsson had been playing. Not only was he the Rangers' leading scorer for the season, but in only five games and one period against the Isles, Ulf had torched them for 11 points. He was a budding Islanders-killer, taken out by a renowned Rangers-killer.

THE MAVEN REMEMBERS: THE INFAMOUS POTVIN-NILSSON EPISODE

Little did of any of us know that what seemed like a routine—yet lethal—Denis Potvin defensive thrust would land into the Rangers' all-time Theater of Infamy.

As it happened, we all knew Potvin as one of the most effective body checkers, not to mention one of the legitimate "mean men" (at least according to Rangers fans) on any blue line in any era.

Ulf Nilsson, by contrast, was one of those light-horse, clean players, of whom it was said you can't hit him because you can't catch him.

Of course, whether your name is Wayne Gretzky, Mario Lemieux, Howie Morenz, or Bobby Orr, everybody gets nailed at one time or another.

Since Nilsson was so important to the Rangers' Stanley Cup hopes at the time, the fact that he suffered a broken ankle was taken personally by the legion of Rangers fans across North America, most of Europe, and the South Sea Islands.

It didn't matter to the Blueshirts Faithful then any more than it does now that Nilsson thoroughly exonerated Potvin and repeated it many times over the years. The damage was done, and decade upon decade, new Rangers fans continue the eternal chant.

As with the check itself, Potvin always seems to deliver the final thud with his deathless quote: "What Ranger fans mean," Denis inevitably chuckles, "is 'POTVIN'S CUPS!'"

The Rangers won the game, 3–2, but the faithful were not satisfied. No referee's decision was going to convince them that what Potvin did back in the first period wasn't dirty.

From that moment on, Denis was booed heartily in the Garden for the rest of his hockey career—both playing and broadcasting.

Then there was "the chant."

Yes, the chant. You know it. Whether at the game, on TV, or over the radio, you've heard a die-hard in the Garden stands whistling the familiar old jingle, "Let's Go Band," with its exultant three-chord refrain, prompting the rest of the crowd to answer—

"POT-VIN-SUCKS!"

It happens at every Rangers game, in perpetuity. And it all began with that innocent play in the corner.

BENCHMARK GAME: ULF NILSSON

February 25, 1979
Madison Square Garden

Islanders 2 Rangers 3
(38–11–10) (34–19–6)

> "Potvin Sucks" is a brand.
>
> It transcends the Islanders, the rivalry, and even Denis Potvin himself. It is, to many Broadway fans, just another way of saying, "Let's Go Rangers."
>
> "My foot stuck in the ice," recalled Rangers center Ulf Nilsson. "It wasn't bad ice. It wasn't Potvin's fault. It was just one of those things."
>
> "It was a hard check," echoed Rangers coach Fred Shero. "You can't penalize a guy for hitting hard."
>
> Well, the referee can't. But the fans can do whatever they want.

Rematch

Heading into the last day of the season, the Islanders trailed the Montreal Canadiens by half a game, or one "point." *Les Habs* were in Detroit taking on the Red Wings, one of the crummiest teams in the league that year, while the Isles were in MSG facing Shero's hungry Rangers. The Canadiens held the tiebreaker, so only an Islanders win coupled with a Montreal loss would bring Long Island its first regular-season crown. It seemed hopeless, and the Islanders played that way.

Arbour's guys did not register a shot until a full 15 minutes were played in the opening frame. They mustered only three shots on net in the second, for a measly two-period total of seven. Potvin took a puck to his right knee, and the crowd cheered heartily while he lay doubled over in pain. As he skated off the ice, he waved back at them facetiously. "I heard those cheers," he said. "They made me very sad for those people."

The game was tied, 2–2, at the second intermission, when up in the press box, the Montreal score was whispered into the ear of scratched Isles defenseman Gerry Hart. "1–0 Red Wings, late third."

Hart nearly choked on his beer!

How can the mighty Canadiens be losing to Detroit with this much on the line?

He slammed his brew, ran down the stairwell (too excited for the elevator), and burst into the visiting locker room. Moments later, Garden staff heard loud screams. For a second, they thought there was some sort of emergency.

"We went bananas when we heard Montreal was losing," said Islanders defenseman Dave Lewis. "We knew it was in our hands at last."

So what happened?

Detroit held on for the 1–0 upset, while back in Manhattan, Bossy scored on a wraparound 16 seconds into the third period, added another gem at 9:23, and assisted on Trottier's power play death knell at 14:27 to secure the 5–2 victory and first-place overall finish.

It was the first NHL regular-season championship by a New York team since the Rangers had topped the six-team league in 1941–42.

Speaking of the Blueshirts, Freddy the Fog and his gritty Garden-men had serious problems. The Rangers had won only two of their final 12 games and were headed for another early postseason exit, or so it appeared.

But—surprise, surprise—things are not always as they originally appear.

JAY-DEEEE! *CLAP-CLAP!* JAY-DEEEE! *CLAP-CLAP*, barked the delirious Garden crowd, as goalie John "JD" Davidson rejected shot after playoff shot. The Blueshirts swept the Los Angeles Kings in the preliminary round, then disposed of the heavily-favored Flyers in five.

How? Two letters, JD. He stopped 212 of 222 shots for an outrageous save percentage of .955 and even achieved a scoreless streak of 168:59, from the beginning of Game Three until the end of Game Five.

That said, Davidson wasn't the only New Yorker with obscene statistics.

After a first-round bye, the Islanders went through the Blackhawks as if they were invisible. Indeed, the Rangers' third-round opponent would be "the anointed ones" themselves.

Potvin had scored 101 points in 1978–79, becoming the second defenseman ever to eclipse the century mark for a season, after the unmatchable Bobby Orr.

Trottier led the league in scoring with 134 points.

For his part, Bossy potted no fewer than 69 goals, at the time second in league history only to the 76 that Phil Esposito scored for the Bruins in 1970–71.

This is what the Rangers were up against, with a trip to the Stanley Cup Finals on the line.

Based on pre-game publicity, the Metropolitan Area was being treated to one of the top sports events ever in local history. The major New York newspapers devoted most of their salient sports space to the "Battle for New York," as did local radio and television.

Even the New York State legislature weighed in, with State Senate Majority Leader Warren Anderson stepping between cable and local television networks in their feud over telecast rights to the series. The cable network won, and local TV was blacked out. So naturally, any Metro area bar with cable became standing room only for all the games, beginning Thursday, April 26, 1979.

Over at Nassau Coliseum, the usual corps of ticket scalpers enjoyed a lucrative evening, with the cheapest seats easily fetching $60 apiece. Other seats were going for $100 and would climb as the series grew in intensity.

The Rangers stormed the Coliseum for Game One and skated circles around the Isles, scoring a 38–22 shots advantage and a 4–1 win before an emotionally charged, bipartisan crowd. John Davidson was the winner. Chico Resch took the loss. It was shocking, but the bottom line was this: Freddy Shero knew what he was doing. The Fog saw through the Islanders' fog bank.

Shero's focus had drifted upon two specific Islanders players—Denis Potvin and Mike Bossy. Anywhere either turned, there was to be a Ranger in his face. So Freddy decreed, and so it was done. Potvin was uncharacteristically off his game all night, and Bossy did not even register a shot!

"They were staring right into my eyes," said dumbfounded Denis, "even after I gave up the puck."

But even with all the pressure, surely the favorites would punish the underdogs moving forward. Game One was like a little sting—so it was believed—and now it was time for the suburbanites to smash the offending mosquito to death.

Well, just 3:12 into Saturday's Game Two, center Walter Tkaczuk gave the mosquito a 1–0 lead. The schizophrenic crowd exploded, or at least half of it did. These Rangers, it was perfectly apparent, were not going anywhere; they were there to win.

The game bounced back and forth in the second and third periods. Wayne Merrick tied it. Journeyman center Bobby Sheehan gave the Rangers a 2–1 lead. Bob Lorimer tied it. Bobby Nystrom gave the Islanders a 3–2 lead.

Finally, with just 4:12 left in the third, Phil Esposito snuck a right-circle shot past Billy Smith, who was alternating starts with Resch, to send this marvelous, energetic, Stanley Cup-caliber game into overtime.

The tension was unbelievable, and it was clear that, unlike in April 1975, the weight of the moment rested largely on the shoulders of the Islanders.

But instead of a conservative, tight-checking, playoff overtime, this period played more like the "fire-wagon" 3-on-3-style extra sessions of modern times.

There were point-blank saves, rebounds, backdoor passes, and semi-breakaways, all in the opening minutes. Davidson made five saves, and Smith made four. At 8:02, Potvin beat a heavily screened JD from the left circle to give the Isles a most dramatic—and needed—4–3 victory. Shots finished at 37 per side, which was fitting, because it was indeed that even a game.

From Shero's perspective, that was okee-dokee!

After all, the "juggernaut" Islanders were supposed to have squashed his club's dreams by now. Instead, this looked like anybody's series heading into Game Three, Tuesday night, May 1, in Manhattan.

Ticket scalpers were taking over $100 just to get people into the building, with top-of-the-line seats going for up to $500 a pop.

Not only was the MSG crowd of 17,375 ready to rock, but another 3,000 boisterous fans watched a simulcast from the Garden's Felt Forum, the adjacent venue colloquially known as "The Theater."

Arbour went back to Resch in net, and Chico rewarded him with eight saves in the scoreless first.

But 3:14 into the second, fleet Rangers center Bobby Sheehan poked home a rebound to open the scoring, and after Islanders speedster Bob Bourne tied the game at 14:04, the Rangers' "Godfather Line" of Phil Esposito, Don Maloney, and Don Murdoch (Esposito and two Dons) went to work on the Public Enemy, Denis Potvin, trapping the cocky savant behind the Islanders cage and stealing the puck.

In true wise-guy fashion, Murdoch and Maloney started shooting, before the Godfather himself, Espo, tucked it in at 16:23.

For Esposito, the bellwether Ranger, it was his sixth goal and 14th point of the playoffs. The Blueshirts received a giant ovation as they left the ice ahead, 2–1, having outshot the mighty Isles, 14–5, in the second period.

Then came JD time.

Davidson made a sprawling save on John Tonelli midway through the third and a nice stick save on Merrick with under eight minutes to go. Soon the league's top defensive tandem of Potvin and Persson were victimized again, this time on an unassisted goal by Steve Vickers at 13:55 to send the already ecstatic crowd into orbit.

By the time the final buzzer sounded, the Blueshirts held a 32–17 lead in shots for Game Three and 107–76 for the series. The most astounding part was that Trio Grande, who had once tallied 26 shots on goal in a Rangers game and 17 points in another one, combined for *zero* shots in Game Three and one point for the series so far.

Game Four, Thursday, May 3, was no picnic for the Isles, either.

It was Smith's turn in the Islanders' net, and Battlin' Billy made 27 saves in regulation to just barely eke the Isles through to overtime tied, 2–2. John Tonelli and Billy Harris struck for the visitors, while the Godfather Line did the damage again for the Rangers, with Maloney scoring on a breakaway in the second and a deflection in the third.

With about three and a half minutes gone by in the extra session, the Nassau-men caught Don Maloney's brother and teammate, Dave Maloney, in a bad line change. Clark Gillies whacked the puck out of the Islanders' end, over the Rangers' blue line, and into "no man's land" between apprehensive John Davidson and speeding Bobby Nystrom.

Time seemed suspended as the crowd wondered who would reach the biscuit first. As Nystrom streaked down the center lane, JD decided to leave his cage and go for it. They both reached the puck at the same time, and the rubber popped up into the air—15 feet high!

"I wanted to call, 'fair catch,'" joked Bobby Ny.

JD went sliding by "Mr. Islander," who patiently waited for the puck to drop, like a leaf falling from a tree, and flicked it into the vacated net at 3:40 of overtime.

The Isles congratulated their hustling hero while the Rangers consoled their goaltender just a few feet away.

But the Blueshirts had once more proven that this series was theirs to lose, even against a team 25 points superior in the regular season.

Gillies's fluky overtime assist was the first point for either him, Bossy, or Trottier since Trots scored back in the first period of Game One. Incidentally, the Islanders were now a staggering 0–18 on the power play.

The Rangers, who were for the past three years virtually ignored by the press and by New York sports fans, were becoming the talk of the town. Meanwhile, the Islanders were losing everything they had built in the four years since J.P. Parise's magic goal.

They got a big Coliseum welcome when they hit the ice for Game Five on Saturday, May 5, though it was apparent that the Rangers had thousands of their fans on hand, as well.

At the suggestion of Chico Resch, Arbour broke his streak of alternating goalies and started Smith for the second straight contest.

Don Maloney stayed hot with a goal and an assist, as did Nystrom for Nassau with a big marker midway through the third, drawing the Isles even, 3–3.

Back and forth the teams traded chances, and wallops, but referee Dave Newell had packed up his whistle long ago. Tension building, the spectators moved to the tip of their seats as the clock ticked under ten minutes . . .

Shot Vickers, save Smith—

Under eight minutes . . .

Save Davidson. Save Smith. Save Davidson—

Under seven . . .

Shot Hedberg, save Smith, shot Hedberg, save Smith—

Under three . . .

Vickers to Greschner, shot, deflected high—

Vickers to Tkaczuk, broken up, Hedberg shot, diving save Smith, back to Hedberg, SCORE!!!!!

The entire Rangers bench jumped onto the ice to mob the jubilant Super Swede, Anders Hedberg, whose backhand scoop put the Blueshirts ahead, 4–3, at 17:47. Their supporters in the crowd went nuts. This time, the lead held up.

Big Apple Upset. The 1979 Islanders were perceived as unbeatable, until they ran into the scrappy Blueshirts. Here, crestfallen fans watch Anders Hedberg (center) and Steve Vickers celebrate Hedberg's game-winning goal with just 2:13 to play in the third period of Game Five of the Stanley Cup semifinals, May 5, 1979, at Nassau Coliseum, which pushed Bob Nystrom (23) and the first-place Isles to the brink of elimination. The Rangers would complete their shocking conquest three nights later in Manhattan. *(AP Photo)*

The long-shot Rangers were a game away from the Impossible Dream, the Miracle on 33rd Street, which they would shoot for in Game Six, Tuesday night, May 8.

Two hours before the 8:35 pm faceoff, the front of MSG looked like the floor of the New York Stock Exchange, as ticket seekers and hucksters traded barbs beside the myriad of newspaper, radio, and television people. Undercover police made 38 scalping arrests.

The Rangers hit the ice to a prolonged ovation that was only subdued once the Islanders came out behind them. Next came a vociferous "LET'S GO RANGERS" chant, which rocked the building for two minutes. Then the fans turned their affections toward their new breakout starting goaltender.

JAY-DEE! *Clap-clap!* JAY-DEE! *Clap-clap!*

Chico Resch started for Long Island.

And hallelujah!—what do you know—the Islanders snapped an 0-for-20 drought on their powerless power play with a Bossy strike at 8:56 and took the 1–0 lead out of the first.

But they were soon done in by the Godfather line one last time. Murdoch spun in a rebound at 5:03 of the second. With the place still buzzing, Esposito almost made it 2–1 but barely missed a feed in front. The fans were roaring at each Rangers touch of the puck. They could sense it, especially when Bob Lorimer of the Islanders was whistled for holding at 7:33.

Esposito and Don Maloney worked the puck free behind the Islanders cage and kicked it out to Ron Greschner for a power play blast. 2–1 Rangers!

Davidson made nine key saves in the second to preserve the slim lead. When the buzzer sounded, the teams came together at center but were eventually separated and slowly made their way to their dressing rooms as the crowd cheered. Old man Espo and his upset kids undoubtedly had the momentum now.

The Rangers came out hard in the opening minute of the third, applying pressure and setting the tone for the remainder of the evening. The Isles began selling out for offense, but their upstart foes were the only ones garnering scoring opportunities, throwing odd-man rush after odd-man rush in the direction of Chico Resch.

With under 13 minutes to play, JD corralled a John Tonelli shot, the Isles' first of the period. Three minutes later, he kicked out a Nystrom try off right wing. With about two and a half minutes left, Tonelli tried a soft shot from the top of the slot, but Davidson dove to smother it. Those were the only three saves Davidson would make in the third period, and the only three he would need.

With the crowd clapping and stomping, "Let's Go Rangers!" the Blueshirts took control of the puck and pinned it deep in the Islanders' zone. Everyone in the building rose to their feet. The clock bled under two minutes . . . under one minute . . .

With 17 seconds to go, Arbour gathered his troops at the bench to talk strategy, while the Garden was filled with an amazingly loud chant of, "JAY-DEE! JAY-DEE!" It was obvious the coach was wasting his breath. His team's confidence was irreparably shattered.

Walt Tkaczuk beat Trottier on the faceoff, whisking the puck into the corner as the clock ticked away. The fans shouted off the countdown and, with the flashing of those final zeroes, bellowed out a howl that echoed through the Garden and possibly throughout the city. The Isles completed this do-or-die period with only three lousy shots on net.

The crowd was delirious, as were, of course, the Rangers, who poured off the bench to mob John Davidson. After the ice was somewhat cleared, the stunned Islanders started the traditional handshake procession, while fans danced, yelled, hugged, and kissed one another—even strangers (hey, it was the '70s).

The pandemonium lasted another 15 minutes inside the Garden and spilled out onto Seventh Avenue afterwards, as thousands of jubilant Rangers-rooters who'd been watching the game around the area forced police to detour any traffic away from the vicinity.

The NYPD was helpless. Fans didn't seem to know or care that they were in the middle of one of the busiest avenues on the planet, while traffic was probably clogged as far uptown as Columbus Circle! After 20 minutes of dancing, shattered beer bottles, and chants of "JAY-DEE!" and "Islanders Suck!" the men in blue and their many horses finally dispersed the masses.

But even as the cars, taxis, and buses came through, hundreds of fans, still not debilitated one iota, continued with their fete in the street, as many of the passing motorists, quite aware of what happened in the circular building to the right, honked their horns and waved back to the celebrants. It was simply unbelievable, but true.

THE MAVEN REMEMBERS: DOOMED BY THE CINDERELLA RANGERS

With the magical touch of Fred Shero, the Rangers advanced to the third round of the 1979 playoffs against one of the strongest Islanders teams in history. Yet I could tell something was wrong with the Nassau-men, and that was even before the Rangers won Game One.

This was similarly evident in Game Two, even though the Isles managed to win the game in overtime.

At the time, I was writing about the series for a new Metropolitan-area magazine located in Times Square. It was a delightful spring afternoon, and when I reached the offices, I distinctly remember telling the editor that even though the Islanders had knotted the tournament at one apiece, they looked doomed. The editor asked me why and I said, "They just look like losers, and the Rangers look like winners."

Well, the Rangers went ahead again, but somehow the Islanders got lucky in overtime once more, this time with a Texas Leaguer that landed halfway between Bob Nystrom and John Davidson.

You'd have thought the Rangers would be doomed by now, but that hardly was the case. Leading the embattled Isles three games to two, they finished Al Arbour's team off in Game Six at the Garden. Tim Ryan worked with me as the play-by-play commentator, and we watched with something of a state of awe as the Rangers simply drew and quartered the Isles.

My most vivid mind-photo was that of five Islanders sitting on the ice with about a minute left in the game during a timeout. They were beyond forlorn because they knew that the score would end 2–1 and, even worse, that they would be accused of choking for the second playoff year in a row.

BENCHMARK GAME

THE STUNNER OF '79
May 8, 1979
Madison Square Garden

Islanders 1 Rangers 2
(2–4) (4–2)

"Nobody with a sane mind last month would have bet on us getting to the Stanley Cup Final," said Rangers captain Dave Maloney. "And that includes me."

So after Coach Fred Shero and the Rangers picked off the favored Isles in six games, the *New York Times* headline aptly declared, "'Impossible' Achieved At Garden.'"

Then-Rangers rookie forward Don Maloney, who broke the Blueshirts record for points in a playoff season with his 12th when he assisted on Ron Greschner's game-winning goal, smiles as he reminisces decades later.

"The Islanders were on top of the league," he waxes. "The best. And we were just this young group of guys that kind of came on the scene and ended up winning to go to the finals."

The scene at the Garden that night made a motivational impression on Arbour's Islanders that previous losses apparently had not.

They sat with blank stares while the overjoyed underdogs celebrated, then got up to shake hands, trudged off to the visiting locker room, showered, changed, departed by bus, and didn't lose another playoff series for five years.

Chapter 4

THE FOUR-YEAR WAR

"It's a real treat to play these guys. Playing Toronto, for instance, there was no emotion. But the guys get fired up for the Rangers."

—Islanders forward Bob Bourne

"There was no fraternizing between the teams. Not once do I recall having even a chit-chat with anybody."

—Islanders goalie Kelly Hrudey

"Nobody played hockey in the third period. I think they were trying to kill each other."

—Rangers coach Fred Shero

"The Islanders were the better players, the better team. But players in Manhattan got a lot of attention."

—Rangers/Islanders forward/Islanders General Manager/Rangers Executive Don Maloney

Perhaps the Rangers didn't need Red Dutton and his famed Curse of the Cup to drop the 1979 Stanley Cup Finals, as they did, to the Montreal Canadiens in five games. Between legendary coach Scotty Bowman and his nine Hall-of-Fame skaters, one could imagine the Habs besting the Manhattan-men without the help of any jinx.

Yet as Montreal cruised to its fourth straight championship, Dutton was in the back of every Rangers fan's mind. It was not lost on the Garden faithful that their team had still not won the Cup since he hexed them nearly four decades prior. Nor was it lost on the Nassau faithful that these Blueshirts, who had smitten the Isles away, were still a cut below championship quality. With back-to-back playoff upsets in 1978 and 1979, Arbour and his Islanders had developed a label even worse than "hexed."

Now they were "chokers."

Two days after taking over the team captaincy from Clark Gillies, Denis Potvin took to the *New York Times* to address the giant elephant in the arena. "The noise and jeers of our final hockey night in Madison Square Garden . . ." he wrote, "are to be resounding in our minds until the day of reckoning, the day we win the Stanley Cup. . . . This is it. This is the season."

He was talking about 1979–80.

Indeed, the 1979 Expressway Series was an ultra-embarrassing loss that left everyone around the Islanders itching to embarrass Big Brother back. Alas, the immediate result was two of the most inflammatory words in the vast Islanders-Rangers glossary—double chili.

A local Wendy's restaurant offered free chili any day after the Isles scored six or more goals at home. Come the very first crosstown battle of the season—Tuesday, November 13, 1979, at the Coliseum—the acrimonious Islanders were spanking the hated Rangers 8–2 late in the second period when a Wendy's executive gave the go-ahead to announce that, should the home club reach 10 goals by game's end, fans would be treated to an extra serving—not one free chili, but two—prompting chants of, "Dou-ble-Chi-li" throughout the building.

The Blueshirts were not impressed with Wendy's generosity nor the Coliseum's announcement. Phil Esposito expressed his distaste with his middle finger.

Was it done maliciously?

Nobody would admit to such a thing, but the fact remains that it was the first and only time the Isles were ever urged to run up the score past six.

A Long Islander would tell you that if the Rangers hated it so much, then maybe they should've stopped the home team from scoring.

That didn't happen. Garry Howatt struck at 9:17 of the third, and under three minutes later, Captain Denis Potvin deposited a wrist shot to make Ranger fans sick to their stomachs, and Islanders fans, well, eventually probably sick to their stomachs, too.

"DOUBLE CHILI!" flashed the scoreboard.

"When they made the announcement, I heard Denis's stomach growling," joked Bryan Trottier. "The next thing I knew, he had taken the puck down the ice and scored."

The Rangers won the next two crosstown matchups, both at MSG—a 5–4 thriller decided by another late Anders Hedberg goal in December and a bloody, brawl-filled 8–2 beatdown in February that even spilled into the dressing room hallway after the game—all while leading the Islanders in the standings virtually wire-to-wire.

But after Bill Torrey added U.S. Olympic gold medal hero Ken Morrow to the Islanders' defense and traded veterans Billy Harris and Dave Lewis to the Los Angeles Kings for thirty-year-old All-Star center Butch Goring in March, it appeared the Rangers—and the rest of the league—were in for a problem.

With the pesky Goring and new bearded banger Morrow, the Isles finished the season 8–0–4 to storm past the Atlanta Flames and Rangers into second place. Equally important, Arbour was finally ready to choose a full-time, number-one goalie. After much consideration, he sat Chico Resch on the bench and plopped Billy Smith in the crease.

The Blueshirts were battered in round two of the 1980 playoffs by the NHL's best team, the Patrick Division champion Philadelphia Flyers. Meanwhile, the Islanders opened against Goring's old mates, the Kings, with the rage of 1979 smoldering in their esophagi, surely not soothed by hearing the same questions over and over.

"Remember what happened last year, against the Rangers?"

Smith backstopped a three-games-to-one romp over the Kings.

"But are you worried about blowing it, like last year, against the Rangers?"

Trio Grande tallied 20 points in a five-game ousting of the favored Boston Bruins. On to the semis—

"Hey, remember the semis last year, against the Rangers?"

The Isles skated past the powerful Adams Division champion Buffalo Sabres in six games and into the first Stanley Cup Finals in franchise history.

The opponent was the Flyers, who finished 12.5 games—or 25 points—ahead of the Islanders in the regular season. Game One was a classic OT win in Philly's beloved Spectrum. Game Two was an 8–3 loss. The Isles won Games Three and Four in the raucous Coliseum to move within one game from glory, but Game Five was a letdown. The bad taste of years prior still lingered in the back of their throats.

Game Six faced off at 2:00 pm on a hot, sunny Saturday afternoon in Uniondale, on May 24, 1980. The Islanders led the Broad Street Bullies 4–2 after two periods but coughed it up early in the third. "Choke, ahem, choke," muttered wisenheimers around the hockey world, particularly those in the five boroughs of New York City. To overtime they went.

Seven minutes in, veteran center Lorne Henning made a brilliant pass through center to Tonelli, who made a brilliant pass down left wing to Nystrom, who deflected it home at 7:11. The Coliseum exploded!

The Islanders leaped on Nystrom, the fans hopped over the glass and leaped on the Islanders, and moments later, the Stanley Cup was presented to a New York team for the first time in 40 years.

Throngs of people ascended on the Coliseum area, and traffic came to a standstill. The familiar "Let's Go Islanders" car horn—*"Honk-honk, Honk-honk-honk"*—blared all night. When the sun came up and the hangover dissipated, it was time to plan a parade.

Parade Predicament

It was widely assumed that, in keeping with tradition, the route would be Manhattan's majestic Canyon of Heroes, this being a major championship by a New York team. But New York City Mayor Ed Koch, along with millions of taxpayers who happened to bleed Rangers blue, saw the matter differently. He decreed that since the Islanders did not play within the five boroughs, his city was not responsible for their parade. *Humbug.*

The sentiment was mutual. When the big fiesta was finally held right outside Nassau Coliseum on Hempstead Turnpike, it was clear there was no place in the entire solar system that any of the revelers—team or fans—would rather be. "Manhattan, you can have the Rangers," read one particularly poignant sign. "We got the Cup."

It was finally true. There was nothing the surly Nation of Blueshirts could do about that. But one thing the Islanders still did not have, to their surprise, was mainstream attention.

By the start of the 1980–81 season, the New York hockey teams' "Q Ratings" were recalibrated to business as usual. The Rangers were still the Big Apple. The Islanders were still the Little Apple, Cup or not.

One ad campaign came to symbolize the pop-culture disparity between the two franchises. The company was Sasson Jeans, the commercials were everywhere, and the jingle, "Oo. La-la. Sas-son," would help score the Islanders-Rangers rivalry for years to come.

The concept was simple, yet provocative. Rangers players such as Phil Esposito, Anders Hedberg, Ron Greschner, wild-haired Ron Duguay, and Dave and Don Maloney skated around in tight jeans, as was the style at the time, dancing and singing the jingle.

"Oo. La-la. Sas-son . . . Oo. La-la. Sas-son . . ." Over and over. To hear it once was to have it in your head for a month, whether you liked it or (more likely) not.

Back home, Arbour's men were stewing while, naturally, winning their hockey pants off.

At 48–18–14, the 1980–81 Nassau-men finished first overall for the second time in three years. The Rangers endured a tumultuous season in which John "JD" Davidson was sidelined with knee surgery and Fred Shero was fired and replaced by the team's operations director, Craig Patrick, as interim coach. They dipped to 30–36–14 and fourth in the Patrick Division.

The teams split a hard-fought, competitive, four-game regular-season set that became so catty that referee Bryan Lewis handed out 148 penalty minutes one night in the Garden in February, including nine misconducts.

The Rangers' Wheel-of-Goaltending spun through the incumbent JD and veterans Doug Soetaert and Wayne Thomas before finally landing on twenty-three-year-old Bostonian Steve Baker, who ultimately led the Blueshirts on another Cinderella journey through the playoffs. Baker and company ousted the Kings and St. Louis Blues—teams that, respectively, finished 25 and 33 points higher during the regular season!—to roll into another semifinal.

And wouldn't you know it—the Islanders were there, too, setting up "The Parkway Series, Part III."

1981 Semifinals

It was the rematch both sides craved. The champs felt underexposed and disrespected off the ice. The challengers had something to prove on the ice. And as in 1979, the stakes would be a trip to the Stanley Cup Finals!

The Coliseum crowd was ecstatic as the Game One opening faceoff drew near on Tuesday, April 28, 1981, and the fans continued to cheer and chant throughout the national anthem—"Let's Go Islanders—Let's Go Rangers—"

Goals by Islanders assassin Anders Hedberg and Ed Hospodar backed the Blueshirts to a 2–1 early second-period lead, but the home team struck four straight times for a convincing 5–2 win. The evening provided quite a contrast—polar opposite, in fact—from Game One in 1979.

Thence the Isles received a long and loud ovation during warm-ups before Game Two on Thursday, April 30, and returned the love with a pair of outbursts for the ages.

Down, 3–1, to start the second period, the champs posted a short-handed goal by Goring, a power play goal by Mike Bossy, and an even-strength goal by Goring in a span of 4:33, then repeated this "man-power natural hat trick" in the third period with a power-play goal by Clark Gillies, a shorthanded goal by Anders Kallur, and an even-strength goal by Bossy, this time in a span of 4:48!

In the process, the Coliseum progressed from hopping to pandemonium. The bedlam that followed Kallur's "shorty" quickly dissolved into a series of brand-new derisive chants, including a thunderous, impro-vised version of "Oo-La-La, Sasson" that seemed to follow Ron Duguay's teeming curly locks around the rink. The song every Islander thought they'd had enough of was suddenly music to their ears as the mockery echoed throughout the building—"OO! LA-LA! SASSON!"

But the next chant was the one that would live on forever. Well, almost forever.

Better than following one player around the ice for one shift, this chant followed a franchise around the league for years. Nobody knows exactly who, but somebody in Nassau Coliseum late in that dominant 7–3 win hollered, "NINE-TEEN-FOR-TY!" and the thing took off like a Blackbird jet.

It was catchy. It was mean. It crammed four decades of Rangers heartbreak into four syllables and five claps of the hand, while implicitly boasting the champion Islanders, as well. It was the perfect chant.

The Islanders' performance was incredible, as confirmed by the over-whelming noise in the building at the conclusion. But the Rangers and their fans felt that with the next two games on Madison Square Garden ice, the series was about to turn their way. They'd beaten their rivals eight of the last ten times at home, including by a combined 12–4 score in the only two Garden clashes earlier that season. When Baker and the Rangers took the Manhattan ice on Saturday night, May 2, the ovation they received was deafening, as were the boos for the Isles, especially Denis Potvin.

While Broadway musical superstar Patti LuPone belted out the final notes of the national anthem, a slew of rubber chickens and dead fish— yes, real, formerly living fish from the sea—were hurled in the direction of Potvin from the Garden stands.

"I guess I'll have to view their reaction to me as a compliment," said the Islanders captain. "I mean, just to preserve my own sanity."

Potvin responded by starting a deft power-play passing sequence with Clark Gillies and Bossy that resulted in Boss's third goal in as many periods. Bobby Bourne added a power-play tally to make it 2–0 after one, then Ken Morrow and Bobby Nystrom buried the Blueshirts with sharp shots late in the second, leaving the audience miserable, lifeless, and defeated. Indeed, there was nothing fishy about Potvin or the Islanders in this game. The teams split a quiet—almost depressing—third period a goal apiece, and the Isles skated off 5–1 victors.

Game Four, on May 5, had begun in the same manner as Game Three. Rangers coach Craig Patrick stuck with Steve Baker in net, Patti LuPone sang the anthem again, and the Garden faithful tossed more dead fish at Denis Potvin.

The other theme was Islanders supremacy. After John Tonelli tallied just 1:02 in, Rangers defenseman John Hughes took a run at Bossy and was called for charging. Bossy scored 15 seconds into the ensuing power play to make it 2–0. On his next shift, Hughes took a run at Bossy and was called for roughing. Bossy scored 55 seconds into the ensuing power play to make it 3–0. Life just could not get any better for the visitors.

Goring buried a shorthanded breakaway at 1:29 of the second. The frustrated fans were fuming. But Ron Greschner and Barry Beck struck late in the period to cut the suburban lead in half, and the place awakened. Play moved back and forth the first nine minutes of the third and tempers began to flare, until young Islanders sparkplug Duane Sutter tucked in a wraparound to make the score 5–2 and send the crowd strolling toward the exits. The Rangers were as dead as a Garden fish flying through the air at Denis Potvin.

BENCHMARK GAME: SUBURBAN SWEEP

May 5, 1981
Madison Square Garden

Islanders 5 Rangers 2
(4–0) (0–4)

If "revenge is a dish best served cold," then the Madison Square Garden ice is every Nassau-man's ideal platter.

The Isles won the Stanley Cup in 1980, but noticeably absent from their postseason racing card were their unfriendly neighbors, who humiliated them in the 1979 semifinals.

Redemption was particularly sweet for one of the most widely criticized goats of the Isles' 1979 debacle, sniper Mike Bossy, who went from breaking sticks in that series to breaking records in this one.

In fact, with one flip of his backhand in the first period of Game Four, Boss set three NHL playoff marks simultaneously. It was his eighth power-play goal of the 1981 postseason and the Islanders' 26th, both records, as well as Bossy's 81st overall goal of the year—regular season and playoffs combined—topping Reggie Leach's five-year-old record of 80.

THE MAVEN REMEMBERS: SWEEPING THE BLUESHIRTS AWAY

One of my neighbors was a diehard Rangers fan who had season tickets and invited me to join him for the fourth game, since I wasn't broadcasting that series.

Even though the Isles were the defending champions, the Rangers always were scary to them, because of what happened in 1979.

Watching that Game Four, I still remained uncertain in terms of this being a series-clincher.

But as the minutes unfolded, it was clear to me this series pitted the boys against the men, and the men weren't going to allow the lads a single victory. And so the series ended in a sweep.

After I dropped my friend off at his apartment, I walked the next few blocks home wondering to myself if what I saw was real or a dream.

Of course it was real, and a dynasty was in the making.

Given the ruthlessness of the Islanders machine and the rival opponent who had just been vanquished, the 1981 Stanley Cup Final against the middle-of-the-pack Minnesota North Stars seemed anticlimactic.

That is, until the end of the fifth and last game, which was the party of the year on Long Island, with deafening chants of "We're Number One!" cascading to the Coliseum ice and reflecting out to Montauk. The city sat quiet while, out in the "burbs," it was once again confetti raining from the rafters by night, and floats rolling up Hempstead Turnpike by day.

Herb Brooks joins the Rangers

But the Rangers recaptured the back pages in short order when they agreed to terms with one of the most celebrated coaches in the game—certainly among those who had never before coached or played in the National Hockey League.

Herb Brooks's hockey legacy goes beyond the NHL, even beyond the sport itself. As head coach of the United States men's national ice hockey team at the 1980 Winter Olympics in Lake Placid, New York, he and his amateur collegiate players defeated those who were perceived as undefeatable—the Soviet Red Army, considered the finest hockey team in the world, NHL included. Brooks and Team USA became instant cold war heroes.

On June 1, 1981, he signed up for a similar challenge—to lead an unspectacular team that wears red, white, and blue uniforms in a clash of cultures with a feared, flawless opponent. Only instead of an ocean away, this enemy was a river away.

Brooks's first year with the Rangers was a success, as the club improved to 39–27–14, good for second place in the Patrick Division. You can probably guess which team finished first.

At 54–16–10, Al Arbour's aces had the greatest regular season of his entire coaching career. What's more, they de-sizzled Manhattan's buzzworthy squad with a 6–2–0 record in the 1981–82 regular-season Battle of New York. The Islanders scored a whopping 35 goals in their six wins over Big Brother, and in the signature fight of the year—December 30, 1981—Clark Gillies painted the Madison Square Garden ice with the blood of Rangers tough-but-apparently-not-tough-enough guy Ed Hospodar.

BENCHMARK GAME: GILLIES VS. HOSPODAR

December 30, 1981
Madison Square Garden

Islanders 4 Rangers 6
(21–11–5) (15–17–5)

Islanders Hall-of-Fame winger Clark Gillies finished an assist shy of a "Gordie Howe hat trick," unless you include assisting young Rangers enforcer Ed Hospodar to the hospital.

Here's Gillies's version of the story, as told at an event nearly 35 years later:

Eddie Hospodar used to sucker me in front of the net. I would say, "You can't do that. I'm going to destroy you if you do that again." Eddie was like, "Oh yeah-yeah-yeah-yeah-yeah . . ."

Then he would spear me in the back of the leg.

"Eddie, I'm warning you. I'm gonna hurt you."

"Oh yeah-yeah-yeah-yeah-yeah . . ."

Then he'd crosscheck me right in the small of the back.

So all these things he would do, for at least two years, and I warned him any number of times that I was gonna get him. And when I got a hold of him, he would kind of go down. And I would just let him up and say, "No, that's not it. That's not what's going to happen to you. It's going to be muuuuch worse."

Well he just kept doing it. And one night we were in the Garden, and Trots got in the middle of something. I went over to straighten it out, and next thing you know, somebody grabbed me by the jersey, and I went, "What the—?!?" I turned around, and it was Eddie Hospodar.

And that's it. That's all I remember.

I had to watch it on replay to see what I actually did. It was pretty nasty but it was everything that I told him I would do and then some.

I went home the next day and the phone rang, and my wife, Pam, said, "It's some guy named Frank Brown."

"Oh yeah, Frank, from the Daily News. *I'll speak to Frank."*

I said, "Frank, what's up?"

He said, "How ya doing?"

"All right. Sitting on the couch, having a beer, just came home from practice . . ."

"Well I just came from Lenox Hill Hospital."

I said, "Oh yeah? What were you doing over there?"

He said, "I was visiting a guy that looks something like Eddie Hospodar."

I think I cut him for about eleven stitches over his eye, broke his cheekbone, knocked out a couple of teeth, and broke his jaw. That was all accomplished with three punches. Eddie told Frank, "He warned me."

Later on in my career, Eddie got picked up on waivers the same year I did in Buffalo, and we became good friends.

One night we were sitting in my house having a glass of wine after dinner, not really talking about anything from the past, just stupid stuff, and my middle daughter—at the time she was probably about six—came over to Eddie and very innocently said, "Mr. Hospodar, can I ask you a question?"

And he said, "Sure honey, what is it?"

She went, "Did you ever get any of your teeth knocked out?"

Eddie looked at me like, "You —hole. You set her up for that?"

I said, "No, to be honest with you I had nothing to do with it, but that's pretty funny." We're still really good friends to this day.

The Patrick Division Final

The Isles narrowly escaped the underdog Pittsburgh Penguins in a classic Patrick Division semifinal, while journeyman goaltender Eddie Mio led the Blueshirts past the Flyers, granting Herb Brooks a chance to pull off the impossible yet again, in "The Expressway Series, Part IV."

Judging by the furious opening 20 minutes of Game One, Thursday, April 15, 1982, at the Coliseum, the Apple was in store for a doozy. There were 23 combined shots, three goals a side, and enough hitting to set off a seismograph.

Brooks replaced Mio with Steve Weeks to start the second period, and the former 11th-round pick from Scarborough, Ontario, made his coach look like a genius, kicking and batting away 14 Islanders shots in the frame. The Blueshirts carried a 4–3 lead into the middle of the third, when Duane Sutter ran into Weeks, sparking another Metropolitan-area melee. All six Rangers on the ice were given 10-minute misconducts, as were four Islanders.

The siege of Steve Weeks continued until John Tonelli redirected Bob Nystrom's pass over his shoulder to tie the game with just 4:16 to play, sending the fans into delirium. But before the cacophony of applause could peter out, Rangers defenseman Reijo Ruotsalainen, the twenty-two-year-old Finnish product playing his first season in North America, blasted a right-point shot through a Nick Fotiu screen and past Bill Smith with 1:58 to go, to put the Blueshirts up 5–4. Now it was the Rangers fans who were dancing in the aisles.

Weeks made one last terrific save—his 28th in two periods—to secure the upset win.

It was the first victory of any kind for the Rangers in Nassau Coliseum since Anders Hedberg's late goal in Game Five of the 1979 semifinals, a series that was now on the Isles' minds again as they looked to avoid Déjà Blueshirt."

Fortunately for them, there was limited time to worry about such things, since Game Two was the very next evening, Friday, April 16. Denis Potvin, Bryan Trottier, and Mike Bossy combined for eight points in a 7–2 slapping that was never close. Westward Ho! We were on to Madison Square Garden, with the series tied at one.

The ticket scalpers were out early, three hours before the opening faceoff of Game Three—Sunday night, April 18, 1982—and the crowd was already loud as the Rangers hit the ice for warm-ups. Brooks went back to Eddie Mio, and the Islanders greeted him rudely, sending 19 rubbers his way through two periods and taking a 2–1 lead to the room.

But in the opening moments of the third, Reijo Ruotsalainen skated the puck past Denis Potvin and blasted a 25-foot slap shot by Billy Smith to bring down the house. Three minutes later, Rangers forward Mike Allison faked Islanders defender Dave Langevin and fired a left-circle shot through Smith's legs to give his team a 3–2 lead. End-to-end action

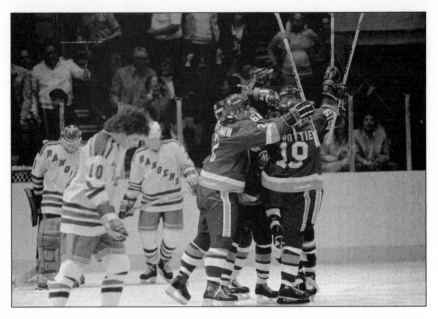

Bryan Trottier and the Isles celebrate after Trottier's game-winning goal in Game Three of the 1982 Patrick Division Finals. *(AP Photo/G. Paul Burnett)*

ensued until a Bob Bourne backhander at 8:26 knotted the matter at three, sending it to overtime.

The homeboys received a big hand and a "Let's Go Rangers" chant at the outset, but the crowd could've saved its breath, since this period of hockey wound up lasting as long as a round of boxing (three minutes exactly). The Sultan of Skates himself, Bryan Trottier, delivered the knockout blow, stunning Mio with a long, spinning, bad-angle backhander to give Long Island a 2–1 series lead.

THE MAVEN REMEMBERS: OH MY, WOE IS MIO

Every champion needs a series-turner to maintain momentum.

Bryan Trottier was the quintessential Islander when it came to that role, and no game epitomized it more than Game Three of the 1982 Patrick Division Finals.

As the overtime began—and ended—I was reminded of the story about the snail that was mugged by two turtles. When the cops came and asked the snail what happened, he replied, "I don't know, it happened so fast."

And so it did. About ten seconds before the three-minute mark, Trottier won a faceoff back to Ken Morrow on defense. Eddie Mio made the save, but the puck dropped on the goalie's doorstep and Trottier was right there to put it in.

Of course we didn't know it at the time, but Trots's goal would catapult the Islanders to a four-games-to-two series win over the Blueshirts.

With Game Four the very next evening—Monday, April 19—Herb Brooks surprised everyone by pulling Mio in favor of the Islanders' kryptonite, John Davidson, even though JD had not played in six months! The hero of the 1979 upset was no doubt being pawned for inspiration. Others called it *des*peration. Either way, the experiment came to an end at 13:08 of the second period, when Davidson re-injured his leg trying unsuccessfully to prevent a Clark Gillies tap-in and a 3–2 Islanders lead.

In one of the most unbelievable "go figure" moments of the series, Blueshirts bruiser Cam Conner, proud owner of nine career NHL goals, beat Denis Potvin to a loose puck in front of Smith and tickled the twine at 6:19 of the third to tie the game. But for the second year in a row, Duane Sutter delivered a Game Four MSG classic for the Islanders, knocking a Wayne Merrick pass out of midair at the Rangers' line, racing in on a semi-breakaway, withstanding a Dave Maloney trip, and sliding the puck underneath goaltender Steve Weeks while falling to the ice at 12:27.

Sutter sat on his knees and raised his arm in a sarcastic victory salute to the quiet crowd. Butch Goring added an empty-netter, and the champions held on, 5–3.

Arbour and his crew looked to finish up two nights later at home, but Eddie Mio made 29 saves in his remarkable return to the Blueshirt pipes, propelling the visitors to a 4–2 win and the series back to Manhattan. Herbie's hustlers had life yet.

On Friday, April 23, 1982, the rejuvenated Garden crowd rued and roared while the Isles and Rangers alternated their way to a 3–3 mid-third-period deadlock. With a tad over six minutes to play, Merrick won an offensive zone draw to Dave Langevin at left point. Not known as much of a shooter, Langevin inhaled, closed his eyes, and let go a high slapper over Mio's shoulder at 13:52. It was the fourth time that the Islanders took the lead in this ping-pong-like game, and for Langevin, it was his second goal of the series while only his third of the season. Shocking.

Time and again, the Rangers gained the Islanders' zone in pursuit of the equalizer, but Billy Smith wouldn't hear of it. With three minutes left, Reijo Ruotsalainen snuck into the low slot from his point position and took a Robbie Ftorek feed for what was sure to be the tying goal, but Smith gloved the 12-foot try spectacularly as the crowd stopped just short of erupting. It was arguably the best save of Smith's Hall-of-Fame career.

Islanders center Bobby Bourne officially ended the 1981–82 Rangers with an empty-net strike from the neutral zone to make it 5–3.

The fans rose in unison to give the Rangers a standing ovation before the ensuing faceoff and a hearty "Let's Go Rangers" after the final horn. It had been a marvelous season for the Blueshirts, but it was the Islanders who ultimately walked away with another championship.

BENCHMARK GAME: LONG SHOTS BY A LONG SHOT

April 23, 1982
Madison Square Garden

Islanders 5 Rangers 3
(4–2) (2–4)

Game Six of the 1982 Patrick Division Finals was a game most Rangers rooters did not expect to see once the Islanders took Games Two, Three, and Four.

Equally surprising was the identity of the man who finally did the Rangers in, and the distance from which he did it.

At the time, Islanders defenseman Dave Langevin had five regular season goals to his name, including only two in the past two seasons, a total the twenty-seven-year-old St. Paul, Minnesota, native equaled during this series alone.

In the first period of the fortnight, Langevin took a routine slapper from just over the red line that hit the ice in front of goal-tender Eddie Mio and skipped past his left pad. And in the final period of the series, Langevin tried a slapper from a tad closer, but still way far—the blue line at left point—and beat Mio again to give the Islanders the "whole kit 'n' caboodle."

Solving the Puzzle

With the dirty work behind them, the Islanders swept a pair of sub-standard opponents, the Quebec Nordiques and the Vancouver Canucks, for the heralded "Cup Trick." To the Rangers, these annual Hempstead Turnpike ticker-tape parades were getting tedious.

Little Brother had not only eliminated Big Brother on back-to-back tries but now summoned a word that was previously reserved in New York sports for baseball's Yankees and the Yankees alone. But now there was no denying it. The Islanders were a dynasty. *And* they still owed the Rangers money.

Worst of all, the Blueshirts fancied themselves good enough to win it all . . . if not for those execrable Islanders, perpetually in their way.

What else was holding the Garden men back? They had deep offense, with perennial point machine Mike Rogers, revitalized heart-throb Ron Duguay, super-scoring U.S. Olympic hero Mark Pavelich, All-Star Eddie Johnstone, and the ever-dependable Don Maloney, not to mention Ruotsalainen's roughly 60-plus points a year from the backline. They had defensive stalwarts like Ron Greschner, Dave Maloney, stout U.S. Olympian Bill Baker, and terrific captain Barry Beck. Their coach was a living legend, an American icon.

The Rangers improved their regular season record to 3–4–0 against the dynasty in 1982–83. It was an improvement, but not enough to snap an eight-year Islanders unbeaten streak in the Battle of New York.

"We're getting closer," warned Coach Herb Brooks. "We're getting closer."

Observers had reason to agree. Goals in the seven-game set were even, 21–21, and the three Rangers wins were momentous. Pavelich buried a hat trick in a 7–3 shellacking at the Garden on November 21. Six days later, Mio became the first goalie to shut out the Islanders on Coliseum ice in almost three years. And with four minutes left on March 16, 1983, Ruotsalainen scored a highlight-reel, game-winning goal in the Garden that Brooks called "a classic."

After sweeping the first-place Flyers in the opening round of the 1983 playoffs, Herb and his elated Blueshirts floated through the midtown tunnel on Thursday, April 14, 1983, to take on the triple-defending champions in the 1983 Patrick Division Finals, "The Expressway Series, Part V."

Billy Smith made 19 stops for the Islanders in Game One—many in spectacular fashion—and the crowd enjoyed them all, chanting his name throughout the game. Any rumbling of "Let's Go Rangers" was immediately snuffed out by "19–40!" Third-period goals by Denis Potvin and the brothers Sutter (Brent and Duane) made it a lovely 4–1 evening for the Islanders.

Game Two came one night later, with the Isles short a pair of injured Hall-of-Famers—Clark Gillies and Bryan Trottier.

No problem.

Smith gobbled 23 shots in a 5–0 whitewashing. More than 15,000 suburbanites sang their tonsils out, with the game at no point in doubt. The third period may as well have been dubbed "Al Arbour & the 19–40 Chorus."

But not so fast.

In Game Three, the Rangers broke their five-game home playoff losing streak against their rivals in scatterbrain fashion, jumping ahead 7–2 after two periods, before holding on for a wild 7–6 win. Bossy actually poked the puck into the net in the final seven seconds to cap a would-be five-goal third-period Islanders rally, but referee Bruce Hood lost sight of the puck and blew the whistle right before Boss's "soda goal" was to make the score "7-Up."

"Ed-dee! Ed-dee!" wailed the crowd one night later, serenading goaltender Eddie Mio minutes prior to Game Four. Mio paid back the Blueshirts faithful with 36 saves and a 3–1 win. *Oh Dio*, that Mio! We were tied, 2–2.

The Islanders ran away with a 7–2 win in Game Five at the Coliseum for a 3–2 series lead. The term "rout" does not begin to describe the effort, as shots through two periods were 35–9 Long Island.

The exclamation point was an end-to-end rush by Islanders speedster Bobby Bourne, who took the puck from teammate Tomas Jonsson behind his own net, flew by two Rangers forwards, blew past Barry Beck at the attacking blue line, undressed Reijo Ruotsalainen in the high slot, and beat Mio from the left circle at 18:35 to make it 5–1.

Bourne's linemate, Duane Sutter, called it "the prettiest goal I have ever seen." Rangers goalie John Davidson called it "a work of art."

The puck's entire trip, from the Islanders goal line to the back of the Rangers net, took exactly six seconds. Bourne was simply a blur. "I went home and watched it 10 or 12 times," Bourne admitted. "And every time I watched it, I got really excited. I looked at where the players were on the ice. I looked at the fans. I'll save that tape for the rest of my life."

THE MAVEN REMEMBERS: MY BUDDY BOURNE BOBS AND WEAVES TO A SCORE

Before the term "highlight-reel goal" was coined, one of the most spectacular of that genre was orchestrated by Bob Bourne of the Islanders.

That it happened in a playoff game, April 20, 1983, and with the series tied at two apiece, made it Special *Deluxe*.

I was fond of Bob for many reasons:

1) He was just an all-around good guy, with no pretensions;
2) He spoke his mind and therefore was a terrific interview, game in and game out. As SportsChannel's interviewer, I needed top talkers like horses need oats;
3) Bourne was the fastest skater on the team, give or take a live rabbit.

Nevertheless, my expectations for anyone—let alone Bob—never included what I was about to see. Kid Lightning weaved around

> the Rangers like a pinball wending its way to the bottom flippers, bisected defensemen Reijo Ruotsalainen and Barry Beck, swooped in on goalie Eddie Mio, and made it look like it was a goal he could score every single night.
>
> Matter of fact, I can still hear the roar of the crowd.

A Drive to Remember

And so the Rangers and Isles found themselves exactly where they'd been one year prior on the fourth Friday night in April, at MSG. Once again, they began Game Six of the second round with the champs looking to close it out.

Instead of an unlikely hero such as Dave Langevin, this time the Isles turned to a usual suspect, Butch Goring, who broke a 2–2 tie with a right circle wrister at 5:21 of the third—his second goal and third point of the contest. Brent Sutter and Ken Morrow added tallies to suck the final breath out of the building and the Blueshirts. For the third year in a row, the Rangers were on the waiting-end of an all-New York handshake line.

Not only had they given their faithful a 43rd consecutive year without the Cup, but in the coming weeks, their rivals rolled through the Boston Bruins and speedy Edmonton Oilers to etch their names in Lord Stanley's silver stein yet again. In just 11 years of existence, the Nassau-men now owned what the Rangers could not gather in 57—a fourth championship. It burned.

1983–84

The Rangers had absolutely seen enough. Early in the following campaign, it showed in their play.

They opened the season on a 7–1–0 tear before bussing into Uniondale to kick off what ultimately would become, game for game, the greatest single season in the history of the Islanders-Rangers rivalry, 1983–84.

- On October 22, 1983, at the Coliseum, the Rangers tallied only their third regular-season victory in Nassau in their last 23 tries!

- The following evening, October 23, at the Garden, the Islanders erased a 5–2 deficit with one of the most amazing rallies in hockey history, only to squander the effort.

Starting at 15:15 of the third, Denis Potvin, Bryan Trottier, and Bob Bourne beat Rangers goalie Glen Hanlon in a matter of 27 seconds.

But in overtime, rookie winger Peter Sundstrom spared the Rangers the embarrassment and their fans an emotional breakdown by converting a two-on-one break with Dave Maloney, improving the Blueshirts to a league-best 9–1–0.

They would quickly cool off.

- On December 17 at the Coliseum, the first-place Islanders went nuts in the final 9:25 of the third period, turning a 2–1 lead into a 7–1 slaughter.

- On January 8 at the Garden, Don Maloney scored with 1:31 to go in regulation to cap a frantic, thrilling, back-and-forth barn burner of a 5–4 Rangers win.

- On January 14 at the Coliseum, Mike Bossy ripped his 400th career goal off a hard pass from Butch Goring in the third period of a 4–2 victory. Vintage Boss.

- On February 15 at the Garden, one of the most popular Blueshirts—the seldom-scoring skull smasher from Staten Island, Nick Fotiu—tipped in the game-winner at 13:08 of the third for a 3–2 Rangers triumph.

Herb Brooks's skaters moved atop the Patrick Division with the win. Before then, they had not held sole possession of first place that late in the season since February 15, 1970.

Also, with their fourth win over the Islanders, the Rangers clinched victory in the regular-season Battle of New York for the first time since 1975.

- On February 18 at the Coliseum, the Isles' Brent Sutter outdid the late-game heroics of Sundstrom, Maloney, and Fotiu by breaking a 3–3 tie with not a moment more than six seconds to play!

His deflection ignited two distinct streaks in New York—a very good one to the east, and a very bad one to the west.

Brooks's boys went 2–7–1 over their next 10 games to drop to fourth place, while Arbour's army finished 15–4–2 to wrap up a hard-earned division title.

The Islanders' secret? A pair of Pats, as in winger Pat Flatley and center Pat LaFontaine, first-round picks in 1982 and 1983, respectively. The youngsters joined the team in late February and spearheaded the Islanders' quest for another championship, or what media folk coined "The Drive for Five."

The "Drive" would begin on Long Island with yet another Rangers grudge match. The difference was, in that it was a first-round series, "Part VI" would be best-of-five instead of seven. Perhaps this would favor the underdogs from Manhattan.

"Thou Shalt Not Covet Thy Neighbor's Goods," read a sign in the Coliseum crowd before Game One on Thursday, April 4, 1984, next to a picture of the Stanley Cup.

In a game of hard hits, high sticks, and plenty of fighting, the Islanders steamrolled the Rangers and goalie Glen Hanlon—Broadway's fourth different *número uno* in five years!—to the tune of 4–1. LaFontaine and Flatley set each other up for goals, while Dave Langevin skipped his father's funeral in Minnesota to play and record two assists.

The momentum carried into Game Two the following night, but twenty-seven-year-old Hanlon played the game of his life, making 45 saves in the 3–0 blanking.

The tone was set 1:19 in, when Hanlon speared what looked like a sure goal off the stick of Brent Sutter. "I was lucky," quipped the marvelous Manitoban.

Minutes later, Hanlon slid across the crease to pluck one of Mike Bossy's patented left-circle wristers out of mid-air, or as the laid-back journeyman netminder described it, "no big deal."

It was the Isles' first postseason shutout loss since 1980, a stretch of 64 games. Asked if he had ever had a day like that before, Hanlon replied, "Once. On a golf course."

A golf course is where the Islanders appeared to be heading after the Manhattan-men crushed them at the Garden in Game Three, 7–2, smothering the quadruple-champions to within a game of elimination. The midtown attack was led by their season's two leading scorers, Mark Pavelich, with a goal and two assists, and Pierre Larouche, with a pair of lamp-lighters.

Arbour put a gag order on his wounded troops after the game, but a few sound bites got out, including this less-than-cryptic message from Bryan Trottier: "I wouldn't want to be the Rangers tomorrow night."

But to the 17,369 fans who spun the Game Four turnstiles on Monday night, April 4, 1984, this was *the* night for them and their Rangers. After three straight years of crosstown humiliation and four straight Hempstead Turnpike parades, something had to give. Right?

When the Garden-men came out for the third period with a 1–0 lead, anything seemed possible. The roar of the crowd reverberated around the stadium: "LET'S-GO-RAN-GERS!"

"Our hearts were in our throats," admitted Islander wiz, Bobby Bourne.

On the second shift of the frame, Patrick Flatley and Brent Sutter went behind Glen Hanlon's net to trap Rangers rookie defenseman James Patrick, who panicked and put the biscuit on the black stick-tape of John Tonelli, to tie the game at 1–1.

Ten minutes later, Flatley drilled Barry Beck into the boards, re-injuring the Rangers captain's shoulder. Adding insult to Beck's injury, Brent Sutter flipped in the game-winning goal while the Blueshirts' burly All-Star defenseman lay face down.

The Isles went on to a 4–1 win, thanks to 29 saves by Battling Billy, setting up rivalry Armageddon, the first winner-take-all Islanders-Rangers playoff game since 1975—this time in Nassau, on April 10, 1984. What nobody yet knew was how this Game Five would somehow match the intensity and drama of the Rangers' furious comeback and J.P. Parise's instant overtime classic nine years prior.

Rangers defenseman Ron Greschner opened the scoring with a genuine beauty at 12:06 of the first, making two All-Time-Great Hall-of-Famers look like children when he spun around Denis Potvin in the right wing corner, cut across goalie Bill Smith with Potvin hooking him, then pulled the puck to his backhand to softly tuck it in. It was the move that widely came to be known as the "Peter Forsberg Team Sweden Olympics shootout," only ten years before Peter Forsberg ever tried it.

Not to be "out-amazing-ed," Mike Bossy stripped Rangers defenseman Tom Laidlaw, slid the puck between Laidlaw's legs, and schooled goalie Glen Hanlon to equalize with just 11 seconds to go in the opening frame.

The Rangers took a 23–10 shots advantage after two periods, but Billy Smith kept the score 1–1.

At 7:56 of the third, Isles winger Duane Sutter curled out of the left wing corner and found weak side blueliner Tomas Jonsson creeping in for an open wrist shot and a 2–1 lead. Just about two minutes later, John Tonelli raced down ice on a shorthanded breakaway, but Hanlon made a sprawling stop to preserve the one-goal deficit.

On the other end, Smith could do no wrong. The spaghetti-thin margin held into the game's final minute, when Herb Brooks pulled his goalie for an extra attacker.

With 45 seconds to go and the crowd screaming its collective head off, Don Maloney found Mark Pavelich wide open in the slot. Pavelich spun and skeeted an almost perfect shot. Smith kicked out his right pad, and the Islanders cleared the puck just over the blue line.

James Patrick carried the puck back in for the Rangers. Ken Morrow decimated him with a hip-check. Yet while falling, Patrick managed to lay the puck off for Pavelich, who streaked through the circles and whipped another low snapper.

Smith popped the puck up into the air . . .

Don Maloney swatted down at the airborne puck and found nothing but net!

Can he do that?!?

Apparently, yes. Referee Dave Newell signaled goal!

The few Rangers-rooters in the audience were beside themselves with glee. The rest of the crowd was furious. The Islanders were certain Maloney's shoulder-height chop was a high stick. Denis Potvin spared none of his adult words while addressing the matter with Newell. It didn't matter. For the fifth time in their now-illustrious postseason history, the Isles and Rangers were headed to overtime. One goal for the series. One goal to end the Drive for Five, or send it racing toward the home stretch. One goal for all of New York.

Oh, and by the way, those four previous overtimes had all gone to the suburbanites. Talk about being overdue.

Neither team stood at the edge of the pool and dipped its toes in. They dove in head first, fast and hard. The action, most hockey historians agree, was as good as the sport has ever offered.

Potvin once again was brilliant, to the dismay of Rangers loyalists. He dove to block a Reijo Ruotsalainen chance from the slot that appeared destined to land a quick Rangers win. Then Bobby Bourne sped through the neutral zone, no doubt eliciting Blueshirts nightmares from the previous season. He galloped past the entire team again, but Hanlon was able to glove his dangerous backhand shot.

Next, Smith made an accidental save while being nearly decapitated by the mass of bodies crashing for the rebound. Bossy wound up for three drives on the same shift, but Hanlon and the Rangers somehow survived. Later, Boss missed the net on a three-on-one break. Both teams were living on the edge.

With over eight minutes played, the Maloney brothers executed a wonderful two-on-two rush, with Dave springing Don for a semi-breakaway.

Smith made an incredible toe-save, robbing the Blueshirts of certain victory. The crowd let out a loud sigh of relief.

Denis Potvin collected the rebound and wisely started the Islanders the other way. The fans again began to get excited . . .

The puck got caught up between Tonelli and Dave Maloney at the Rangers line, so the two old warriors tackled each other.

The three principles—Tonelli, Maloney, and the puck—slid into the left wing corner, taking down Rangers center Larry Patey in domino fashion. The noise got louder . . .

As Patey stumbled over the pileup, he turned the puck over to Brent Sutter on the half-wall. The anticipation grew even louder . . .

Sutter fought through Patey's trip to crank a one-legged slapper that made a SMACK off Hanlon's goal-stick. The crowd groaned, "OHHH!"

Ruotsalainen quickly cleared to the weak side, but alas, the weak side had no Rangers. A hopeful roar . . .

Heady Islanders stay-at-home defenseman Kenny Morrow one-timed the puck off the boards, like a squash player—a roller—under teammate Pat Flatley's screen, and under Hanlon's pads. CRESCENDO!!!

The escalating energy erupted as the Islanders sealed the 3–2 victory.

THE MAVEN REMEMBERS: SURROUNDED BY RANGERS, GOAL BY MORROW

Many savvy observers have said that the decisive Game Five of the Rangers-Islanders playoff at Nassau Coliseum ranked among the finest NHL games ever played.

Broadcasting for *SportsChannel*, I saw most of the game from my arena perch. But with the Islanders leading 2–1 in the third, I had to repair to our studio.

But you know what they say about the "best laid plans." With less than a minute remaining, Don Maloney scored for the Rangers, and the game went into overtime.

You have to understand that my interview room at the Coliseum was located a mere twenty yards from the Rangers' dressing room. And since our room had the only monitor from which to watch the game, the Rangers players who were either injured or scratched for the match drifted into our little alcove. And since we were broadcasting for the Islanders, we wanted no part of any Ranger in our abode.

That's easy to say, but the two Blueshirts who planted themselves in front of the TV monitor happened to be Nick Fotiu and Barry Beck. Both men were conspicuously large, tough, and also friends of mine. There was no way they could be escorted out the door.

So, when Maloney delivered the tying goal, Beck and Fotiu invited themselves back to watch the overtime.

The overtime began, and as it unfolded there were screams of joy and sadness as saves were made by Billy Smith and the Rangers continued to press the attack, almost scoring several times.

When Ken Morrow's shot eluded the Blueshirts' defenders and goalie Glen Hanlon, Fotiu and Beck bolted from the room as if shot from a howitzer. Once they were out of earshot, those of us who were part of the Islanders' TV crew finally vented our exultation.

Morrow, the unsung hero, was mobbed by his ecstatic teammates, newly christened winners of 17 playoff series in a row, including four over the Rangers.

It was one of hockey's best plays. It was one of hockey's best overtimes. It was one of hockey's best games.

But the Rangers had no appetite for the romance of this remarkable moment. As the Isles congratulated one another in the home dressing room, the Blueshirts sat quietly down the hall, pondering familiar questions. Or, to paraphrase William Shakespeare, "There is much virtue in if."

What if a half-inch here? What if a quarter-inch there?

And what, oh what, in the wide world of Red Dutton, do we have to do to get past the Islanders?

BENCHMARK GAME: THE PUCK WILL COME OUT, TO-MORROW

April 10, 1984
Nassau Coliseum

Rangers 2 Islanders 3
(2–3) (3–2)

There are good games, great games, classic games, and legendary games, and then a rung above all that—amid a handful of others in a compression-sealed, gold-plated, Burmese-crystal container on the top shelf of the beautiful armoire that is NHL history—is Game Five of the 1984 Patrick Division Semifinals.

"It was the best game I've ever seen," gushed celebrated sports anchor Warner Wolf on his CBS local news recap. "Without question."

How first-rate, discipline-loving head coaches such as Al Arbour and Herb Brooks ever allowed their teams to play so fast and loose in a deciding extra session was a wonderful mystery.

Here is how three of the men who were there—Maloney, Flatley, and Isles third goalie Kelly Hrudey—describe the thrilling conclusion of "The Classic":

Flatley: *In that 1984 series, Billy Smith had to have a bodyguard when we went to the city to play in the Garden.*

Maloney: *The Islanders were winning Cups. You just wanted to beat them so badly at the time because they were so good and won so often.*

Flatley: *The Rangers always had good teams under Herb Brooks. And we had good teams, too. It definitely amps up the intensity when both teams have a legitimate chance to win the Stanley Cup.*

Maloney: *Al Arbour thought that was as good a played five games as there ever was the entire time he was with the Islanders.*

Hrudey: *It was frantic and intense hockey.*

Maloney: *Tying the game late the way we did—that was pure ecstasy. For 15 minutes, while it lasted.*

Flatley: *I remember exactly what happened. Brent Sutter and I were behind the net. The puck went back to Kenny Morrow. He had a very heavy shot. Thank God it went in. The crowd was insane.*

Hrudey: *That's why that Islander team could perform so well for so long, because they could handle that. And they didn't get caught up in the emotion of it. You look at some of the Islanders' amazing comebacks during their four consecutive Cup streak, and they found every way to win. It wasn't just always leading. They had to come from behind. They had to win in overtime. They had to win trailing series. That was a remarkably tough team mentally.*

Chapter 5

TRANSITION

"The fans in the Garden get your energy boiling. The momentum of an Islander-Ranger game builds all day. You can feel it in the streets. They're always Game Seven playoff environments."

—Islanders/Rangers forward Patrick Flatley

"When you go out on the ice, it's the Islanders against the Rangers, period. The people in the stands feel it, and they make you feel it."

—Islanders defenseman Denis Potvin

"I understood very quickly how intense the rivalry was."

—Rangers defenseman Randy Moller

"I tried to make a trade with the Islanders, but I couldn't trade with them, because the Islanders didn't want to trade with us, and really, we didn't want to trade with them."

—Rangers forward/General Manager Phil Esposito

"This being my final game here, it crossed my mind several times what kind of farewell address to give them. Then I decided that kind of message wasn't appropriate."

—Islanders defenseman Denis Potvin

The 1984 Rangers failed to halt the Nassau Dynasty Machine. But they did leave a significant dent, for what that was worth.

Consecutive Series Victory Number 17 was physically grueling and an emotional purge on the wounded Islanders, who gutted out Series Wins 18 and 19 and returned to the Stanley Cup Finals for a fifth straight year, where they were dethroned by hockey's new dynasty—the Edmonton Oilers, led by "The Great One," Wayne Gretzky, and his sidekick, Mark Messier.

Thus died the valiant "Drive for Five." Long Island fans were disappointed, yet proud of all their team had accomplished. Across town? Relief, with a natural dose of *Schadenfreude*.

On paper, the Islanders and the Rangers attacked in 1984–85 with virtually the same teams. But the players who had dueled so beautifully in the marvelous ice-poetry that was the 1984 Patrick Division Semifinals could not find that gear just six months later.

The season was a dud, on both sides of the river. The Islanders finished third in the Patrick—7.5 games behind the second-place Washington Capitals.

As for the Rangers, their season was in jeopardy from the start. Through the first 14 weeks of the season, 23 Rangers suffered 37 different injuries—everything from torn knees to broken legs. One defenseman, Tom Laidlaw, lost his spleen.

This did not bode well for Coach Herb Brooks, who was in the final year of his contract. Every loss brought only more pressure, and he finally lashed out, criticizing his veteran players in a January 7 *New York Times* article. The piece claimed two sources heard Brooks call defenseman Barry Beck a coward.

Beck read the article.

He went to practice, found Brooks, and yelled his lungs out. The coach yelled back. The Rangers captain broke a bunch of hockey sticks and chucked a garbage can onto the ice. It was officially a bad season.

On January 21, 1985, Rangers general manager Craig Patrick fired Brooks and took over. That didn't work, either. The team soon went through a long drought that dropped their record to 17–30–9.

The Rangers hadn't been that bad since 1975–76. The Islanders hadn't been so average since 1973–74. With frustrations mounting, the teams fell back on something they'd always been good at—bopping each other.

Four of the seven crosstown meetings in 1984–85 spun certifiably out of control. Leading the way early for the Rangers, surprisingly enough, was 170-pound rookie forward George McPhee, who jumped up in weight class to fight the Isles' 195-pound Pat Flatley on October 30 in Uniondale, 215-pound Dave Langevin on November 9 in Manhattan, and 200-pound Bobby Nystrom on February 7 at the Coliseum, in one of the most frenetic, freewheeling fistfights you'll ever see.

At the end of the battle, Nystrom was ejected for headbutting McPhee, like a ram in the wilderness, though McPhee had headbutted Nystrom first. It was a scene more befitting *National Geographic* than *SportsChannel*.

THE MAVEN REMEMBERS: THE BOUT OF THE CENTURY, BOB NYSTROM VS. GEORGE MCPHEE

Rangers forward George McPhee may have been a second line player, but he was notorious as a first-class fighter (and this on a relatively small stature). If one labeled McPhee "The Toy Bulldog," it wouldn't be a bad description.

The Islanders found this out soon enough when the much larger Dave Langevin engaged Little George in a bout that the Isles' defenseman would love to forget. So, you can imagine that McPhee's boxing rep was held in the highest regard in the Islanders' room.

Of course, the Nassau-men had a few fair pugilists of their own, not the least of whom was Bob Nystrom. So when Nystrom and McPhee dropped their gloves on the night of February 7, 1985, at Nassau Coliseum, the capacity crowd would see a fight to end all NHL fights.

By any estimation you would have to call it a draw, except for one thing—the bout was broken up by linesmen right after Nystrom uncharacteristically headbutted his foe.

Knowing Nystrom as I did, I was somewhat annoyed by the fact that Bobby would resort to such a tactic. Then again, as they say, "All's fair in love and war," and we all know that hockey is a war game on ice.

As the years drifted by, I would tell hockey fight fans that I saw one for the ages but always added a postscript about my dismay over the headbutting.

Then, one day I was in Washington, D.C., for an Islanders game and guess who was GM of the Caps—none other than George McPhee. Since George had some time on his hands, we started to talk about this and that, until I brought up the fact that his fight with Nystrom was a classic. Then the conversation went like this:

"I have to tell you, George, I was disappointed that Bobby ended it by headbutting you."

Then, a pause and a smile curled across McPhee's face.

"Why are you smiling?"

"Because what you didn't know is that I headbutted him first!"

But all that was nothing compared to the anarchy of February 17, 1985, at Madison Square Garden.

Young Islanders goaltender Kelly Hrudey was beaten by seven different Rangers in the first two periods. The home squad was up five goals. The visitors were fed up. So at 19:25 of the second, a tussle between Steve Patrick and Bryan Trottier at John "Beezer" Vanbiesbrouck's right post quickly escalated to a ten-man pileup.

In the eyes of Trottier's linemates, 6-foot-4, 205-pound Patrick was an unappealing suitor for the 5-foot-11 Hall-of-Famer, and they crashed the party—hard—turning Vanbiesbrouck's crease into an amateur game of rugby (without the ball). After 20 seconds of horseplay, foes began to disperse, but Tomas Sandstrom would not let go of Clark Gillies. Terrible idea.

POP! Down went Sandstrom—his nose a bloody souvenir of Gillies's right hand.

Passions were reignited. Steve Richmond grabbed Gillies for a tangle in the left-wing corner. Duane Sutter paired off with Sandstrom, Paul Boutilier with James Patrick, and Stefan Persson wrestled Mike Rogers.

Beezer was a *voyeur*, while Hrudey stood at center ice, waiting for any excuse to pounce.

"I was right at center," he remembers, "because the goalie can't cross center ice. When he does, something bad is going to happen."

But Hrudey *wanted* something bad to happen. Having surrendered seven goals, the twenty-four-year-old Edmonton kid was ready for a shower.

Vanbiesbrouck started a conversation with Duane Sutter at the top of the crease. "That grabbed my attention," says Hrudey.

Sutter felt the same, so he grabbed Beezer's facemask and yanked him toward the goal line. Next, to everyone's surprise, the typically well-mannered Beezer swung!

Sutter was irate. *The nerve of this goalie!* He reached for his attacker, but Sandstrom intervened. The crowd noise grew to a sonorous pitch. Vanbiesbrouck had no idea why. He stared Sutter down, turned to his left, and . . .

The last person in the building to notice Kelly Hrudey charging John Vanbiesbrouck was John Vanbiesbrouck. By the time he looked up, Hrudey was two feet away, skating about 150 miles per hour.

CRACK! One right cross under Beezer's cage. WHOOSH! Ripped the thing off! The bandana-wearing bopper dragged Beezer into the left-wing corner, landed three right jabs, and tackled him.

On the Rangers bench, George McPhee stood barehanded in the open door. He and his teammates were ready to charge. Meanwhile, Steve Richmond tried to get at . . . anyone, but linesman John D'Amico managed to pull the feisty defenseman all the way to center by tugging at his jersey.

Back at the goal line, linesman Ron Finn helped referee Andy Van Hellemond peel Hrudey and Vanbiesbrouck apart. The goalies were still chirping. They were hot. Worst of all—they had dinner plans!

"John and I were represented by the same lawyer," explains Hrudey, "and my wife came to New York for that game, and we were going to go have dinner, all of us, after the game.

"So, of course, that was not going to happen anymore."

Van Hellemond handed out 53 penalty minutes and six ejections in one of the lengthiest line-brawls in Islanders-Rangers history. Ultimately, he postponed the final 35 seconds of the period, sent the teams to their locker rooms, and handed out four minors, nine majors, plus game misconducts for Steve Patrick, Gillies, Richmond, Sutter, Hrudey, and Vanbiesbrouck. The third period was quick and relatively relaxing, with plenty of extra room on both benches. The Rangers won, 9–3, handing the Islanders their seventh straight regular season loss in Madison Square Garden. The Isles would break that streak five weeks later, pasting the Rangers 5–2 in the rubber match of the seven-game Battle of New York.

BENCHMARK GAME: HRUDEY AND THE BEEZ

February 17, 1985
Madison Square Garden

Islanders 3 Rangers 9
(30–23–4) (19–30–9)

It was one of the lengthiest line-brawls in Islanders-Rangers history, punctuated by Nassau goalie Kelly Hrudey's 30-yard dash at his unsuspecting counterpart, John Vanbiesbrouck.

But if you thought referee Van Hellemond was in a tough spot, imagine this game from the perspective of Hrudey's and Vanbiesbrouck's attorney, Lloyd Friedland, who suddenly went from enjoying a nice evening with his wife to watching two of his clients punch each other with cages on.

The Friedlands had plans to dine with the goalies and their wives after the game. But this was the furthest thing from either netminder's mind as Kelly was slapping Beezer upside the head.

"All I know is how uncomfortable it would have been after the game," recalls the Isles' bandana-wearing, fist throwing crease-custodian. "We all just thought, 'Maybe tonight's not the best night.'"

A Teaspoon of Magic Left for the Isles

But perhaps the most remarkable—and simultaneously forgettable—factoid from the 1984–85 season was that the 26–44–10 Rangers actually finished fourth in the division, and therefore qualified for the playoffs! It lasted 76 hours, before the first-place Flyers skated off with a three-game sweep.

Meanwhile, Al Arbour's aging soldiers showed they had a teaspoon of magic left in them yet.

Down a pair of games to the favored Capitals, the Isles became the first team in NHL history to come back from 0–2 down in a five-game series. Then they, too, caught the Flyers bug, as the soon-to-be Stanley Cup Finalists from the City of Brotherly Love severed Long Island's streak of Wales Conference championships in round two. For only the second time in 11 years, the Isles would watch the semifinals from home. It appeared their finest days were behind them.

Aside from the incredible Mike Bossy, whose 117-point season included 11 goals and seven assists in seven games against the Rangers, the Islanders' most exciting players were now youngsters Brent Sutter, Flatley, Hrudey, and Pat LaFontaine.

There was turnover across the river, as well. Two days before the start of the next season, new Rangers head coach Ted Sator sent five popular, generally productive veterans—Glen Hanlon, Pierre Larouche, Mike Rogers, Nick Fotiu, and Steve Richmond—to the minor leagues. It was no wonder Craig Wolff of the *New York Times* called it "a transition year" for both clubs. But one thing that hadn't changed was the intensity of the crosstown contests. The games—which they split 3–3–1 in 1985–86—provided more than their share of memorable moments.

- On October 19, 1985, at the Coliseum, budding phenom LaFontaine beat Rangers rookie goalie Terry Kleisinger from the high slot for the game-winner with just 24 seconds left in a 5–4 Islanders home-opening thriller!

- On November 24 at the Garden, the city crowd's hate affair with Islanders goalie Billy Smith reached a passionate peak.

First Battling Billy earned a roughing penalty for administering the ol' stinky-glove face-wash to one Ranger. Then he took a swipe at another and got away with it. Later Smitty jumped up and punched Tomas Sandstrom—to the great surprise of no one, except maybe Sandstrom—after the winger smacked, hacked, and whacked away at his pads, digging for the puck and a go-ahead goal late in the third. "I had to do *something*," reasoned Smith. "Didn't I?!?"

James Patrick attacked Smith. Gord Dineen attacked Patrick. For the rest of the game, the Rangers faithful yelled at Smith with their every last vulgar ounce of spirit. Some threw coins. Some threw worse. Smith kept playing.

Early in overtime, Islanders winger Greg Gilbert intercepted Steve Richmond's ill-advised D-to-D pass and beat rookie goalie Ron Scott for the winner. 4–3 Islanders.

Smith skated out from his goalmouth and waved his stick to the angry crowd. "An insult for an insult," he explained. That's when the jeering really took off.

- On December 20 at the Garden, one particularly unpopular suburban defenseman enjoyed a special evening.

Denis Potvin had tied Bobby Orr's NHL record for most points by a back-liner on December 7, 1985, early in a game against Quebec. But Potvin failed to record another point in the balance of that game, and four others. He was stuck on 915, and the moment was starting to get stale.

It was as if he were waiting for Broadway.

Those fans who trekked through the snowy night prayed *"Please don't let him do it here."* But early in the first, Denis head-manned the puck to exactly the right guy—Bossy—who carried it through the neutral zone and slapped it past John Vanbiesbrouck at 3:38 to give his buddy point number 916, and the record. The Islanders piled on Potvin.

Half the crowd booed their favorite villain heartily. A few stood and cheered. "It's sort of ironic I did it here," joked the jocular defenseman after the game, a 2–2 draw.

But eventually, the midtown fans laughed last in 1985–86.

Winter melted away, the playoffs came around, and the teams finally swapped fortunes, with the Rangers outperforming Potvin, Smith, and the Islanders for the first time since 1979.

The Capitals swept the Isles in the first round, while across town, Ted Sator and 1986 Vezina Trophy winner John Vanbiesbrouck led an upset binge for the ages.

Never mind that first-place Philadelphia finished with 110 points—32 better than the Rangers!—and had won 18 of the previous 19 battles between the teams. The Rangers beat them in five games. And never mind that Washington had 107 points. Sator's Soldiers dismissed them in six, before succumbing to Patrick Roy and the eventual champion Montreal Canadiens in the Wales Conference Finals.

The wonderful performance elevated the Rangers' stature, and with it, expectations for 1986–87. So imagine the surprise when, by November, both Sator and GM Craig Patrick were ex-Blueshirts.

Patrick's summer firing stemmed from personal issues in his family life, which seeped into his work life. The man Madison Square Garden president Jack Krumpe chose to replace him with was the team's TV color commentator, the Godfather himself, Phil Esposito.

Espo tinkered like a man possessed. Out were Reijo Ruotsalainen, Glen Hanlon, Mike Allison, Bob Brooke, Mike Ridley, Kelly Miller, and Bob Crawford. In were Kelly Kisio, Lane Lambert, Walt Poddubny, Tony McKegney, Curt Giles, and the great Marcel Dionne. In November, Esposito fired Sator and replaced him with forty-two-year-old Windsor Spitfires coach Tom Webster. Two months later, Webster stepped down for health reasons. Espo took over for games, while Wayne Cashman and Eddie Giacomin ran practices.

Coaching instability may have been common in the City, but it was virtually unheard of on Long Island, until the summer of 1986, when after 13 remarkable seasons, Al Arbour finally stepped down. GM Bill Torrey hired Terry Simpson, the forty-two-year-old coach of the Prince Albert Raiders.

1986–87

The Islanders and Rangers deadlocked 3–3–1 again in another scintillating regular season series.

Fabulous forward Tomas Sandstrom led the charge for the Rangers with eight points in their three wins, including Garden hat tricks in a 4–3 New Year's Eve overtime thriller and a 7–5 March 4 punch-fest that featured seven fights, two ejections, and 145 penalty minutes.

By March 21, the Blueshirts were in the Coliseum trailing the second-place Isles by only two games and leading the final crosstown contest 3–2 midway through the third period. But LaFontaine struck on a power play at 9:47 and even strength at 15:05 to win the game and spin each team's season in opposite directions.

Thanks in large part to that 4–3 loss, the Rangers drew the powerful Flyers in the first round and were vanquished in six games. Meanwhile, Kelly Hrudey and the Isles went to Washington, where they would color NHL history royal blue and orange yet again, winning the longest Game Seven of all time on a goal by LaFontaine at 8:47 of quadruple overtime. Following that famous "Easter Epic," Simpson's soldiers were edged by Philadelphia four games to three in the Patrick Division Finals.

1987–88

The next rider on the Rangers' coaching carousel was former Quebec Nordiques front man Michel Bergeron, the sixth Broadway bench boss in two and a half years.

At 36–34–10, the 1987–88 Rangers finished with a winning record for the first time since 1983–84 but also missed the playoffs for the first time since 1976–77! Go figure.

The New Jersey Devils took fourth place over the Rangers on the strength of a tie-breaker and took on Terry Simpson's 39–31–10, Patrick Division-champion Islanders in the first round, meaning one more Rangers point in any game that year would have meant Expressway Series number seven.

Instead, New York had to make do with another tight, exciting regular-season series—split 2–2–3 this time—that offered plenty of highlights.

- On November 29, 1987, at the Garden, Rangers goalie Bob Froese became only the second netminder to score a goal . . . at least for five days.

Then on December 4, the league reviewed the tape, stripped the twenty-nine-year-old former Flyers backup of his goal, and awarded it to defenseman David Shaw. "I'm glad it's all been rectified," said Froese. "I never had a secret desire to score a goal."

Ironically, the player who cared most was the man who'd vacated the Islanders net, Billy Smith, who happened to be the first goaltender to ever score. When Isles forward Brent Sutter's errant pass eluded its intended target and went the distance at 8:59 of the second period, it not only stretched the Rangers' lead to 3–1—the eventual final—but it also gave Battling Billy unwanted company in the record book. . . temporarily.

"If he touched it, fine," groaned the ever-surly Smith. "But if he didn't, it shouldn't be allowed."

- On December 29 at the Coliseum, the Islanders rallied for a 3–3 tie with two goals in the final 11 minutes, including one of the hallmark dazzlers of Pat LaFontaine's dazzle-full career.

Patty took a Potvin pass on right wing, split defensemen Jari Gronstrand and Michel Petit with one hand—like Moses parting the sea with a righty-bladed staff—and tore Vanbiesbrouck apart with a backhand deke to tie the game at 17:47.

Potvin called it "one of the prettiest plays I've ever seen."

- On February 2 at the Coliseum, the teams skated, hit, and saved their way to a 2–2 tie in a game both sides described as their most exciting of the year against any opponent. The thriller culminated when Walt Poddubny batted the tying goal past Billy Smith with 40 seconds to play.

- On December 14 at the Garden, Marcel Dionne moved past his own general manager, Phil Esposito, into second place all-time in goals scored with his 718th early in the first period. The faithful were appreciative.

Dionne also closed the scoring with just 6:12 remaining in the third, earning the Blueshirts a 4–4 tie. His career total of 731 has since been surpassed by Wayne Gretzky, Brett Hull, and Jaromir Jagr.

- On March 2 at the Garden, the crowd arrived early to bid a crude, rude, New York farewell to Denis Potvin, who had announced his retirement during training camp and was therefore likely playing in his final game at Madison Square Garden.

"I was convinced there was going to be something original," Potvin goofed after his team was beaten 3–1. "I'm quite disappointed."

The event became less of a hockey game than a mass-group therapy session of 18,000 people getting their deepest, ugliest feelings off their chests. "I never promised anybody that after I played them they would love me," said Denis.

If Potvin's final trip to Broadway didn't by itself signal the end of the rivalry's golden era, then his team's play in subsequent months certainly did.

The aforementioned 1987–88 Devils ambushed Simpson's Islanders in six games in round one. Then Bossy, who had missed the entire season with a back injury, joined Potvin in the retirement circle. The team entered the 1988–89 campaign with a rink-full of question marks, and in pretty short order, those questions were answered in the negative.

1988–89

This next generation of Islanders learned the NHL the hard way, one loss at a time, en route to a 28–47–5 campaign that ended in "LAST-PLACE! *Clap, clap*! LAST-PLACE! *Clap-clap*!" as fans at Madison Square Garden would remind them.

After Bergeron's Blueshirts swept the Isles in a Thanksgiving Weekend home-and-home, Bill Torrey called Al Arbour in the middle of the night and begged him to return to the Islanders bench. On December 6, 1988, Terry Simpson was fired and replaced by Radar.

A week later, Rangers forwards John Ogrodnick and Brian Mullen each beat Billy Smith within a 32-second span to key a 2–1 home win and send the Nassau-men to their 11th consecutive defeat, one shy of the franchise record, which was easily attained the following evening. For the first time since their birth year, the Islanders were at rock bottom.

In fact, the team almost finished with the worst record in all of hockey—and would have, if not for a 6–4 win in the Garden on the last day of the season. With the win, the Islanders swapped draft positions with the Quebec Nordiques, who picked Hall of Famer Mats Sundin first overall. The Islanders took Dave Chyzowski second. *Who?* Exactly. The winger scored 15 career goals for the Islanders.

The third-place Rangers topped the Islanders in the standings for the first time since 1974–75, beat them 5–2–0 in the regular season series, finished with their second-straight winning record at 37–35–8, and boasted the NHL's Rookie of the Year in defenseman Brian Leetch. But general manager Phil Esposito was not close to satisfied.

Espo and Michel Bergeron were not getting along. Espo fired Bergy and took over for the playoffs, where the Blueshirts were cruelly swept by Mario Lemieux and the Pittsburgh Penguins. By the time the final buzzer sounded, it was clear the fire-er was about to become a fire-ee.

An Old Islanders Friend and an Old Islanders Foe Come to Broadway

Esposito was let go in May and replaced by thirty-five-year-old Detroit Red Wings scouting director Neil Smith, a former 13th round Bill Torrey draft pick who had spent eight years in the Islanders organization.

Who could have imagined that this ex-Islander would become among the most hated to Isles fans?

The thin, unobtrusive Smith was charged with finding the Rangers' 15th coach in 16 years. The man he eventually chose, fifty-five-year-old Roger Neilson, had old ties to the Isles as well, though on a decidedly less friendly basis.

See, before the Dynasty Islanders were the Dynasty Islanders, they were perennial upset-bait—considered Softies who cowered to tougher, albeit less talented, clubs such as the 1979 Rangers or the 1978 Toronto Maple Leafs, coached by one Roger Neilson, who some believed oozed with mystical powers, hiding a tough interior.

How physical were Neilson's Leafs in that bitter 1978 quarterfinal series? After Game Two, Clark Gillies told reporters, "It's getting out of hand." Mike Bossy left Game Six on a stretcher. The terms "cheap shots," "chippy," "dirty," "goons," "intimidation hockey," and "violence" were thrown around by players and media throughout. Neilson lapped it up. "We're going to be as rough and mean as we can," bragged the rookie coach. Seasoned media types called it one of the most vicious playoffs. Al Arbour took the high road but never forgot.

In 1982, Neilson used the same methods to coach the Vancouver Canucks—a team with arguably less talent than even the '78 Leafs—all the way to a Stanley Cup Finals date with Arbour's Nassau-men. Again, Bossy was pounded and butchered all over the ice, mostly by Vancouver's Dave "Tiger" Williams. "You know how a Roger Neilson team plays," bemoaned Denis Potvin. The Isles swept, but the games were ugly, to the point George Vecsey of the *New York Times* called the series "as tasteful as a bunch of mugs mauling one another in the alley after too much beer." Torrey described it as "a rugby match," and "the way Roger teaches."

This is what the Islanders thought of Roger Neilson *before* he became head coach of their arch-nemeses.

By now, the Blueshirts had not finished better than third place since 1982 and had not claimed first place since 1942. The Islanders had just missed the playoffs for the first time since 1974. But the rivalry was about to get its edge back, and then some, with one of the rowdiest, cruelest, most entertaining editions yet in 1989–90.

1989–90: The Epitome of Hatred

The fun began with a home-and-home set the final weekend of October. Down 5–2 in the third period Friday night in MSG, the homeboys staged a stunning three-goal rally, capped by a long rush from an unlikely hero, twenty-eight-year-old rookie defenseman Miloslav Horava. The lefty-shooting Czech streaked down right wing and faked out Rich Pilon so badly, the stocky defenseman stopped and dropped as if his Islanders jersey was on fire. Horava walked around Pilon, deked to his backhand, and beat rookie goalie Mark Fitzpatrick at 14:26 for the first goal of his NHL career.

Such grace was starkly contrasted the following night in Uniondale, where Islanders fourth-liner Mick Vukota, himself a "goon" by even the most generous standard, caught top-line Rangers center Carey Wilson with a dangerous knee-on-knee check away from the play. Wilson was sidelined for two months.

The Rangers took revenge by skating circles around the stumbling Islanders, routing their hosts 4–1. But the spice of the evening was a pair of ejections in the final two minutes of the game. Brent Sutter was tossed for cutting Tony Granato with a high stick, and Rangers rookie winger Troy Mallette was given a match penalty for gouging the eye of Islanders defenseman Dean Chynoweth.

Incredibly, this was Chynoweth's second brush with eye-gouging in one year. He had missed the previous season with blurred vision, suffered at the hands—literally—of the Flyers' Rick Tocchet.

Now exactly one year and one day after the Tocchet incident, the 6-foot-3, 220-pound Mallette tackled 6-foot-2, 190-pound Chynoweth at center ice and started punching him in the face. Chynoweth yelled, "Hey, watch it!" Mallette said, "Sorry," and skated off, pointing his fingers at the crowd in a victory sign. But what really happened down in that scrum at center ice? It's a he said-he said situation.

Chynoweth claimed he felt fingernails scratching around his eye. According to Mallette, "His face was right there. I was trying to get some shots in."

The eye was scraped and purple afterward, but the brawny Blueshirts brawler maintained there was no intent to injure. Many viewers doubted that.

Either way, Vukota was not impressed with Mallette or his smug, *WrestleMania*-style celebration. So Big Mick squared off with, and walloped, Rangers tough guy Kris King at 19:36. Then Arbour and Neilson took a minute to catch up . . . right there on the ice.

Al claimed it started with Neilson "yapping" at him after the Mallette incident. So when the game finally ended, he hopped off the bench and turned toward Roger. "You've got a lot of nerve!"

Neilson charged back. Linesman Ray Scampinello grabbed him, while Pat Dapuzzo grabbed Arbour. "Your guy's trying to gouge my guy's eye out," shouted Radar. Referee Denis Morel pushed the coaches apart.

"Roger's a frontrunner," Arbour later snapped. "When his team's doing well, he's great. And when it's the other way, forget about it. He's got a guy who gouged our player again, and he's yapping away."

"It's unfortunate when a team shows their frustration in fisticuff-type ways," mocked Rangers goalie John Vanbiesbrouck. "And it's a proven fact an Al Arbour team will never go down without a fight. The big boys come out and things happen."

Beezer was referring to bruisers like Vukota, Pilon, and Gary Nylund taking shifts in the final minutes of a blowout game. The Rangers believed that Arbour would often dispense these ruffians with malice aforethought.

This would become a major theme in the months ahead.

"That's our style," explained Pilon. "To say, 'You might beat us but you're not going to kick us when we're down.' We wanted to make sure they know that next time."

Mallette was fined $500 but not suspended. The Islanders were not happy.

The next match—November 12 at the Garden—was less physical, though intense and bizarre in its own way.

It started when the Islanders noticed something they thought they could use to their advantage. The great Blueshirt power play quarter-back Brian Leetch was wearing skates that said "Graf," but the Graf brand had not paid licensing fees for the season. So with the Rangers on a man-advantage, Arbour begged referee Bill McCreary for a penalty on Leetch. No sale. He then asked McCreary to at least send Leetch off to change his skates. McCreary wouldn't do that, either. Instead, the game was delayed a minute while the Rangers taped over the offending logo.

Arbour was getting annoyed. With the score 2–2 midway through the second period, a brawl broke out behind goalie Mark Fitzpatrick's cage involving Gerald Diduck of the Islanders and the Rangers' Brian Mullen and Rudy Poeschek. Two against one. McCreary called it even.

When he went to explain his decision to Arbour, the coach removed his glasses, which the ref took pejoratively, as in, "You need glasses!" So McCreary issued a bench minor. "I was just taking them off!" Al contested. Too late. Now Radar was enraged.

Jan Erixon scored the game-winner at even strength six minutes later, and the Rangers held on, 4–2. "I guess we have to battle everybody," Arbour whined of McCreary.

But to Arbour's chagrin, the buzz in town was not over the offici-
ating, but the performances of the first-place, 11–4–3 Rangers, and the
last-place, 4–12–3 Islanders.

The suburbanites needed a spark, if not an outright miracle. They
skidded all the way to 5–18–3 before Torrey dealt former 36-goal man
Mikko Makela to the Los Angeles Kings for a pair of depth players—5-
foot-9 center Hubie McDonough and the "Blond Bomber," a 6-foot-1,
205-pound Kurt Cobain-look-alike named Ken Baumgartner, widely
regarded as one of the toughest S-O-Bs in the NHL.

The move was viewed as waving a white flag on the season. But
instead, what followed was one of the most insane ten-week runs in the
history of the storied Arbour-Torrey duo.

Makela's departure was followed by four consecutive Islanders
wins leading up to December 9, when the first-place Rangers came to
Uniondale to skate with the still very much in last place Nassau-men.

It was the first Coliseum sellout of the season, and thanks to goalies
John Vanbiesbrouck and Mark Fitzpatrick, the 16,297 boisterous, bipartisan backers were treated to a classic.

The checking was fierce—and clean. The defense was stout, the
skating crisp, the passing tight, and the goaltending superb.

Shots were 16–8 Rangers in the first period (no goals) and 9–8
Islanders in the second (no goals). By the third, the place was a powder
keg.

"Let's Go Islanders-Let's Go Rangers!"

Fans roared with every rush, anticipating that big play that would
carry the night. Up and down they came—the first-place visitors going
one way, their rejuvenated hosts back the other. As the minutes ticked
away, emotions heightened.

"Nine-teen-for-ty"—

CLANK! Rangers sniper Darren Turcotte rang one off the post!
"Oooooooohhhhh" sighed the Blueshirts faithful, then "Oooooooohhhh"
shrieked their suburban counterparts, as Beezer stoned Pat Flatley on a
rebound.

Shots were 8–7 Rangers in the third and 2–1 Isles in overtime, for
a game total of 33–26 Broadway. Beezer and Fitzpatrick got them all en
route to the only 0–0 tie in Islanders-Rangers history.

Fitzpatrick called it "probably the best hockey game I've seen this year."

The rematch took place exactly one week later in the Coliseum, and naturally Vanbiesbrouck and Fitzpatrick were back in net. The Rangers took a quick 2–0 lead, but a breathtaking stretch of hockey from Pat LaFontaine—two goals and a brilliant assist—helped the Isles rally for a 4–3 win.

Neilson's diagnosis: "We weren't able to check him." That, too, would become a major theme in the months ahead.

The loss knocked the Blueshirts off the top of the remarkably close and volatile Patrick Division for the first time all season.

How volatile?

Well, three weeks later, the Rangers were in *last place*. And ten days after that . . . the Islanders were in *first*!

In 29 games immediately following the trade for McDonough and Bomber, the once incompetent Islanders went 23–6–2. The Rangers, on the other hand, suffered a miserable 1–11–3 stretch that had Neil Smith phoning Los Angeles for a season-saving trade of his own.

On January 20, he sent Tomas Sandstrom and struggling sophomore Tony Granato to the Kings in exchange for All-Star sharp-shooter Bernie Nicholls, who'd scored an incredible 70 goals and 150 points one year prior. The deal worked. Nicholls produced 37 points in 32 games after the trade, and the Rangers took back first place.

The Blueshirts carried a 13–4–3 streak into the next crosstown match—March 2 at MSG—sitting just 2.5 games up on the third-place Islanders. The stakes were gigantic, but early on it was clear this contest would be remembered not for high-quality play, but for low-quality ice.

Cracks and ruts abounded as the Rangers jumped out 2–0 in the first. This was Madison Square Garden, but one would have an easier time skating in an actual Garden. Full chunks were popping out. In some spots, it was down to the concrete. Intermission was extended by twenty minutes so the zamboni could circle twice.

The Islanders fought back and took a 3–2 lead in the second, but Turcotte tied it at 19:28. Meanwhile, four straight calls went Manhattan's way to end the period, and Arbour lost his mind, giving referee Rob

Shick such a verbal going-over that the young ref slapped him with a bench minor for unsportsmanlike conduct at 20:00.

John Ogrodnick scored the game-winning goal on the ensuing power play—his team-leading 38th—and the Homesters ran away, 6–3. Then Islanders brass threw a hissy fit.

With about two minutes left, Arbour sent out his usual muscle crew—Baumgartner, Vukota, and Gerald Diduck. Neilson noticed and countered with a few of his bigger boys. Sure enough, Bomber went after Mark Janssens, who refused to fight him, then Normand Rochefort, who obliged.

As Shick walked through the hallway after the game, Arbour spotted him . . . and charged! Thankfully, security and Torrey were there to restrain him, and the altercation never got physical.

The visitors were so upset, they kept their locker room closed. Torrey was the only Islander available to reporters, and all he wanted to talk about was the ice. "It shouldn't have been played!" he complained. "I've got three guys waiting to see the doctors because of ruts in the ice. The place is a joke!"

"We know where the ruts are," cracked Neilson, when asked how his team was able to play so well.

The curly-haired quipster had one more dig for his adversaries, with a threat, to boot. "They just wanted to put on a show of toughness, I guess," Neilson remarked of the end of the game. "It wasn't our time for a showdown of toughness, but that time may come."

As if things weren't heated enough, the seventh and final game of the regular season series was probably the worst time and place to put fans of both teams under one roof: 2 o'clock, St. Patrick's Day, at the raucous Coliseum.

The Isles hadn't won in exactly five weeks, a streak of 14 games—one shy of the franchise record set in the expansion year of 1972–73.

That '73 team was one of the worst in NHL history. These 1990 Islanders, however, were still in the playoff hunt, just one game back of the final spot with two weeks remaining.

The Rangers were comfortably in first again but had their own issues. Stud defenseman Brian Leetch was ruled out for the year with a broken ankle suffered three days prior.

To little surprise, fights broke out all over the jam-packed stands. But on the ice, it was an afternoon of clean play and sparkling performances. Darren Turcotte scored three points for the visitors, including one of the superior individual efforts of the season. Early in the first, the rookie center took a Kevin Miller feed in stride at center ice, withstood a hooking back-checker, moved over the middle of the blue line, and split Dean Chynoweth and Jeff Finley with such precision that the pair collided. Chynoweth spun away, but Finley managed to swipe Turcotte off his feet. No problem. On the way down, Turcotte jabbed at the puck and pinballed it past stunned Islanders goalie Mark Fitzpatrick to give the Rangers a 1–0 lead.

Unfortunately for Rangers fans, Turcotte's teammates could not match his effort. Brent Sutter recorded a hat trick and LaFontaine added three points in a 6–3 Islanders triumph.

The huge win gave the Isles life in the standings, but subsequent losses to the Capitals, Kings, and Flames put their postseason hopes on a respirator. While they were getting beat in Calgary, the Rangers were in Quebec City making magic. Down 4–2 to start the third, the visitors reeled off five unanswered goals and clinched the regular season Patrick Division championship.

It was the first time the Rangers had won any division since 1942! Three meaningless games remained, then on to the Patrick Division playoffs. But whom would they face?

Well, the Islanders, *if* Arbour's clan could make the playoffs. But this was a monstrous if.

The Isles needed two straight wins, plus two straight Penguins losses and a Capitals win or tie in Philadelphia, just to eke out the final spot.

On Wednesday, the Islanders beat the Maple Leafs in Toronto. One down, four to go. On Thursday, the Flyers blew a pair of leads against the Caps and the Penguins blew a two-goal lead to the Blues. Three down, two to go. Barely.

On Saturday March 31, 1990, a sellout crowd filed into Nassau Coliseum ready to root for their Isles against the Flyers, and at the same time, for the Buffalo Sabres against the Penguins.

A sign taped behind one goal said, "LET'S GO BUFFALO."

Brent Sutter's four-point performance gave the Islanders a 6–2 victory, their first win of the season against Philadelphia in seven tries.

But the Pens were having a good night, too. The great Mario Lemieux returned from a back injury and scored in the third period to knot the game. A tie is all his team needed to eliminate the Nassau-men.

So the Islanders scurried into their locker room to watch the end of the Penguins game, while fans stayed and watched on the scoreboard, chanting, "Let's-Go-Buff-a-lo!"

The game went to overtime. The Isles were 300 lousy seconds from elimination. The Coliseum went quiet. But one minute in, Sabres defenseman Uwe Krupp scored! The fans erupted. Their prayers had been answered.

Twenty miles west, news spread around the Rangers locker room. The Isles won. The Pens lost in OT. The "Expressway Series, Part VII" was finally upon us.

The Expressway Series, Part VII

It was a matchup the Big Apple craved, and hadn't seen in six years. When longtime-Ranger-current-Islander Don Maloney was asked if it might take the fans a while to get readjusted, he responded, "Yeah, about six minutes."

"People take these series quite personally," warned Rangers defenseman James Patrick. One such person was former Islanders minor league player and scout, Neil Smith. "I'm going with an Islander Stanley Cup ring," he said, "sitting around trying to watch my team eliminate them."

Game One was Thursday, April 5, at the Garden. Neilson surprised many by going to rookie goalie Mike Richter over Vanbiesbrouck. Arbour tapped his rookie, Fitzpatrick.

This was a new flavor for the Arbour-Neilson soap opera, as opposed to that of the late '70s and early '80s. Now it was Roger with the more gifted team. But that would not change how he wanted to play. "It's going to be a hard work series," he foretold. "Physical."

This proved to be a self-fulfilling prophecy, as Neilson started Chris Nilan on the Nicholls line in place of playmaker Mike Gartner. The coach's "time for toughness" prediction from back in March was about to come to fruition.

Right off the drop, Nilan charged Hart Trophy candidate Pat LaFontaine behind the play and elbowed him in the left temple. Later in the period, defenseman Randy Moller caught him in the chin. But LaFontaine's was far from the only royal blue helmet getting rattled. The Rangers were credited with 86 hits on the night. Nicholls led the way with ten.

Richter was fabulous, with ten saves in the opening frame. Fitzpatrick went five-for-six, the lone goal coming on Nicholls's rebound of a Moller shot at 5:14. 1–0 Rangers.

Midway through the second, Islanders winger Randy Wood went crashing into Richter after Blueshirts defender Normand Rochefort slipped on the notorious Garden ice and tossed his stick at Wood's feet in desperation. Referee Don Koharski pointed to center for one of the easiest penalty shot calls of his career.

So Wood collected the puck at center, skated quickly through the right circle, faked forehand, and pulled the rubber backhand for a stuff-in. Richter dove left, went into a split, and blocked the puck with his foot. The crowd was in love.

Four minutes later, Chris Nilan fed lefty-shooting Mark Janssens across the slot for a terrific one-time finish. 2–0 Rangers.

The Rangers took the game away in the third period, limiting Long Island to just five shots. Then at the end, with the score 2–1, the sides went from fed up with each other, to utterly incensed.

It started at 18:43, when LaFontaine chased down a Don Maloney head-man pass at the top of the Ranger zone.

BOOM! James Patrick knocked him off the puck. Chris Nilan knocked him on his behind—a quasi-dirty double-dip. Patty's neck whiplashed hard, and the back of his head SMACKED! the ice. It was Lights. Out.

LaFontaine was unconscious for 30–45 seconds according to Islanders trainer Mark Aldridge, who had to slip a tongue depressor in the superstar's mouth to ensure proper breathing. "His eyeballs were nowhere to be found," testified Maloney.

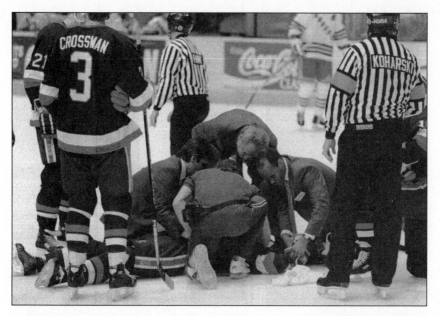

One of the rivalry's scariest moments. Islanders superstar Pat LaFontaine lies unconscious after a pair of controversial hits late in Game One of the 1990 Patrick Division semifinals, April 6, 1990, at Madison Square Garden. *(AP Photo/ Mark Lennihan)*

A scary portion of home fans cheered while LaFontaine lay motionless and heckled as he was wheeled off on a stretcher. Koharski said he saw the entire play and that neither hit was a penalty. But there were doubters on the Isles' side. For them, it was a matter of principle. The game had started with a high hit on LaFontaine. Now it was ending with a high hit on LaFontaine. They were furious.

Fitzpatrick left for an extra attacker, but his team couldn't score, and with two seconds left they faced a draw deep in their defensive zone. No way to tie the game now.

So Arbour put Fitzpatrick back in, along with Baumgartner, Vukota, Nylund, Diduck, and Trottier.

Then it was Neilson's turn. Would he give the Islanders the fight they were clearly looking for?

King, Nilan, Janssens, Jeff Bloemberg, and Ron Greschner lined up. Roger threw Mallette out, too, but Janssens sent him back to the bench.

Janssens and Trottier stepped in for the faceoff to Fitzpatrick's left. The other four Rangers stood way behind Janssens, while the Isles came right up to the line, ready to attack. Baumgartner was so juiced up, he couldn't stay still. The Blond Bomber kept skating circles all over the Islanders half of the zone, staring the Rangers down like a bull looking for his matador.

On the drop, Baumgartner skated to Kris King and popped him in the mouth. King didn't see it coming because he was distracted by Vukota, who had gone right after Bloemberg and mauled him.

"Oh, look at Vukota!" yelled MSG play-by-play announcer Sam Rosen. "Oh, look at that jerk!"

Bloemberg turtled. Though at 6-foot-2, 200 pounds, he seemed like fair game, the twenty-two-year-old Ontario native was a Born Again Christian, and, as such, did not believe in fighting. Vukota didn't have the memo and must have thought this was the easiest duel of his life. He hit him with about 25 rights before the Rangers pacifist finally decided to grab his assailant's arms.

"The Islanders look like garbage on this play!" screamed Rosen's partner, former Rangers goalie John Davidson.

Nylund and Nilan squared off in a tussle that was more Greco-Roman wrestling than hockey-fighting, but it escalated to an 11-man melee by the Islanders bench, where fans rained down as much garbage as they could find.

Richter straddled Fitzpatrick as though performing the Heimlich maneuver. Baumgartner, meanwhile, was not finished with King. He followed him all over until linesmen Mark Pare and Dan Schachte let them go in the right wing corner.

When it was over, officials escorted the main miscreants away one at a time. The crowd jeered loudest at Vukota, singing "aaaaaaaaaaaaaaaass . . . hole" while he skated to the tunnel.

Off the ice, Rangers scratches Lindy Ruff and David Shaw cursed at Arbour and called him classless. Al and Battling Billy Smith—now the Islanders goaltending coach—had to be held back by security.

BENCHMARK GAME: BLOOD FEUD

April 5, 1990
Madison Square Garden

Islanders 1 Rangers 2
(0–1) (1–0)

A superstar player knocked unconscious. His archrival crowd cheers while the trainer keeps him breathing. A mob harasses his ambulance as it leaves the arena.

An all-time great general. His coaching nemesis. A bunch of guys who love to fight. And a Born Again Christian who refuses to.

Debate over this 1990 Patrick Division Semi-Final—specifically Pat LaFontaine's head injury and the ensuing melee—dominated New York and the hockey world.

Who was out of line? Who, if anybody, was not? Everyone had an opinion.

Fans of both teams flocked to the mailboxes to send their thoughts on the controversy to local newspapers. The papers ran those angry letters for weeks.

Here's how a pair of key players from that night's Garden sizzler—Isles captain Patrick Flatley and Rangers defenseman Randy Moller, who belted LaFontaine in the face early in the game—recall this infamous Seventh Avenue slapdown decades later.

Moller: *We weren't going out there trying to kill Patty, obviously. But if we had an opportunity to be physical, hit him, we were going to take that opportunity. We knew that if we were going to be successful we would have to neutralize him.*

Flatley: *I don't think that was a deliberate attempt to injure Patty. It was just a fluke hit. James Patrick's not that type of player. And he would've been upset about that—the effect that it had on Pat. It was just an unfortunate accident really.*

> **Moller:** *Jeff Bloemberg got jumped—that was a little surprising and a little disappointing.*
>
> **Flatley:** *That got a little ugly. After the fact, one of the guys that Mick Vukota grabbed—Jeff Bloemberg—was a Born Again Christian who was against violence. I think that if Mick would've known that Jeff Bloemberg was a Born Again Christian who was against violence, he wouldn't have grabbed him.*
>
> **Moller:** *I think that one of the reasons we came out on top was because we were much more successful physically in that series. We all expected it would be a physical, borderline chippy series, and it lived up to its expectations.*

Again Arbour kept the locker room closed to the media, and the visitors had no comment on the fight. The hosts, on the other hand, talked plenty.

"If Al Arbour ever leaves the Islanders, he'll be welcome in the Eastern League," cracked Neilson.

Neil Smith, once given a job by Arbour, took it further. "I'm disgusted," he scoffed. "I never thought I would see the day he would do that. Ever since I worked for Al and Bill I tried to emulate them, but maybe I should think again. They should be ashamed of themselves. I'm embarrassed for them."

The next day, the Islanders shot back, taking aim at the Garden, its staff, and its customers. Bill Torrey sent a report to Neil Smith accusing the arena of mishandling LaFontaine's medical care, stating that his trip to the hospital was unnecessarily delayed because officials insisted on an in-house examination. The Isles also claimed the ambulance lacked sufficient equipment, and that it was rocked and pounded by fans as it left the Garden. The Garden acknowledged that the ambulance was attacked by a mob of Blueshirts backers but denied all other claims.

The Islanders were docked $25,000 and Arbour was hit separately for $5,000. Vukota was suspended for ten games. Baumgartner got one.

In his statement, NHL President John Ziegler used the terms "shameful," "disgraceful," and "degrading."

Torrey issued a statement of his own. "We not only question the president's decision, but even more so, his comments attacking the integrity of the team, its coach, and the franchise. While we do not condone the events that took place just prior to the end of the game, to place all of the guilt on just one team is clearly unjust and arbitrary."

THE MAVEN REMEMBERS: MAVE VERSUS THE MAD DOG

In the late 1980s and early 1990s, broadcaster Bill Mazer hosted one of the best sports radio shows in New York. The program on WFAN lasted from noon to 3:00 p.m. on radio and took place in Mickey Mantle's Restaurant on Central Park West.

Mazer had me slotted to come on with him at 1:00. More important, it was the day after the bitter Game One of the 1990 Patrick Division Semi-Finals.

Near the end of my segment with Mazer, Bill would hook into the next show, which featured Mike Francesa and Chris Russo, alias Mike and the Mad Dog. As soon as Mazer introduced them, Russo went into a diatribe about how bad a guy Al Arbour was for sending out all his goons to beat up all those poor defenseless Rangers.

Infuriated, I shot back that Arbour was simply making a statement and that Russo has no idea about hockey thinking or history. I added that Russo's idea of history was contained in a comic book, and the insults flowed from there.

Suffice to say that the Russo–Francesa vs. Fischler airwave battle caused a furor that lasted through the weekend and into the following week. But it didn't end there.

Although I didn't actually hear Mike and the Mad Dog's diatribes, I was told that they were hammering me hard enough that my nickname could have been Flathead. Of course they had the program, so there was not much I could—or wanted—to do about it, but the sour melody lingered on into spring and would have dissipated on its own had something unusual not taken place.

SportsChannel, for which I had been working many years, decided they wanted to exploit Russo's radio popularity and created a show for him that would launch in late spring.

Capitalizing on our feud, a marketing person at SC came up with this bright idea of having a Mad Dog versus Stan floor hockey contest, and sure enough, our marketer found a gym out in Nassau, got nets, and set a date.

When I arrived, there was Chris, already lacing on his sneakers. We shook hands and at least temporarily laughed off the feud, only to move it into the realm of floor hockey.

I beat him by a goal. We shook hands and, not too many years later, cemented the peace when Russo and Francesa had me on their show, proving that my mom was right when she said that time was a healer.

LaFontaine was diagnosed with a moderate concussion and discharged from the hospital in the morning. The team dubbed him "questionable" for Game Two, but this was just playing coy. Everyone knew he'd need time.

Game Two was a bitter, testy affair. Even with Bomber and Big Mick absent, each team was called for 15 minor penalties—and chippy ones. Referee Denis Morel whistled coincidental malefactions on eight occasions.

Yet while the Manhattan-men netted three power-play goals, their counterparts managed to score zero. That turned out to be the difference in the 5–2 Rangers triumph.

Then there were the ejections.

Already down 4–2 in the second, Fitzpatrick wound and butt-ended Troy Mallette with his goalie stick—viciously—earning an early shower. Early in the third, Normand Rochefort stuck wood to Randy Wood yet again, this time hooking him in the mouth and getting tossed. Later, Morel banished Jeff Norton for high sticking Jeff Bloemberg in the forehead.

"Pure stupidity," deadpanned Isles goalie Glenn Healy, when asked to summarize his team's mental approach to Game Two.

The series moved from city to suburb, where staff and law enforcement braced for rivalry Armageddon. Coliseum officials had already decided to implement the earliest last call in the history of the building—beer sales would be cut off after the first period.

"We've had some problems at Islander-Ranger games," reasoned the Nassau County Police Department.

Despite Richter's terrific play, Neilson switched to John Vanbiesbrouck for Game Three. Healy started for the Islanders.

Fans mixed it up—a shove here, a punch there—but overall were better behaved than on St. Patrick's Day. A greater battle of emotions played out in the rink.

The Rangers answered an early tap-in from Isles captain Brent Sutter with three straight goals of their own—a first period wrister from Mallette, capped by a Radio City Rockette-like celebratory jig, and power-play slappers by James Patrick and Nicholls 80 seconds apart in the second.

The home team chased those two goals zealously, taking a huge lead in the shot department, but Beezer made save after save. Time was melting away.

With under nine minutes to play in the third, the Islanders finally caught a break, as Kelly Kisio was whistled for a controversial slashing. The Isles' Patrick Flatley cashed in with a creative redirection of a Brent Sutter pass along the goal line at 11:47. The Coliseum came alive. 3–2 Rangers.

1:22 later, Hubie McDonough lifted a backhand rebound over a seated Vanbiesbrouck to send the building into a frenzy and the game into overtime. Hubie's celebration made Mallette's look tame.

Shots in overtime were 10–9 visitors. Healy and Beezer were perfect. The play was clean and exciting. But right before the fourth intermission, the series took another ugly turn.

With under ten ticks left, Jeff Norton, Long Island's best defenseman, fought through a Chris Nilan hook in the left-wing corner of his own zone and played the puck safely up the boards. But Nilan's clutch left Norton vulnerable to a hard forecheck from Mallette, who barreled in and drilled the 53-point blue-liner from behind.

Norton crumpled, face down, and lost consciousness for about ten seconds. He was eventually taken off on a stretcher and spent the night in the hospital. "Groggy," attested trainer Mark Aldridge, "and his face was swollen badly enough that it was distorted." For the Islanders and their fans, this was too familiar.

Mallette was penalized with a boarding major and a game misconduct at 19:52. The home team would have a long power play to start the second overtime. They were eager to win it for their fallen friend.

Czech playmaker David Volek drew a double team at right point, then dished across the slot to defenseman Jeff Finley, who slammed a hard pass between Patrick and Vanbiesbrouck—a laser—finding Sutter at the far post for an easy tip at 00:59 of double overtime. The Isles took Game Three, 4–3. The Rangers led the series, 2–1.

After the game, the clubs were especially chatty, but on different topics. The Rangers wanted to talk about the slashing call on Kisio. The Islanders were upset over the Norton hit.

"When you hit a guy from behind like he did you can cause serious injury," said winger Alan Kerr. "It's a dangerous hit."

"There are certain things that aren't done," said Patrick Flatley. "You do not put another player's career in jeopardy."

"That hit on Norton was vicious," barked Baumgartner. "The potential for injury is much higher than anything Mick and I did in that fight."

"They are always lily-white," remarked Arbour of the rivalry's portrayal, "and we're the guys in the black hats."

"I wanted to make contact, take the puck," Mallette explained. "He was looking right at me, and at the last second, he bailed out, turned his back. You can't just put on the brakes because a guy turned his back."

"There wouldn't have even been a call if he wasn't hurt," argued Neilson.

Torrey and Arbour called for Mallette to be suspended. The league reviewed the tape and ordered no further discipline.

Norton was listed as "doubtful" for Game Four. LaFontaine was upgraded to "probable." But come game time, neither suited up. The Islanders were in trouble.

Vanbiesbrouck was back in goal for the Rangers. Healy opposed him. The home crowd ached to keep momentum going off the thrilling Game Three rally. But the Rangers shot that down in cold blood.

Brian Mullen scored on a power play just 41 seconds in and Darren Turcotte made it 2–0 at 10:53. Flatley cut the lead in half, but goals by Wilson, Moller, and Ogrodnick in a span of 2:32 mid-second period signaled a blowout.

"Beezer! Beezer!" chanted the visiting fans throughout the third. "Let's Go Rangers!" Kisio scored shorthanded at 16:31 for the exclamation point, 6–1. It was a statement win.

The only bickering in this one was between Baumgartner and Nilan. Early in the first period, Bomber charged him, so Nilan threw his arm against his assailant's stick for protection, breaking the ulna in his forearm.

Nilan stayed in the game, and Baumgartner followed him all over, trying to start a fight. But his prey refused to tangle with a broken arm. Instead, Nilan did his jousting in the media afterwards.

"The only time he plays is when I'm on the ice," he said of the excitable Blond Bomber. "He's out there to hit and cause stuff. Maybe someday he'll be a player."

"Is *he* out there to score goals?" retorted Baumgartner. "Was it a coincidence that he was out there both times our players were injured?"

In his book *Fighting Back*, Nilan says Baumgartner approached him the following season and apologized for trying to fight him, explaining that he did not know about the injury.

It all ended on an uplifting note, as the teams played a clean Game Five at the Garden, with a lot of excitement and a lot of goals. Arbour tried to send one last desperate message to his team, scratching living-legend Bryan Trottier as well as Alan Kerr and scorer Derek King in favor of Rob DiMaio, Tom Fitzgerald, and Derek Laxdal. Richter started against Fitzpatrick.

The series' most noted casualties both returned to the Islanders lineup and connected at 9:51 of the opening frame—Norton from LaFontaine—to answer an early Mike Gartner power-play breakaway strike. Just seconds after the Norton goal, Laxdal stole the puck from Lindy Ruff and DiMaio scooped it, breezed through the neutral zone, and roofed a slapper over Richter's glove. Arbour's moves were paying off . . . until the hosts scored four straight goals.

Ogrodnick tipped one past Fitzpatrick on a power play at 15:47 to tie the game. The Nassau-men were then awarded 40 seconds of 5-on-3 time to start the second, and not only did the Isles fail to take the lead, but when Rangers winger Paul Broten left the penalty box to make it a 5-on-4, he stole the puck from Norton, carried deep into the Islanders zone, and fed Kisio, who found Rochefort for a shorthanded wrist shot at 1:02. 3–2 Rangers.

Gartner notched his second power play goal of the game at 8:40, and Carey Wilson finished off a pretty passing play with Turcotte and Ruff, even strength, at 11:34. Healy then replaced the man who had replaced him two nights earlier. Fitzpatrick had only 15 saves on 20 shots. It was 5–2 after two.

The Garden was ready to party like it was 1979—the last time Big Brother had beaten Little Brother in a playoff series. But a nice and easy third period would not behoove the wackiness of the 1989–90 season.

Wayne McBean scored at 1:50. 5–3. Randy Wood scored at 11:18. 5–4. The home-backers fell silent, while pockets of Long Islanders in the stands came alive. But on the very next shift, righty-shooting Gartner cruised in on a 2-on-1 with Nicholls, looked up from the top of the right circle, and fired a slap shot past Healy's stick side. The Rangers faithful roared. The man who'd been scoreless for four games had a Game Five hat trick! 6–4.

There was no quit from the other side. The Islanders pushed and pushed, and with 3:07 to play, Flatley beat Richter with a wrister. 6–5! Tension in the building reached max capacity, and 16,651 fans were biting their nails to oblivion.

Healy was pulled for an extra attacker, and as time wound down, the Islanders got where they wanted to—the low slot. It was a mad scramble. With five seconds left, Sutter found a loose puck, took aim, fired . . . and missed *just* wide right.

The Rangers cleared. Their excited rookie goalie leaped around, hugging Moller and Nicholls at once. The rest of the team followed soon. The 1990 Islanders were finally vanquished. And the first man at the head of the handshake line on the losing side . . . was Ken Baumgartner.

"Relief, relief, tremendous relief," sighed Neil Smith. "We were a worried team in the third period," echoed Neilson. "The consequences of losing in this city to the Islanders when we were the heavy favorite made it tense."

"I couldn't believe what was happening at the end," said James Patrick. "Something is special about series between these two teams. Things happen. Crazy things. Bad things."

The difference was power play and goaltending. The Blueshirts scored 12 special-teams goals, while the Islanders potted only four. Long Island racked up 175 penalty minutes in five games, and Manhattan sat for 139. Richter and Vanbiesbrouck combined for a save percentage of .922. Fitzpatrick and Healy stopped only .853. Shots were 167–150 in favor of the Islanders, but they were outscored, 22–13.

They were also out-concussed, 2–0.

On the way out, reporters asked Jeff Norton if it could be the year the Broadway Blueshirts finally bring the city the Stanley Cup. Norton gave a thoughtful pause . . .

"I hope not."

Chapter 6

1940

"The chants made it seem like there were two sides to the rink. You couldn't help but get charged up."

—Islanders/Rangers forward Bill Berg

"I like to play against the Rangers. I like it when people hate you. You get in a fight on the ice and you get a fight going in the stands. Games between the Rangers and the Islanders are like Dynamo against the Red Army."

—Islanders/Rangers defenseman Darius Kasparaitis

"It's not like going to Winnipeg on a Tuesday night."

—Islanders/Rangers goalie Glenn Healy

"Those were our playoff games."

—Islanders/Rangers forward Bill Berg

"To have lost to the Islanders would have been a disaster," admitted Rangers coach Roger Neilson.

Instead, his 1990 regular season Patrick Division champs fell in the second round to the underwhelming, sub-.500 Washington Capitals—who even played without leading scorer Dino Ciccarelli—marking the 50th straight year of disappointment in Manhattan. "If they ever sold milk at Madison Square Garden," teased Bill Scheft in the *New York Times*, "there would be a picture of the Stanley Cup on the side of the carton."

Speaking of disasters, the Islanders' run to the 1990 postseason, seemingly a miracle at the time, turned out to be one of the worst curses in franchise history, and not only for the injuries suffered by Pat LaFontaine and Jeff Norton. By overtaking the Pittsburgh Penguins on the final day of the season, the Isles cost themselves the fifth slot in that June's draft, a pick the Pens used on future All-Time great left wing Jaromir Jagr. With the next selection, the Isles took a center named Scott Scissons, who played two games in the National Hockey League. "I'll take the playoffs," declared Bill Torrey at the time, though 750 Jagr goals later, he may reconsider.

The un-checkable Czech was not the only new Penguin giving Islanders fans heartburn during the 1990–91 season. Bryan Trottier's contract was bought out in July 1990, and the thirty-three-year-old legend headed west, but not before making it known that he was in talks with—*gasp!*—the New York Rangers.

Trottier was so upset at the Islanders for dropping him, he was ready to don red, white, and blue. Rangers general manager Neil Smith flirted back. The speculation carried on for three weeks. Luckily for Torrey, Trots finally signed his Penguins deal and never suited up for the Blueshirts . . . as a player.

The saying "Absence makes the heart grow fonder" proved hollow for these Islanders and Rangers. After a five-month offseason, the clubs were back at each other's throats at the first opportunity, during training camp. The breakout brawler of the 1990–91 preseason was 5-foot-10 200-pound Rangers winger Tie Domi, acquired from the Toronto Maple Leafs in June. This stocky Windsor-boy with an oversized cranium packed a punch, which Ken Baumgartner found out at the Garden on September 23.

BOMBER-DOMI I:

Following their scrap, Baumgartner poked fun at his assailant's over-sized melon, picking up Domi's enormous helmet and spinning it atop his own head like a *dreidel*. Not to be outdone, Domi crafted his own Ken "Bomber" Baumgartner wig by slicing a white towel into long strips with scissors he found in the penalty box. Everyone had a chuckle when Tie exited the bin with this new "flow" streaming out the back of his helmet, whisking his faux blond locks to and fro as if he were Madonna.

The 1990–91 Islanders had bigger problems than Tie Domi. They finished dead last in the Patrick Division at 25–45–10, their worst record since 1973–74. The lone bright spot was their 4–2–1 performance against a strong Rangers squad that finished 36–31–13 for the second year in a row. It was a series full of combative, dramatic hockey.

On November 2, 1990, Islanders goaltender Glenn Healy stopped future Hall-of-Famer Mike Gartner on a breakaway with 20 seconds remaining to preserve a 3–2 upset, handing the Manhattan-men their first home defeat of the season.

Three weeks later, it was a night of stars at the Coliseum, as Brian Leetch, Mike Gartner, and Pat LaFontaine all converted highlight-caliber individual efforts. LaFontaine's frolic around the Rangers defense and goalie Mike Richter was so extraordinary it drew applause from fans of both teams. Brent Sutter tied the game with just 1:31 to go in regulation, and it ended 2–2.

The third meeting of the season—January 22, 1991, at the Coliseum—was remarkable in other ways. With two minutes to play and the home team up a goal, Randy Wood tripped Bernie Nicholls near the Rangers' bench, separating the crafty center's shoulder. Bernie turned and punched his attacker in the back of the head. Referee Bill McCreary caught him and raised his arm for a delayed penalty. The home fans roared.

But not so fast . . .

As Healy left his crease for an extra skater, Jeff Norton collected the puck and calmly slid it back to his defensive partner Craig Ludwig.

Except there was no Craig Ludwig. He was across the blue line, and the biscuit glided toward the empty cage.

Over 16,500 hearts dropped at once, as half the crowd tried yelling the puck into the empty net, while the rest tried yelling it away.

It hit the left post. The Isles won, 3–2.

BOMBER-DOMI II, III

Two weeks later, February 6 in the city, Tie Domi and Ken Baumgartner wasted no time writing their sequel.

About two seconds into their first shift, the pair grabbed each other and spun around clockwise.

On his next shift, Domi drew a high-sticking major on Islanders winger Brad Lauer, leading to three Rangers goals. Fans started to mock the Isles with chants of "LAST PLACE! *Clap-clap*, LAST-PLACE! *Clap-clap!*"

Rivalry within a rivalry. Despite surrendering three inches to the Islanders' Ken Baumgartner (24), Rangers forward Tie Domi (28) held his own in five consecutive bouts with the "Blond Bomber" between September 1990 and February 1992. Here the pair battle in "Bomber-Domi II," February 6, 1991, at Madison Square Garden. *(AP Photo/Steve Freeman)*

Later, Domi went flying into yet another Kris King-Mick Vukota scuffle already in progress, at which point Baumgartner chased him through the neutral zone and smashed him like a tackling dummy, setting the stage for Bomber-Domi III.

Tie stood his ground and wrestled Bomber to the ice, picked him up, landed a left, two rights, then tackled him again. Advantage Domi.

On his way to the box, the Windsor Warrior looked across at Baumgartner and did his patented "speed bag" hand gesture, air-swinging his fists about each other at eye level, to wit, "I used your face as a punching bag." The crowd was ecstatic.

Domi was a star of the 5–2 win, having drawn five key penalty minutes on the Isles and 22 hard-earned ones on himself. But he was not available to the media, for his father John Domi had passed away in Ontario during the game. Tie was not told until after the final horn. Neil Smith gave him a game puck and Tie put it in his father's coffin. He missed two games but was back to making trouble when the teams faced off at MSG on February 18.

The Rangers were still angry about the trip by Randy Wood on Bernie Nicholls back in January. Nicholls swore revenge and made good on that promise early in the second period, skating up to the winger and suckering him from the side. "You'd like to take your stick and shove it right in his teeth," Bernie later mused.

The Islanders were an unholy mess. LaFontaine was unhappy about his contract and publicly acknowledged that he had formally requested a trade. Torrey held a press conference to express his disappointment. The other players were caught in the middle. Yet amid all that, the way-last-place Isles stunned their first-place rivals, 5–4. LaFontaine had two assists and a brilliant goal from his backside.

On March 9, the Rangers took another disappointing trip through the Midtown Tunnel for the second of what would become a season-threatening eight-game losing streak, which lasted all the way to the next and final crosstown matchup, March 24 at MSG. This time the Rangers took care of business, 3–1, to finally clinch a playoff berth. Of course the clubs engaged in one last line brawl with seven seconds left. "It's a good thing we don't play them again 'till next year," joked Rangers rookie Ray Sheppard.

The Islanders' season was so poor, even Bill Torrey and Al Arbour were under fire. Roger Neilson was on the hot seat, too, after his team was defeated by an inferior Capitals squad for the second straight year—this time in the first round. To many, this Rangers lineup's lack of guts was illustrated by their performances in Uniondale, where they had not won a regular season game since October 28, 1989. Optimists blamed the streak on the fact that, by this point, the rivalry was all the Islanders had going for them. The team was losing and their only home sellouts were against the Blueshirts. For example, only 10,412 fans would show up for the Islanders' 1991–92 home opener! But every Rangers game was a guaranteed 16,297. The Isles were always juiced up. And as the streak grew longer, chants of "19–40!" grew louder.

The Rangers needed alterations in the summer of 1991. Smith dropped his own captain, Kelly Kisio, and signed Edmonton Oilers free agent forward Adam Graves, who had never scored more than 9 goals in an NHL season. Per that era's rules, Smith and Edmonton general manager Glen Sather had a week to negotiate compensation for Graves. The subject of those discussions gradually turned to the future of a different Oiler.

Isles and Rangers Go Moose Hunting

Mark Messier was thirty years old, and at the pinnacle of his career. Four times a champion as Wayne Gretzky's sidekick, the legend of "Mess" grew even greater when he captained the Oilers to a fifth Stanley Cup in 1990, sans "The Great One."

But like Gretzky, Messier had to move on. The Graves signing was further proof that the Oilers could no longer afford to win. So Mark demanded a trade.

Here's the best part . . .

Every team wanted Mark Messier. But as the season approached, the final three in talks with Sather were the Chicago Blackhawks, the Rangers, and the Islanders.

Neil Smith was desperate. He'd spent all offseason criticizing his team's heart, and he knew Messier had plenty. But the Islanders had LaFontaine, a more attractive chip than anything Smith could offer. Patty was a training camp holdout. It was a messy, bitter divorce, but a Messier deal would surely make nice alimony.

By October 1991, Chicago was off the table. "Moose" was coming to New York. But to which team?

The sooner Torrey could deal LaFontaine, the better. But the Rangers had two things the Isles didn't—prospects and money. Their system was stacked with hot youngsters like Tony Amonte, Louie DeBrusk, Alexei Kovalev, Steven Rice, and Doug Weight. On October 3, Smith sent Bernie Nicholls, DeBrusk, Rice, and a sum believed to be between $1.5 million and $5 million to the Oilers for Messier and future considerations. Messier was named captain after three days. The future consideration turned out to be one of the most beloved stay-at-home defensemen in Rangers history, Jeff Beukeboom.

On the surface all was jolly in Rangers land, but beneath that surface was a fundamental difference of theory between two very proud and stubborn hockey men, Moose and Neilson.

Messier was an Oiler and, as such, believed in playing fast and aggressive. Neilson wanted to maintain his defense-first mentality, even with a team as insanely talented as the 1991–92 Rangers. At least for the regular season, that talent concealed the organization's behind-the-scenes warts. Messier won his second Hart Trophy as league MVP, and the Rangers won the Presidents' Trophy handily with a record of 50–25–5—their best since 1971–72.

But they still had trouble with the locals, going 2–4–1 against Little Brother for the second consecutive time.

BOMBER-DOMI IV

The first Islanders-Rangers game of the season was a wild one, October 9, 1991, at the Garden, in which Messier scored the first goal of his Rangers career. Two minutes later, Domi and Baumgarner grabbed each other along the boards.

"Well I guess it was inevitable," muttered MSG Network's Sam Rosen. "OooohhhBaaaby," mused his partner John Davidson, as Tie spun Bomber around, threw him down, and hammered him with southpaws.

Kris King scored to break a 3–3 tie with 15 seconds left in the game. The Rangers tacked on an empty netter to win, 5–3.

On October 25, Pat LaFontaine's holdout was resolved, as Torrey packaged Patty, Randy Wood, and Randy Hillier to Buffalo for twenty-two-year-old stud center Pierre Turgeon, two-way winger Benoit Hogue, hulking defenseman Uwe Krupp (the same Uwe Krupp who had shot the Isles to the playoffs 19 months earlier), and checking center Dave McLlwain. He also sent Captain Brent Sutter and Brad Lauer to Chicago for sniper Steve Thomas and center Adam Creighton. In true Torrey style, both deals were completed at 2:45 in the morning.

The new Isles were taken aback by their first taste of the rivalry. "Half the crowd was for the Rangers," said Thomas after a brawl-filled, ejection-laden November 16 home victory over the Blueshirts. "That's a little weird."

Hogue even had to ask reporters why Islanders fans were chanting "19–40."

On December 28 in Uniondale, the Suburbanites shocked the Urbanites with a dramatic buzzer-beater of their own. Tom Fitzgerald's long distance wobbler beat John Vanbiesbrouck with 2.7 seconds remaining. 5–4 Isles.

The Blueshirts bounced back at home on February 14, an ironic date for a 9–2 beat down featuring an Adam Graves hat trick and exactly 100 penalty minutes combined. *Newsday* dubbed it "The Valentine's Day Massacre."

Early in the third, Vukota went after Kris King—a standard ritual—but Domi zoomed in and sucker-punched Big Mick hard. So Baumgartner fought through two linesmen to get at Tie, setting up Bomber-Domi V.

Bomber-Domi V

Baumgartner got a punch in, but the shorter Domi was able to wrestle the big Blond Bomber to the ice yet again. "I heard if I hit him, I could put him out for the season," mocked Domi, a reference to an injury suffered by Baumgartner in a fight against the Flyers back in December.

Six days later, the Isles scored a blowout of their own, 6–2. Turgeon dazzled his new fans with a hat trick and five points, helped largely by a series of foolish penalties by Domi. "I got frustrated," he confessed. "That '19–40' stuff really gets on your nerves."

The final two games of the series were a 1–1 tie in the City and another 4–1 blowout on the Island, which extended the Rangers' Coliseum regular season winless streak to ten, at 0–8–2. Fans took it as an omen that the Blueshirts couldn't win big games. The team went into the playoffs and validated that fear with a six-game, second-round upset defeat to the Penguins, featuring poor performances by everybody, especially Messier and Richter.

By the time the final horn sounded, the once-private rift between Moose and Neilson was the worst kept secret in sports. Mess could hardly say Roger's name without shuddering.

Neilson kept his job, though—more than could be said for Bill Torrey, who was fired and replaced with Don Maloney. So now, amusingly, the general manager of the Rangers was a longtime Islander, and the general manager of the Islanders was a longtime Ranger. Would this help mend the relationship?

No. Not with players like Tie Domi, Joey Kocur, and Mick Vukota still in town, and not with Islanders fans screaming "19–40!" every time they saw a blue sweater. And though Ken Baumgartner had been traded, the Nassau men had a new blond pest, a twenty-year-old Lithuanian defenseman named Darius "Kaspar" Kasparaitis.

1992–93: The Coliseum Drought Continues

The only thing worse than Kaspar's English was his manners. During the Garden end of a weekend home-and-home in October 1992, he knocked Messier into the Islanders' net and refused to let him out, like a hallway bully collecting a toll. Then late in a 6–4 Islanders win at the Coliseum December 26, the pair took turns swinging sticks and gloves at each other in the corner. The Rangers captain was unraveling, while the Islanders were reveling.

"It's great to beat these—," spat Steve Thomas, catching himself just shy of an adult word . . . "Guys."

With Turgeon and Thomas soaring up front and rookies Vladimir Malakhov and Kasparaitis transforming the blue line, the Islanders were in the playoff conversation. The buzz around the Patrick Division was over a pair of surprising New York teams. The Islanders were not that bad. The Rangers were not that good.

Furthermore, the discord between Messier and Roger Neilson was becoming unbearable. Finally, with the Rangers eight games out of first on January 4, 1993, Neilson was fired and replaced by Ron Smith of the club's AHL Binghamton affiliate.

But the Blueshirts' Nassau Coliseum drought was not going anywhere. They coughed up three leads in a quarrelsome 4–4 tie at the Coliseum February 1 and were embarrassed in a 5–2 loss there on February 13. The streak was at 14 games.

The clubs emerged from that Valentine's Eve battle tied for the final Patrick Division playoff spot. Back and forth that spot went, until the final meeting of the season, Friday night April 2, 1993, at Madison Square Garden.

It was game 76 of 84 for both teams. The Isles carried a two-game winning streak and a half-game lead. The Rangers carried a three-game losing streak and had just lost Brian Leetch to a freak accident in the street. But history was on their side, as the home team had won all but two of 27 Islanders-Rangers games since the beginning of the 1989–90 season.

This one felt like a Game Seven playoff matchup. Desperate energy permeated through the Garden.

The home team trailed, 2–0, late in the second period, but Rangers goals by recently acquired veteran center Eddie Olczyk and Swedish defenseman Peter Andersson tied the game.

The Blueshirts had a glorious chance to perhaps save their season with 1:43 of four-on-three power-play time to close out regulation, which they squandered. Messier's cross-crease pass barely skipped over Mike Gartner's stick in the final moments. It would've been an easy slam-dunk winner.

Instead, we moved to overtime, where Rangers sophomore sniper Tony Amonte would make a fatal mistake.

He curled at the faceoff circle in his own zone and blindly fired a cross-ice pass that was easily intercepted by Vladimir Malakhov at the right point. Seconds later, Turgeon wiggled free at the top of the crease and one-timed Brad Dalgarno's centering feed past Richter at 3:41 to send the Isles to the playoffs, and the Rangers to oblivion. It was his 50th goal of the season.

The next day's *New York Times* called Turgeon "the best center in New York this season," a petty, almost bitter shot at Messier, of whom so much had been expected. Turgeon was twenty-three years old and finished the season with 58 goals and 74 assists. Messier was thirty-two and finished the season with 25 goals and 66 assists. Maybe it was actually the Islanders who won out in the LaFontaine-Messier drama.

BENCHMARK GAME: TURGEON'S 50th

April 2, 1993
Madison Square Garden

Islanders 3 Rangers 2 (OT)
(37–33–6) (33–32–11)

"It was more like a classic playoff game than a regular-season game," recapped Al Arbour.

Pierre Turgeon laced up only 255 times in the regular season and 15 times in the playoffs for the Islanders, yet remains one of the few most popular players in franchise history. This game is a major reason.

At 3:41 of overtime, he sent the "bridge-and-tunnel" patrons into a frenzy.

"I shot it," said ever-modest Turgeon. "It hit Kevin Lowe's skate and went in. It was kind of lucky, but I'll take it."

Islanders playoff tickets went on sale the following morning.

While the Isles prepared for the playoffs, the Rangers spent their final three home games being booed mercilessly by their own customers. Messier, who had played hurt for much of the season, bore the brunt of it. "SAME. OLD. S—!" was a persistent chant, as was, amazingly enough, "19–40!"

That's how frustrated people were.

The team was officially eliminated on April 12 with a 1–0 loss to lowly Philadelphia, clinching a playoff berth for the Isles. A Flyers fan shouted "1940!" at Smith after the game. The Rangers GM yelled back "F— you!" Everyone had heard enough.

"They should be ashamed," wrote the *Times'* Jennifer Frey. "Even for a franchise legendary for its Stanley Cup futility, these Rangers are an embarrassment of epic proportions. With the biggest payroll in the National Hockey League, with more talent than most general managers dream of, the Rangers could not make the playoffs."

What that underachieving talent needed, Smith reasoned, was a strict, drill sergeant-type bench boss. Thus, he turned to a man so dour that he'd already been jettisoned by two other franchises despite amazing success.

On April 17, 1993, "Iron" Mike Keenan was in Manhattan signing up to be the highest-paid coach in the NHL, and for the pressure that would surely accompany the role.

"He's a winner," Smith said of Keenan. "And I'm infatuated with winners."

That winning included trips to the Stanley Cup Finals with the Philadelphia Flyers in 1985 and 1987 and the Chicago Blackhawks in 1992. In only eight years of head coaching, Keenan had been to the semifinals five times. But none of his teams had carried the Cup.

Asked why he chose Keenan—and for so much money ($3 million over four years)—Smith joked, "I didn't think the Islanders were going to give me Al Arbour."

Keenan's preferred methods were manipulation, degradation, and intimidation. He did not seem to care if his players liked him, and many didn't.

Iron Mike called his new gig "the biggest challenge in hockey." Few disagreed. The Rangers had loads of talent, but they were a mess, both with a lowercase "m" and a capital "M," as in, Mess was still captain, and whether there was room in the same building for both his alpha personality and Keenan's was anybody's guess.

Worst of all, the 1992–93 season wasn't over yet. The Rangers and their tortured fans had to watch Little Brother sweep the rest of the Metro area off its feet yet again, as Arbour took his underdog Islanders back to the Wales Conference Finals by upsetting the Capitals and the two-time defending champion Penguins, even without Turgeon, who was injured late in the first round.

With the emergence of young players like Malakhov, Kasparaitis, Derek King, and the incredible Turgeon, things on Long Island looked promising. Don Maloney's lone major addition in the summer of 1993 was one of Mike Keenan's favorite goalies, twenty-nine-year-old former Flyers playoff hero Ron Hextall, acquired along with the 23rd overall pick for Mark Fitzpatrick and the 14th overall pick.

Across town, Smith traded John Vanbiesbrouck for a seldom-used defenseman named Doug Lidster and signed Islanders playoff hero Glenn Healy as Richter's backup. The joke around hockey was that the Rangers finally found a goalie who can win at Nassau Coliseum.

Otherwise, the Rangers stood still entering the 1993–94 season. Smith's hope was that with a new coach and a new philosophy, 1992–93 would not repeat itself. And he was right.

1993–94: The Rangers Enter a New Era

Under Keenan, the Rangers were like a brand-new team. By Thanksgiving weekend they were headed to Nassau Coliseum at 16–5–2 with a 14-game unbeaten streak—a perfect time to break the dreaded Nassau hex. At 7–12–2, the Isles were drowning. It felt like they couldn't beat anybody.

Except still, apparently, the Rangers.

"If we played every team in the league like we play against them," grumbled Steve Thomas after netting a hat trick in the 6–4 win, "you'd be looking at a first place hockey club."

The problem was, they didn't.

And the Blueshirts weren't on the schedule for another two months— February 2 at the Garden—by which point Arbour's slumpers were four games back of the final playoff spot in the East.

The Rangers were the best team in hockey by far, at 33–13–3. They were also so sick of Kasparaitis, they spent a total of six roughing minors going after him twice in the middle of the second period. "Those guys hate me," grinned Kaspar.

As for the puck, the home team netted it four times thanks to an Adam Graves hat trick. But Ray Ferraro found the equalizer with just 1:02 to go in regulation.

The dramatic 4–4 tie spun the Isles in the right direction. They heated up, got right back in the playoff race, and set sail for another City-Island weekend March 4 and 5.

Meantime, for a Rangers team with an enormous lead over everyone, there were only two goals remaining in the regular season: stay healthy, and beat the darn Islanders already.

It was a referendum on their credibility as Cup contenders. Rangers players felt it, and certainly so did their fans. Any Islanders-Rangers game is a playoff simulation, so it was time to find out—was this team ready to win big games, or not?

Well, the first match at the Garden was a pretty bad sign. The homesters held a 3–0 lead in the middle of the second period, but the Isles got two back. The crowd began to boo. The Rangers stopped skating. The fans kept booing. Kasparaitis upended Messier with a hip-check. They booed louder. King tied it with 6:27 to go in the third. They booed even more. The game ended 3–3. They were exasperated.

The clubs packed up and headed east, 1,589 days after the last regular-season Rangers victory in The Land of 19–40!

This Saturday night crowd was particularly unruly. The "19–40!" chants were thunderous and the fighting in the aisles and hallways excessive, even for an Islanders-Rangers game. But the most exciting feud was the ongoing one on the ice between Rangers captain Mark Messier and Islanders nuisance Darius Kasparaitis.

Kaspar chased Messier all around the rink and even flipped him over on his head yet again. As a result, Mess took three minor penalties against him. The Nassau-men cashed in on two.

Richter coughed up three bad goals and was benched just 45 seconds into the second period.

That's when an anomaly occurred . . . something rarer than a Blueshirts victory in Nassau Coliseum. A New York Rangers player—in uniform—was given a standing ovation by Islanders fans. It was Glenn Healy.

Nine months prior, "Heals" had backstopped the Isles to a pair of major upsets over Washington and Pittsburgh. Now, he was taking over for the Blueshirts and received a huge round of applause.

Healy stopped the first two shots he saw, but with the contest tied, 3–3, and his team shorthanded, the overzealous former Islander whiffed on a hard rim-around behind his cage. Benoit Hogue popped it in—4–3—and shockingly, Keenan had seen enough. After 11 minutes and 11 seconds, he sent Richter back in for Healy. That's how badly Keenan wanted this game.

Heals entered the bench and went straight for Keenan. Iron Mike didn't back down. For a few moments, the duo engaged in a heated argument in front of everybody.

The Islanders fans stuck up for their old goalie. HEA-LY! *Clap-clap*! HEA-LY! *Clap-clap*!

"I'm not going to repeat what I said," Healy disclosed after the game. "A kind 'Hello' is all it was. Just exchanging greetings." Mike Richter heard differently. "I remember it involved body parts," he recalls. "And where he can put certain things and all kinds of other things."

Healy finally took off his helmet and sat down, though he did keep muttering aloud.

But Keenan's second goaltending change of the middle period produced the momentum swing he wanted. The visitors finished that frame strongly, then blitzed their suburban hosts in the third and tied it on a goal by, of all people, Jeff Beukeboom, at 10:05.

The Rangers kept peppering Hextall and earned a power play with 1:27 left in regulation. At 18:57, brilliant second-year Russian defenseman Sergei Zubov, the team's leading scorer, corralled a feed from Graves near the blue line, stepped into a low slapper that Hexy couldn't glove, and dropped to his knees in glory, pumping his fists in the air while slowly spinning along the ice.

This time—finally—there was no late Islanders equalizer. The streak was mercifully over.

BENCHMARK GAME: ONE HEX DOWN . . .

March 5, 1994
Nassau Coliseum

Rangers 5 Islanders 4
(42–18–5) (27–30–7)

"The 1993–94 Rangers were 0–1 in this building coming into this game," charged Mark Messier in the victorious locker room. "That's all that matters."

Really though?

The Blueshirts of the early '90s were an enormously talented team. Overall, the Islanders of that era were sub-mediocre. So how did they run off a streak of 12–0–3 in 15 straight regular season home games vs. the Rangers?

"The Islanders come out really gung-ho," believed Rangers general manager Neil Smith, "and these are real motivating games for them. For whatever reason, we are not on the same high that the Islanders have."

"It was important psychologically," said starting goalie Mike Richter. "Get a win in their building before the damn playoffs start."

"It was not another win," admitted Brian Leetch. "It was special."

With a key victory over the Isles under their belt, the Rangers headed into the second half of March in a good position. All seemed right with the Rangers, but Neil Smith and Mike Keenan had no use for complacency. They made five trades on deadline day, March 21.

Out went Gartner, Amonte, Peter Andersson, depth winger Phil Bourque, and center prospect Todd Marchant. In came a pair of Keenan favorites from the Blackhawks, wingers Brian Noonan and Stephane Matteau, as well as a pair of Messier favorites from the Oilers, thirty-four-year-old legend Glenn Anderson and thirty-five-year-old center Craig MacTavish.

Cheeky Islanders fans took to calling their rivals the New York OilHawks.

The refurbished Rangers had one Islanders game left in the 1993–94 regular season—April 10 in Uniondale. To the newly minted Presidents' Trophy winners, this nationally televised Sunday matinee meant zero, but for their upstart neighbors, there could not be more on the line. The Isles were tied with the Florida Panthers for the eighth and final Eastern Conference postseason spot with just three games remaining.

Arbour's Army took care of business, 5–4, and clinched the playoffs three nights later, setting up the "Expressway Series, Part VIII."

Crosstown Crushing

"I don't think there's a more challenging opponent we could face in the first round," shared Richter. Many agreed.

Despite a 14-game difference between the teams, it was hard to find a pundit from counties Suffolk to Sullivan who didn't view the series as a toss-up. Some even gave the Islanders a slight edge. They had their reasons:

1) Big-game goaltending.

Hextall had won the Conn Smythe Trophy as postseason MVP in 1987. Richter still wore the stigma of the 1992 Penguins series, specifically a pivotal Game Four Ron Francis dump-in from the neutral zone that somehow squeezed between his legs.

2) Head to head.

Since their defeat in the 1990 playoffs, the Isles had dragged the Rangers up, down, and sideways, to the tune of 14–7–4.

3) Momentum.

The Islanders would not have qualified for the playoffs if not for an eight-game unbeaten streak in April.

4) Luck.

How else could one explain the on-ice fortunes of these two franchises? The Islanders crest had mystical powers, so it seemed, while the Rangers logo was infected by Red Dutton and the Curse of the Cup.

At least up until that point—Sunday April 17, 1994, at 1:00 p.m.—when the Islanders and Rangers took the Garden ice for Game One before another national television audience.

Whatever pressure was on the home team—and there were mounds of it—was eased by a Brian Leetch power-play goal just 3:34 in. It was 2–0 Rangers after one.

Then with the teams skating four-a-side midway through the second, Messier took a left-wing drop pass from Graves just inside the blue line and trickled an unassuming wrister through Hextall's five-hole. The crowd didn't know whether to clap or laugh. Even Moose admitted he had no intention of scoring with the shot. "Obviously, it was a terrible goal," admitted Hextall.

From then on, fans gave the veteran Hextall a series of Bronx cheers that seemed to never end. Every time he caught a long dump-in with his goalstick, he received a sarcastic standing ovation. It happened a handful of times.

And they sang, "Hehhhxxxx . . . taaaalll, Hehhhxxxx . . . taaaalll." The game was slipping away from the Islanders.

Three minutes after the Messier goal, Graves made it 4–0. Two minutes after that, Kovalev embarrassed Kasparaitis, Krupp, and Hexy to make it 5–0. Three minutes after that, Zubov scored the final goal of the day. Hextall was finally pulled for Jamie McLennan. 6–0 was the final. For those in royal blue and orange, it was the afternoon from hell.

Game Two was the very next night. In a surprising move, Arbour started McLennan, his backup. It felt a little panicky. Still, everyone expected a closer contest than that of the previous day.

The Rangers led only 1–0 after the first, but the Isles surrendered four goals in the second period again, and another 6–0 rout was on. Richter made 29 saves to secure his second shutout in a thirty-three-hour span.

The Series Shifts to Nassau

Unlike their heroes, the home fans at the Coliseum were ready when called upon. Chants of "LET'S GO ISLANDERS" and "19–40!" drowned out any murmur of "Let's Go Rangers" leading up to Game Three in Uniondale on Thursday, April 21.

"WE CAN DO IT!" said one banner.

Arbour went back to Hextall to start. He also made changes on offense and defense, making the lineup bigger and tougher.

The Coliseum boiled to full froth. The puck was dropped. The game began. Esa Tikkanen scored at 2:08 on a slap shot from the top of the left circle. Leetch scored on a power play 1:38 later—another point slapper past Hexy's leg. 2–0 visitors.

Low, long goals by the Rangers were now *the* theme of Hextall's season. He had only one save in the first period. Graves beat him from the slot midway through the second. 3–0.

Long Island's first goal of the series was more embarrassing than it was therapeutic. Ferraro chipped in a rebound at 15:28, and the place exploded, as if they never thought they'd see another goal for the rest of their lives.

After all, the Isles had gone almost 204 minutes without scoring, going back to the regular season. That's over ten periods. Ferraro smacked the boards behind the net—his way of venting a series' worth of frustration.

"LET'S GO ISLANDERS" echoed around the building, until Kovalev scored on a power play 3:20 later.

Zap! The wind was sucked right out of the gut of the home crowd again. Now those "LET'S GO RANGERS" chants were on the map.

Blueshirts captain Mark Messier (11) beats Islanders goalie Ron Hextall (72) for the 22nd and final Rangers goal of their triumphant sweep in the 1994 playoffs. Hextall surrendered 16 red lights in only 158 minutes of action during the series. This patented Messier right-wing wrister put the Broadway-men ahead, 5-2, in the third period of Game Four, April 24, 1994, at Nassau Coliseum.
(AP Photo/Ron Frehm)

Graves blasted another long one midway through the third. Hextall finished with only 13 saves on 18 shots. Richter made 21. 5–1 was the final.

The series was officially a massacre in progress, and nobody could stop it. Arbour stuck with Hextall for Game Four. It wasn't going to matter.

Armed with little broomsticks and big voices, more Rangers fans came out to this Sunday matinee than to any other Islanders home game outside the first two years of the Long Island franchise. Any Islanders fan would have to be a masochist to show up. Most just didn't have the stomach for it.

Even when the Isles scored on their first two shots of the game, the result was hardly in doubt. Kovalev cut the lead to 2–1 in the first, then Zubov and Messier put Manhattan ahead to stay in the second. In keeping with habit, all three shots beat Hextall from beyond the circles.

The Rangers added a pair of goals in the third period, including Messier's fourth of the series, for a 5–2 final.

"SWEEP! SWEEP! SWEEP! SWEEP!" Blueshirts-backers had taken over the building.

Coliseum Conquerors. The Rangers enjoy one of their greatest moments on Long Island ice, as they celebrate their four-game dismantling of the upstart Islanders, April 24, 1994, at Nassau Coliseum. *(AP Photo/Ron Frehm)*

Giddy fans threw their brooms on the ice as their heroes celebrated the win. On the other end of the rink, not one Islander held his head high, nor deserved to.

"It's embarrassing, really, to us and our fans to go out there and play this way," said Steve Thomas.

Even Kasparaitis was rendered ineffective. The Rangers didn't fall for his shenanigans, and he wound up a minus-six for the series.

With an aggregate margin of 22–3, this 19-goal Rangers blowout is second only to the 1972 Boston Bruins' 28–8 semifinals advantage over the St. Louis Blues. The Rangers led for a total of 198 minutes and 17 seconds, while the Islanders led for 22:14 overall. The score was tied for 19:29.

Several stars contributed to the team's success. Brian Leetch had eight points, Alexei Kovalev and Mark Messier each had seven, Sergei Zubov had six, and Adam Graves had five.

"I honestly do not believe the gap between the Rangers and ourselves is as severe as this series showed," said Don Maloney. "But on the other hand, you have to bow to them. They absolutely humbled us . . .

"It went from bad, to worse, to disaster."

BENCHMARK GAME: URBAN SWEEP

April 24, 1994
Nassau Coliseum

Rangers 5 Islanders 2
(4–0) (0–4)

Like the upset of '75, the sweep of '94 was a turning point in the relationship between New York's hockey fan bases. Seven weeks later, the Rangers were finally champions, and their fans *still* hold the sweep over Islanders fans.

Arbour's loyalty to Hextall in Games Three and Four surprised a lot of newspeople. Al surprised them further Monday when he ditched clear-out day, heeding the old advice, "If you've got nothing nice to say, say nothing at all."

"He doesn't want to see any of the players," explained second-year Islanders general manager and former Broadway man Don Maloney. "He is that upset."

Maloney was asked which Islanders in his estimation did not play up to their potentials. His answer: "Who *did*?"

THE MAVEN REMEMBERS: TENNIS, ANYONE?

Islanders fans chanted "19–40!" with so much zest and for so long, it seemed as if the anti-Rangers ribbing would go on forever. But it ended abruptly in the Spring of 1994 when the Rangers dominated the Isles in the playoffs.

The "tennis tourney" went by scores 6–0, 6–0, 5–1, and 5–2, and Isles goalie Ron Hextall was worth every bit of the negative critiques he received.

Needless to say, one series does not make a Stanley Cup winner, but it sure catapulted the Blueshirts into the postseason stratosphere.

Among other things, it muted a once-audible shout that went something like this—"19–40!"

Yet while certainly the Rangers and their supporters held short-term bragging rights in the battle of the Apple, general bragging rights still lived in Nassau, with all the records and hardware and lack of documented hexes.

Back in preseason, Keenan had showed his new team a video compilation of past ticker-tape parades in Manhattan's famous Canyon of Heroes. He wanted them to visualize the moment they were working toward. To date, the only New York hockey ticker-tape parades had been on Hempstead Turnpike in Uniondale.

The Blueshirts trailed in the Eastern Conference Finals, 3–2, after five tenacious games with the young New Jersey Devils. Keenan's crew was in disarray. Key guys were hurting. Coach and players were squabbling. Rookie goaltending sensation Martin Brodeur and his Devils teammates were the toast of the Garden State . . . and Long Island.

The Devs manhandled the Rangers for most of Game Six and led, 2–0. The Jersey faithful chanted "19–40!" and the Canyon of Heroes seemed a million miles away.

But New York stormed back behind terrific play from Richter, a goal by Kovalev at the close of the second period, and a natural hat trick by Messier in the third.

Two nights later, the Rangers led Game Seven, 1–0, into the final minute . . . final half-minute . . . final ten seconds. The Garden was going bananas!

But Devils winger Valeri Zelepukin just *barely* slid a rebound under Richter's left pad. The clock showed 7.7. It was as if the puck had been pushed across the line by the ghost of Red Dutton himself.

Now the 1994 Rangers were staring that ghost in the face. One slip-up and the ticker-tape was dead—their first-place season, their sweep of the Islanders, their Game Six comeback in Jersey all for naught.

They defied the ghost—and the Devils—with a dominant sudden-death performance and a double-overtime wraparound goal by Keenan's guy, Stephane Matteau. The Rangers graduated to a Stanley Cup Finals matchup with the Vancouver Canucks, while Isles fans graduated from the first stage of grief—denial—to the second stage—anger.

The Blueshirts moved out to a three-games-to-one advantage, but in Game Five, the Canucks spoiled a magical, three-goal, third-period Rangers comeback.

Then they blew out the Manhattan-men in Game Six. On to a seventh game!

"There are 23 million people in New York today," joked Glenn Healy, "who have already dialed the nine and the one."

After the final practice of the season, Keenan dusted off his ticker-tape parade video and popped it in the VCR one last time. A lot of players were hardly speaking with him at that point, but they all respected the video.

The Game Seven MSG crowd hid their nerves as best they could. By the time Garden staple John Amirante belted out the national anthems, fans were screaming their hearts out. Miles east, rival-rooters were equally anxious.

The Blueshirts took a 3–1 lead into the third period. The Canucks scored 4:50 into the third. The tension was unbearable. With six minutes to go, Vancouver center Nathan LaFayette sent a ten-foot one-timer towards a yawning net . . . and hit the post. It was pure luck—the type of thing Rangers fans hadn't seen in 54 years.

"NO MORE CURSES!" screamed Sam Rosen, as the Blueshirts held on, 3–2!

That's when Islanders fans attained the fourth level of grief—depression. For most, the final stage—acceptance—hasn't set in to this day.

Back in Midtown, jubilant Adam Graves screamed "19–40!" into the closest camera.

On Friday June 17, 1994, a steady stream of modern-day ticker-tape—not unlike the confetti that would often spray from the Nassau Coliseum crowd in their glory years—fluttered across the clear New York sky, glistening in the early summer sun and landing on floats carrying Keenan, Messier, Conn Smythe winner Brian Leetch, and the 1994 Blueshirts, while 1.5 million people lined the Canyon of Heroes.

Chapter 7

SIDESHOWS

"It doesn't seem to matter where anybody is in the standings. The Rangers fans don't like the Islanders. So the game is always an emotional game and it's always an exciting hockey game."

—Islanders forward/coach Butch Goring

"Even in the locker room, you can hear the chanting and everything. Sometimes there's more fights in the stands than on the ice."

—Islanders/Rangers defenseman Bryan Berard

"It's a rivalry, we're close in the standings, but it's more than that. It's personal."

—Rangers forward Theoren Fleury

Your typical head coach won't get run out of town six weeks after winning the Stanley Cup. Mike Keenan, however, was never your typical head coach.

Alas, by July 25, 1994, Iron Mike was general manager and bench boss of the St. Louis Blues, leaving Neil Smith happily in search of the New York Rangers' fourth head coach in twenty months.

Smith learned firsthand about the "baggage" following Keenan from Philadelphia to Chicago to New York. He had been called four things—ambitious, cantankerous, conniving . . . and a winner. In only fourteen months with the Rangers, Keenan demonstrated all four.

Whereas in 1993, Smith eagerly signed up for Keenan's act, by spring of 1994 he regretted it, even as the Blueshirts skated toward their first Stanley Cup in the modern era of hockey.

Throughout that run Smith made tongue-not-quite-ensconced-in-cheek remarks to reporters about his head coach, such as "He doesn't have an escape clause, but if he wants to go, I'll drive him to the airport," and "If we win the Cup and he leaves, it will be like winning two Cups."

In the end, Smith had his two Cups, though he never did personally drive Keenan to the airport.

Like their on-ice product, the parting of this coach-GM duo was a thing of beauty. Keenan was too successful to fire, nor could he quit, because there were four years left on his contract. So when his Stanley Cup bonus check arrived one day past the July 14 deadline, he stood up and proclaimed the entire deal void. Commissioner Gary Bettman dissolved the contract, and on August 9, 1994, a forty-one-year-old former journeyman blue-liner, Colin Campbell, was introduced as the next head coach of the Rangers.

Area fans of some vintage remembered Campbell as the fellow who nearly stopped one of the greatest goals in Islanders history—Mike Bossy's mid-air masterpiece in Game Three of the 1982 Finals, when Campbell, then of Roger Neilson's Vancouver Canucks, slid desperately across the goal line in a failed but noble attempt to block Boss's pinpoint backhand.

In that way, Campbell's name was an echo of a bygone era of Islanders dominance that had withered almost completely away, a reality reinforced when Al Arbour stepped down as coach on June 1, 1994, to be replaced by an original Islander, forty-two-year-old Lorne Henning.

Then in August, Cablevision purchased Madison Square Garden. Charles Dolan and his New York cable television giant had agreed to purchase the Islanders from John O. Pickett back in 1992, but the closing deadline came and went without a sale.

Still, when it came to making Islanders fans miserable, losing Arbour to retirement and Cablevision to the Rangers placed distant second and third to the outbreak of Blueshirts Stanley Cup Fever sweeping across the region.

It was the Summer of Stanley in New York. The Cup was everywhere. The players were everywhere. Starter brand official Rangers championship caps were everywhere. It was inescapable.

Not even the Keenan controversy could derail the love-fest, nor could the labor strife that hampered the National Hockey League all year. Hockey went on hold—a process that ultimately bit a three-month chunk out of the 1994–95 season—but the Big Apple hardly bickered. Islanders fans were down on their club anyway, and for the first time in over five decades, Rangers fans were incapable of anger.

The season began in January, 1995. Blueshirts Nation had a blast, especially when it came to the rivalry.

The Isles and their supporters knew what was coming. They found Rangers fans quite arrogant already, even before the team had won anything. Now? Forget it. As the season crept closer, Uniondale braced for the worst.

In fact, it was only a week before the lockout that Islanders general manager Don Maloney—a longtime veteran of Isles-Rangers from both sides—decided there was one thing he never, ever, ever wanted to hear again . . .

"Hehhhhh . . . xtaaaaalllll . . . Hehhhhh . . . xtaaaaalllll . . ."

So he traded his beleaguered goalie, Ron Hextall.

"It bothered me," Maloney admitted. "The effect it has on a team when a bad goal goes in on the road, and the Hextall chant goes up. That's rattling."

"Well, I've been booed before," the spirited Hextall shot back. "Was I the whole reason we lost? I don't think so."

He was sent to his original team, the Philadelphia Flyers, in exchange for twenty-five-year-old netminder Tommy Soderstrom.

And naturally, when the Isles and Rangers met for the first time in 1995—March 23 on Long Island—the most electric chant of the night was "WE-WANT-HEX-TALL! *Clap, clap, clap-clap-clap!*" care of those in blue and red.

Coincidentally, Soderstrom made 37 saves in a 1–0 Islanders victory that night, including a dandy on Brian Leetch in the final seconds.

The suburbanites fared well for the entire 1995 season series, going 3–1–0 against Big Brother, yet for their fans, the games were still torture. After decades of taunting directed east to west, it was time for Islanders-rooters to pay the piper, and the city-backers weren't offering any discounts.

Rangers fans had a newfound air of aplomb. They were out for comeuppance, walking around the concourses with an angry pride in their eyes, looking for Islanders fans to terrorize. "19–40!" was nowhere. "We-Want-Hextall!" was everywhere. During a timeout in the third period of the March 23 game, a fan near section 315—upstairs behind Mike Richter—tied a mini-replica Rangers 1994 Stanley Cup banner to an inflated helium balloon and let it go. Blueshirts fans stood and cheered and whistled as the banner floated into the Nassau Coliseum rafters, triumphantly in their eyes, helplessly in those of the home-backers.

The second crosstown meeting of 1995 was April 7 at Madison Square Garden—a low point in the Rangers' season, and a low point in Islanders history.

The Isles Get Stood Up in Midtown

Pierre Turgeon had only 27 points in 34 games and was minus-12. Those in charge were not happy with his effort. So Maloney put the superstar on the trading block and on April 5 got fleeced. Sneaky Pete and Vladimir Malakhov were dealt for the captain of the Montreal Canadiens, playmaker Kirk Muller, as well as defenseman Mathieu Schneider and forward prospect Craig Darby.

"From a fan's point of view, they're probably wondering how the heck we could ever trade Pierre Turgeon," admitted Maloney. "We need to find competitive people and leaders here."

"Competitive." "Leader."

That's what Muller, the twenty-nine-year-old six-time All-Star and former captain of the New Jersey Devils, meant to the Isles. What did the Isles mean to him? They were about to find out.

The trade was completed by 1:30 p.m. Wednesday. Turgeon and Malakhov flew to Montreal and scored five points combined in a 6–5 win that very evening. Meanwhile, Muller and Schneider were to fly out at five. Neither did.

Instead, Muller was on Montreal TV expressing his grief—tears and everything. He walked out on the interview.

So Maloney told the press they can expect the boys Thursday. Schneider showed, but Muller didn't.

Muller asked to be flipped at the trade deadline, 3 p.m. Friday. Maloney balked.

Maloney pleaded, "Please, give us a chance." Muller balked.

By Friday evening, Maloney had to face reporters in Madison Square Garden and answer the obvious question: "Where's the other guy you traded Turgeon for?"

"Personal time," he responded.

It was official. Kirk Muller ditched the first Islanders-Rangers game of his career, though he did have the decency to show up two games later.

What was left of the team (Benoit Hogue had been traded, too) took the ice on April 7 to a deafening new post-'94 Cup brand of Garden hatred and somehow prevailed, 4–3, after trailing, 2–0, early on.

THE MAVEN REMEMBERS: KIRK MULLER TRADE

I was unimpressed with the Kirk Muller trade. I vividly remembered how he snubbed Lou Lamoriello and jumped ship on the Devils. What's more, I'd become enamored by Pierre Turgeon's play and hated the idea that he was leaving the Islanders.

But that was small potatoes compared to what would follow. A deal was a deal, and I looked forward to the change of personnel, merely for the sake of change. What's more, the idea of Muller and Matt Schneider coming aboard hours before a Rangers game at the Garden really whetted my broadcasting appetite.

So there I was, two hours before game time, standing in the cramped corridor outside the visitors' dressing room at the Garden. All manner of media types established their own personal turf anticipating a media scrum with Muller and Schneider. As the minutes ticked off with neither showing up, I felt an uneasy pain in the pit of my stomach, anticipating that something had gone wrong, but I wasn't sure what.

When Matty Schneider finally appeared, I knew what it was all about. Islanders P.R. director Ginger Killian finally allowed that there would be no Kirk Muller on this night. But there was no explanation as to why—whether he had the flu, missed his flight, or simply developed a dislike over the idea that he would be an Islander.

Eventually Muller relented, arrived on the Island and appeared before the media, and supremely unconvincingly said he was ready to give his all for the Nassau-men.

As a musicologist, I was reminded of Frank Sinatra's classic rendition of the song, "All or Nothing at All." In the end, the Islanders got nothing at all from Muller.

The star of the 1995 season series was Soderstrom—brilliant in four starts with a .944 save percentage and 2.00 goals against average. Unfortunately for Lorne Henning, the soft-spoken Swede and his teammates were not nearly as effective in their other 44 games. The Isles finished next-to-last in the entire NHL, besting only the relatively brand-new Ottawa Senators. Maloney canned the popular coach after only one year.

Meanwhile, former Islander Glenn Healy was becoming the first man to play the role of postseason hero for both New York teams.

Freed from the pall of his tormentor (Mike Keenan), the 1993 Isles' Upset Kid played so well in 1995 that Colin Campbell started him over Mike Richter three times in the Rangers' first round matchup with the top-seeded Quebec Nordiques.

Healy helped the Rangers turn the series around with huge victories in Games Two and Three. Richter finished off the Nords in six. Late in the clincher, the Garden faithful turned their attention to the next opponent, the second-seeded Philadelphia Flyers.

"WE-WANT-HEX-TALL! *BOOM, BOOM, BOOM-BOOM-BOOM!*"

"WE-WANT-HEX-TALL!*BOOM,BOOM,BOOM-BOOM-BOOM!*"

If they'd said it once, they'd said it 10,000 times—Rangers fans wanted Ron Hextall.

"We had his number last year," said Colin Campbell in what appeared to be an understatement.

For the second year in a row, the Rangers and Hextall collided in the playoffs, and for the second year in a row, it was a one-sided sweep. Hexie stopped 109 of 119 shots and got the last laugh. For at least one member of the 1994 Islanders, there could be a modicum of redemption.

Milbury—Love at First Whack

The heroics of Healy and Hextall reflected poorly on Don Maloney, who had gotten rid of them both. Throw in the public relations nightmares that followed the Turgeon trade, and it was fair to say Maloney needed a home run with his next move.

On July 6, 1995, he brought in the man considered the best available coach in all of hockey, a forty-three-year-old Walpole, Massachusetts, native who would surge to the forefront of the Isles-Rangers conflict and stay there a long time—perhaps too long, in the opinion of many.

The sixth coach in Islanders history had guts galore and a mouth to match. His name was Michael James Milbury.

Milbury was well received on Long Island. For one thing, he'd taken the Boston Bruins to the 1990 Stanley Cup Finals and the 1991 Wales Conference Finals in his only two prior seasons as an NHL head coach. Pretty good.

Even better, in the eyes of many—during a postgame melee on December 23, 1979, Milbury, then a Bruins defenseman, climbed into the MSG stands and wailed on a Rangers fan with the man's own shoe.

To Islanders fans, it was love at first whack.

New York stations showed old clips of "The Shoe Incident" for days after the hiring. But two weeks later, the Rangers administered a blow of their own.

Ray Ferraro was one of the most popular remaining New York Islanders—if not *the* most. The thirty-year-old, 5-foot-9 fireball led the team in scoring for the 1993 playoff run, plus the entire 1995 season.

He was also a free agent, and as would become a common refrain for years to come, the Nassau-men didn't have the money.

Neil Smith chimed in with $5 million over three years and a team option for a fourth. Ray made the Isles and their fans feel every penny's worth of pain. Whoever penned the expression "Words will never hurt" could not have foreseen the words Ferraro would come up with for his July 19 press conference at the Garden.

"I'm coming to a team that's not happy just to get through the first round of the playoffs," he cracked, a scantily veiled shot at the team he was leaving. "I don't want to go through that again."

Ferraro also touched the most sensitive nerve in all of Islanders Country. "The year we went to the semifinals," he explained, "the Rangers hired Mike Keenan. There it was again! We were the only team playing, and Keenan was the main story. I wanted to go somewhere where hockey is on the front page.

"I know people are going to view it like I fled the store, but it's not like we didn't give the Islanders ample opportunity to match the offer."

"We'd have liked to keep Ray" was Don Maloney's response. "But we're not going to cry over it."

Perhaps they should have.

The 1995–96 Islanders were comprised almost exclusively of players who were before their prime, past their prime, or never had a prime. Throw in Muller, who didn't want to be there, and it was no surprise they were still winless when Ferraro came back to town on October 17, 1995.

As an Islander, Ray had loved the intimacy of Nassau Coliseum. Now he got to hear it from the other side. "I've been called a lot of things today," he joked.

The first time he touched the puck there was hardly an Islanders fan in the building not screaming "BOOOOO!" There was also hardly an Islander on the ice in Ferraro's vicinity.

A dump-in would end all the booing. Ferraro chose to bask in the moment.

He carried down left wing. The booing intensified. He undressed Dean Chynoweth forehand to backhand and unleashed a wrister past rookie goalie Tommy Salo. The Islanders fans finally shut up. The Rangers fans erupted. Time of the goal was 1:23 of the first. That's how long it took Ray Ferraro to shove it down the Islanders' throats.

Only five games in, the 1995–96 Islanders season felt like it was already over. "It looks like the worst-coached team in hockey," groaned Milbury.

It also looked like the worst-dressed team in hockey, at least in the court of public opinion.

New Uniforms, Same Rivalry

Back in December 1991, absentee Islanders owner John O. Pickett abdicated operational control of the franchise to a crew of season ticket holders who had loaned the team money.

They were known as the "Gang of Four," and on June 22, 1995, they unveiled the Isles' brand new series of intellectual property, their magnum opus of absurdity.

There was a new uniform pattern, new colors, two new logos, and even a mascot—a giant, creepy, red-bearded, middle-aged man named Nyisles in full hockey gear with a goal-lamp on his head, as if the Turgeon-less power play weren't enough to give local children nightmares.

The stated purpose of the switch was to better connect the team to the community. The Gang believed the Islanders' old style was not "Long Island" enough. For the record, that original blue and orange are the official colors of Nassau County, and the logo is a map of Long Island.

The designers went deep into the Crayola box on this one. There was some really dark blue, some tangerine, some teal, and some light gray. It was busy. In addition, instead of stripes around the waist, there was a large wave. Across the shoulders was a small wave. Each sleeve had a medium wave. The logo was an elderly hockey stick-toting fisherman— albeit with an impressive physique—above a wave. The shoulder patch was a lighthouse in front of a wave. There were so many waves.

"The Islanders were living in the shadow of the Rangers," designer Ed O'Hara later told *Newsday*. "We all agreed that a strengthened tie to Long Island was important."

Guess who did not agree.

"I've gotten 500 negative letters already," said the Gang of Four's Stephen Walsh at the press conference. "We get threatened every day," concurred his colleague Robert Rosenthal.

But Maloney stood by the company line. "New fans will love it," he said, "casual fans will love it, and for the traditional fans, we'll have to teach them how to love it."

The fans who loved it most were those of the Broadway Blueshirts.

Especially since by the time the 2–10–2 Isles visited the 9–5–1 Rangers on November 10, every hockey fan in the area had noticed that the new logo bore a hysterical resemblance to that of a prevalent frozen seafood company called Gorton's.

Yep, there was a Gorton's Fisherman.

He wore a banana-colored raincoat, whereas the Isles' Fisherman preferred Caribbean green. Otherwise they were quite similar, from their bucket hats to their chiseled features and their gray beards.

Thanks to these unlikely doppelgangers, Madison Square Garden had its new favorite chant:

"WE-WANT-FISH-STICKS! *Clap, clap, clap-clap-clap!*"

The crowd ridiculed the Islanders for the duration of an easy 4–1 win. In the third period, two fans put on yellow ponchos and fake beards and went marching through the arena. The bit tickled the crowd.

An Ex-Ranger Becomes an Ex-Islander

Maloney couldn't find the right trade for Kirk Muller, who became such a cranky, divisive force that his coach couldn't even take it anymore. Two days after the loss in the Garden, Milbury kicked him off the team. The situation sealed Don Maloney's fate.

Islanders fans—the few that still watched in person—started chanting "Don-Must-Go!" at every home game. Many joked that Maloney must still be on the Rangers' payroll. Some with even more vivid imaginations yelled he was a Rangers mole all along, sent to sabotage the Islanders' roster and uniforms. Maloney was finally fired on December 2, 1995. He went to work for Neil Smith and the Rangers the following season.

Mike Milbury was elevated to the dual role of coach and general manager and finally traded Kirk Muller to the Toronto Maple Leafs in January. Things felt calmer, but the Islanders' nightmare season was far from over.

THE MAVEN REMEMBERS: MAGNIFICENT—OR MAD— MIKE; TAKE YOUR PICK

I befriended Mike Milbury when he was a defenseman for the Boston Bruins. I liked everything about him. He was a New Englander, brash, hardworking, and didn't mind an occasional fight. I especially enjoyed our interviews. Milbury was such a good talker that *Newsday*'s sports TV columnist at the time, Stan Isaacs, wrote that he should be on between the second and third, as well as the first and second, periods.

The other thing I admired was the fact that Milbury had the guts to fight Alan Eagleson, who not only ran the NHL Players' Union, but was the number-one agent in the business for a long time. In those days, it was not healthy to go to war with Eagleson, but Mike didn't care. In the end, Milbury was not the lone Eagleson critic among the players. Eventually—under pressure from his constituents—Eagleson resigned from his role as executive director.

To some observers it was surprising that Mike lasted eleven years as general manager on the Island. There were, however, reasons. For one thing he was—and still is—a persuasive charmer and master of the "schmooze."

For another, whenever a new owner took command, he was willing to give Milbury an opportunity to make the team better, rather than bring in someone less conversant with the organization.

Ultimately, Mike became an acerbic analyst for *NBC* and still remains a friend whenever we meet.

Same as he was as a player, Mike has remained a spicy character among too many vanilla types in our business.

In early February, Ray Ferraro recorded 3 goals and an assist in a home-and-home Blueshirt sweep of their lowly neighbors, giving him 6 points in 4 games against his ex-mates, all Rangers triumphs. And he wasn't the only former suburbanite on a Broadway roll; the wins were Healy's third and fourth against the Isles on the season.

After enduring five years without a regular season win at Nassau Coliseum, the Manhattan-men now had 3 in a row—6 of 7 including the postseason. "I think I'm dominating Roger's and Mike's records now," teased Campbell about his predecessors Neilson and Keenan, curators of the late, dreaded 15-game Uniondale winless streak, which now felt like a century ago.

"We've kind of erased a lot of those bad memories," said Brian Leetch.

Spittin' Mad

The back end of that midweek set—February 8 at the Garden—was a rocker from start to finish. The Broadway faithful constantly reminded the Islanders that they were in "LAST-PLACE *Clap-clap*! LAST-PLACE, *Clap-clap*!" and of course, that they, the fans, wanted fish sticks.

In an effort to one-up the Gorton's Fisherman rain slicker costume guys from back in November, somebody threw an actual fish onto the ice with 4:45 to go in the third, causing a delay.

All the taunting clearly got to the Islanders. With 7:51 gone in the second, 6-foot-3 rookie power forward Todd Bertuzzi took a reckless charging penalty on Rangers defenseman Ulf Samuelsson along the endboards. It was the type of hit the 6-foot-1 Swedish sandbagger was accustomed to doling out, but this time he got flattened.

Ulf Samuelsson and Milbury already had a dubious history, dating back to the 1991 Bruins-Penguins Wales Conference Finals, when Ulf took out Boston's superstar Cam Neely with a knee-to-knee open ice collision, a hit that famously left Coach Mike slapping the boards maniacally and smashing a hockey stick across the glass in protest while play continued.

Now five years later, Milbury was watching the aftermath of Samuelsson's scrum with Bertuzzi and could swear he saw Ulf jab "Bert" with the butt of his stick.

So as Samuelsson skated past the Islanders bench, Milbury leaned over and shouted at him. Ulf turned around and went past the Isles again. "I shouldn't have done that," he'd later admit of the second lap.

That's when the match took the tone of the classic 1992 Keith Hernandez *Seinfeld* episode. A bunch of Rangers all claimed they saw Milbury do the same thing. . . .

He spit at him.

"I don't recall," said Milbury. "I *do* recall a severe butt-end by Ulf on Todd Bertuzzi. Did they mention that?"

"No, it was an elbow," replied Samuelsson. "What planet is he on?

"Obviously you do stuff in the heat of the moment, but right now I'm trying to teach my two kids not to spit at each other at home. It's going to be tough now that they saw it on TV."

"If I wanted to spit at somebody, I'd probably hit him," answered Mike. "I'm a pretty good spitter."

The game got further out of hand in the final minute, when Milbury put out a line of toughies and Campbell answered with his own. A brawl ensued between Rangers Joey Kocur, Samuelsson, and Jeff Beukeboom, and Isles Dan Plante, Brent Severyn, and Bertuzzi.

Worse yet for Milbury, Samuelsson wasn't penalized, so with 15 seconds left and the score 5–2, he was free to jump deep into the offensive zone, where he scored a goal. Campbell admitted he'd had Ulf out there because he specifically wanted his prime agitator to score. Milbury called it "the twist of the knife."

The humbled, humiliated Isles sought revenge in the Garden on February 22, 1996, with the fish and spit of two weeks prior barely scraped off the ice.

But what good is motivation without a lineup? The Islanders' best player, twenty-three-year-old Slovakian phenom Zigmund Palffy, would miss the game with a concussion, as would their next leading scorer, Travis Green, with a sprained knee.

Meanwhile, the Rangers entered with a 24-game home unbeaten streak, tied for a franchise high set in 1970–71. One more and these Blueshirts had the team record! It seemed like a sure thing, especially after Bertuzzi left the game in the first period, courtesy of a high-stick from Samuelsson.

Yet somehow the Fish Sticks skated out with a 5–3 win, the highlight of their season. "We are a lot of points out of the playoffs," leveled winger Marty McInnis. "But this is a feather in our cap." Down the aisle, Colin Campbell called it "a good slap in the face."

Speaking of slaps in the face, Milbury was steamed by the one Bertuzzi took from Samuelsson. "I think it's worthy of a suspension," he snapped. "This is getting ridiculous!"

Ulf claimed the high-stick was an accident. "He's still a jerk," answered Milbury.

Colin Campbell upped the ante, mocking the Isles and Milbury, who had spent the previous season as a TV analyst critiquing the work of coaches around the league. "All the coaches watched him on ESPN last year," Campbell smirked, "and we're waiting for him to come through with the goods."

Needless to say, they would have to keep waiting.

The 1995–96 Isles finished last in the Atlantic Division, second-to-last in the Eastern Conference, and third-to-last in the NHL. Meanwhile, the Rangers had a bounce-back year, posting a record of 41–27–14.

They also got their fourth straight Coliseum win, 4–1 this time, in a nationally televised Sunday afternoon grudge match on March 31.

The Isles finally held Ray Ferraro off the board in the Coliseum, but only because he'd been traded to the Los Angeles Kings at the deadline.

Late in the third, the Bertuzzi-Samuelsson tit for tat spun off into some of the most rowdy, crude, borderline inappropriate fisticuffs in Isles-Rangers history.

The teams came together around a spat between Brent Severyn and Darren Langdon. Ulf and Bert found each other, and the rambunctious winger popped the devious defender with a left.

Veteran puncher Shane Churla snuck behind Bertuzzi, put him in a chokehold, and dragged him to the Islanders' net. Bertuzzi pile-drived Churla to the ice. The duo rolled around along the goal line in alternating headlocks, like a pair of adolescents giving each other "noogies."

When Churla got up, he was missing his jersey and most of his shoulder pads. And apparently, he didn't care for undershirts.

Then the pads slipped off. He was naked from the waist up. Fans of both teams were going wild, especially the women.

The tussle dragged on and on. All three officials tried to break it up, but they quickly became collateral damage. The players could not care less.

Linesman Jean Morin stepped between Bertuzzi and Churla. Bertuzzi tugged and they all came tumbling down, like a *Three Stooges* routine. Then Big Bert and Churlish Churla spent a minute punching each other around Morin and his partner Kevin Collins.

Collins escorted Churla to the box. Morin was supposed to take Bertuzzi, but they took a detour.

Bertuzzi wanted Samuelsson. Morin held on for dear life. Eventually he, Bertuzzi, and Islanders rookie defenseman Bryan McCabe went toppling over one another.

"Here we are on national television," said Colin Campbell. "You can't toss a linesman."

The league agreed. Bertuzzi was suspended for three games and Churla for two.

The incident shined a FOX TV spotlight on the warts of New York hockey. The Isles were a complete circus. And in just two years, the Rangers had gone from a tough, smart, disciplined championship team to the type of team that gets pulled into that kind of garbage.

After another lopsided second-round exit—this time at the hands of the Pittsburgh Penguins—Rangers fans missed Mike Keenan.

And Islanders fans missed, well . . . the Islanders.

At that moment, a pair of white knights rode into town.

The Great One and the Great Con

First, Wayne Gretzky.

The newest Rangers free-agent center turned down higher offers from other teams to come play with his old pal Mark Messier. Not that it was dirt cheap. The Rangers gave the thirty-five-year-old Gretz a two-year deal worth $8 million, plus incentives.

The Islanders, on the other hand, couldn't even afford to keep their own captain. Thirty-two-year-old Patrick Flatley was bought out in July. To Isles fans, his departure was disheartening. Where he ended up was sickening.

"I specifically called the Rangers for that reason," remembers Flatley of his one-year deal in Midtown. "I was anxious to get some retribution against the Islanders and Milbury because they bought out my contract. I wanted to prove that they had made a mistake. So I was primed for the reverse side of the rivalry."

It was yet one more indignity for Nassau-rooters who'd already watched Glenn Healy and Ray Ferraro hammer the Islanders in 1995–96, beneath chants for Ron Hextall and for Gorton's fish sticks.

On October 10, 1996, John Spano appeared, a flicker of light at the end of the long, dark Hempstead Turnpike.

The Islanders announced that Spano, a thirty-two-year-old Dallas, Texas, businessman and Manhattan native, had agreed in principle to buy a substantial portion—believed to be 82%—of the team and its cable rights from John O. Pickett.

It was the Isles' 25th anniversary season celebration, and Spano walked around the home opener shaking hands and mingling like a celebrity.

"Save-Us-Spano!" chanted the desperate crowd, as well as "Last-Place-Ran-Gers!" whenever the out-of-town scoreboard flashed updates about a certain 0–3–2 club and their developing 5–2 loss in Montreal.

Indeed, the Gretz 'n' Mess reunion tour was not the cakewalk that Neil Smith had hoped, even though both were off to flying starts. The Rangers came into the Coliseum on November 6 at only 6–7–3 and left no better off after a fierce 1–1 tie.

The game was so competitive, Milbury even prefaced his obligatory postgame Rangers putdown with a quasi-compliment. "That's not a bad hockey club we were playing," he said. "They get paid a lot more than we do."

It was $38 million to be exact, the highest payroll in the league. Yet the Blueshirts finished only fourth in the Atlantic Division at 38–34–10. Equally frustrating was their inability to dominate Little Brother the way they had in 1995–96.

After the tie in November, the teams alternated victories and finished 1996–97 in a 2–2–1 standoff. Here are the highlights:

- On December 11 at the Garden, Tommy Salo dazzled with one of the superior goaltending shows in the history of the rivalry, a 37-save binge in a stunning 5–3 Islanders win.

Midway through the third, he slid right to left across the goalmouth to snag a Gretzky opportunity that was so ripe, the Garden lighting director put a spotlight on The Great One and the sound guy blasted off the goal horn!

They had both been fooled, along with more than 18,000 other people in the building and millions watching on TV.

- On January 2 at the Garden, the Rangers finally solved Salo with a late third-period comeback.

In a furious matter of moments, Messier assisted on defenseman Alexander Karpovtsev's game-tying goal at 13:12, then scored the game-winner at 16:30.

- On January 13 at MSG, the Rangers debuted their new third uni-forms—darker blue, red, and silver sweaters adorned with the face of the Statue of Liberty.

"Yuck," critiqued Mike Milbury.

"They didn't overdo it," rebuffed Rangers star winger Luc Robitaille. "Some teams did. I'm not going to name names."

Incidentally, the Rangers' Lady Liberty jersey and the Islanders' Fisherman jersey were created by the same designer, Ed O'Hara of the Manhattan company SME.

Milbury's Isles spoiled the evening with a 4–2 win.

- On February 8 at the Coliseum, Messier embarrassed the Isles in cold blood before a Saturday afternoon FOX Network audience, scoring goals 30, 31, and 32 on the season—one in each period—for the first-ever Rangers hat trick in Uniondale.

Moose's last goal delayed proceedings with 3:20 to go while Islanders staff scurried around the rink picking up all the hats that had rained from the crowd, unusual for a visiting player and also not a great look for national TV—at least from the home team's perspective. They cleared the ice as fast as they possibly could.

Less than three and a half minutes earlier, Patrick Flatley had attained the highlight of his personal grudge against the Islanders by stealing the puck from Kenny Jonsson and roofing it over skinny Eric Fichaud for a big insurance goal.

Thus concluded the crosstown season series for 1996–97.

The white knights, however, were just getting started.

John Spano was talking as if he were Santa Claus and all of Long Island had been good. The man had plans.

He claimed to have private investors for a new $180 million arena. He wanted to outbid the rest of the league on every free agent star the roster could hold. Plus he cleaned and repainted the Coliseum bathrooms, a feat that, to Islanders fans, was worth more than a division title.

Milbury even got the go-ahead to boost the league's lowest payroll, so he added quality veteran scorers such as Bryan Smolinski and Robert Reichel, and the Isles almost made the playoffs.

There was a buzz. John Spano and his vision blew a tornado of hope from Manhattan to Montauk Point.

Then there was Gretz.

What was so amazing about Gretzky and his 97-point regular season and 20-point playoff run in 1996–97 was not how his now thirty-six-year-old body defied aging. It didn't. He was slower and less agile in Manhattan than he'd been in Edmonton and even Los Angeles. Gretzky led the Rangers in points almost solely because of his smarts—that supernatural hockey intellect that was already world famous but had always been wrapped in tremendous physical gifts. With those gifts diminishing, The Great One set out to see how far he could go on basically guile alone. The answer was the Eastern Conference Finals.

So the underdog Rangers hopped on Gretzky's back and captivated The Big Apple again, scoring postseason routs of the Florida Panthers and Devils. They even awoke a dormant chant—"We-Want-Hex-Tall!"

Again, the crowd wasn't careful what it wished for.

Ron Hextall relieved Flyers goalie Garth Snow and won Games Three, Four, and Five of the Conference Finals against the Rangers, giving him four straight playoff victories in the Garden since his personal disgrace of April 1994. "When they chant my name, I get all warm and fuzzy," he said.

Despite tip-top seasons from Messier and Leetch, who won his second Norris Trophy, the reunion tour fell seven wins short of the goal.

And the other white knight? Forget it.

In hindsight, we should apologize for mentioning Spano and Gretzky in the same context.

But at the time, Spano felt that important. In fact, he *was* that important. But only in some faraway reality that exists nowhere except in his own head.

Back on earth, here's how it played out. Buckle up:

On February 24, 1997, the NHL had approved the sale of the Islanders to John Spano. All seemed ginger peachy.

On April 7, 1997, the deal was closed, though Spano had failed to tender the first of five $16.8 million installments he owed Pickett for the cable rights. He assured Pickett that the check was on its way.

The cable payment was delayed—inexplicably from Pickett's perspective—for months. The money, it seemed, was everywhere but Long Island—held up by Spano's accountants and trustees, or by bankers in the Cayman Islands, or by clans in South Africa, or even an IRA bombing in London.

Next came the bounced checks and wires.

All the while, Pickett received letters from the banks reassuring him of Spano's accounts. But Pickett would not be appeased until he had the actual dough.

Eventually—and incredibly—Spano offered half the team to the owner of the Garden City Hotel in exchange for just this first $16.8 million payment. Pickett was about to get the money after all. But by then, the FBI and the U.S. Attorney's office were involved. There was no way Spano would be allowed to run an NHL team.

On July 11, 1997, Spano agreed to walk away from the purchase. John O. Pickett reassumed control. The dream ride was over. The Islanders had not been saved after all. Rangers fans had yet another laugh.

Over the next few weeks, the truth came out. Spano's letters were forged. The documents used to obtain Spano's loans were forged. His supposed rich ancestors did not exist.

On July 23, 1997, Spano was arrested for almost every type of fraud extant.

Pickett made out okay, though. He sold the team for about $15 million more than he'd agreed to sell it to Spano, this time to a group headed by forty-six-year-old CEO Steven Gluckstern, along with real estate brothers Howard and Edward Milstein.

1997–98

The Rangers underwent a pretty drastic transformation, as well, not of ownership, but of captaincy. Mark Messier signed with the Vancouver Canucks after a bitter stalemate with Neil Smith and the Garden, during which even Mike Milbury flirted with Mess in the mistaken belief that Moneybags Spano was still his boss.

Speaking of switching sides, on September 29, 1997, Pat LaFontaine was traded from the Buffalo Sabres to the Rangers for a second-round pick.

Yes, *that* Pat LaFontaine, from two chapters ago.

The 1990 playoffs resulted in Patty's first concussion. Unfortunately, it was gradually followed by five others. The Sabres couldn't stomach it anymore.

"I think I'm the only player in history who has been traded twice and hasn't had to change his license plate," joked Mr. New York—State, that is—of his Long Island to Buffalo to Manhattan journey.

The Rangers were set to open their season at home four nights after the trade, against—who else?—the New York Islanders.

Of course, LaFontaine thrilled the crowd with a huge third-period goal. He deflected Alex Karpovtsev's shot past Tommy Salo to knot the matter at two, which is how it ended.

Patty went on to have a good year, with 62 points in 67 games. He scored his 1,000th point on January 22, 1998, at the Garden and was given a long standing ovation. Years earlier, they had rocked and pounded his ambulance. Now he was their hero.

The second Islanders-Rangers game of the season was Halloween Eve at the Coliseum. The hosts had Mike Richter under a spell, while the visitors had themselves under a "misspell."

Of all the names to get wrong, how do you flub Wayne Gretzky? Or, as he was known that evening on the back of his Lady Liberty jersey, "Gretkzy."

The moment of the night was a sensational power-play goal by Isles defenseman Bryan Berard, who toyed with Richter hard—almost obnoxiously—pulling the four-time All-Star farther and farther out of his net with a series of fake shots and passes, like a left-point puppeteer. The reigning Rookie of the Year then smiled at Richter and floated a wrister over his shoulder for a 4–2 lead. Richter was immediately pulled. The homeboys won, 5–3.

The next matchup—Thanksgiving Eve in Nassau—put referee Don Van Massenhoven's patience to the test, as well as Neil Smith's.

The second period was standing room only in the penalty boxes. Of particular unrest were Rich Pilon and Rangers tough-man P.J. Stock, who fought twice on the night.

The Isles breezed by the Blueshirts, 4–1, behind Robert Reichel, who scored three goals and an assist. Like Reichel and Pilon, the crowd was merciless, pounding the sub-.500 Rangers from the anthem to the end.

Smith took issue with Islanders executives about a pair of videos that ran on the scoreboard during TV timeouts. One was "Two Could Play That Game," Bill Smith's famous Hockey Night in Canada 1983 Conn Smythe Trophy acceptance speech in which he mocked Wayne Gretzky for diving. The other was a clip from a September 1997 episode of *The Simpsons* in which Homer insists, "Nothing good has ever come out of New York City." If only cartoons were Smith's biggest problem.

THROUGH THE EYES OF AN ANONYMOUS NASSAU COLISEUM SECURITY GUARD

The hardest part of working Islanders-Rangers games was the major brawls up in the 300 sections.

When you had a mild game against some other team, we security were more of a "Meet-&-Greet." But during Islanders-Rangers games, we were patrolling. There's just a lot of animosity between the two teams. And you'd have groups of Rangers fans in the stands—that's like putting fire near a gas tank. The Islanders fans would go and start a conversation with them, and you know where that ends up—with 10 security shirts up there dragging people out.

We'd always talk about areas that were going to be "hot areas," sections inside that we knew there were tickets sold, so we knew there were going to be Rangers fans. We'd get a heads up from the Islanders that this section or that section was going to be full of Rangers fans, so we'd put a guard on each side at the top and another guard or two at the bottom. Then we'd walk up and down the stairs at the breaks, just to kind of show that we were there. Because all it starts with is someone saying something to someone else, and it just escalates from there.

We'd go over to both of them and say, "Guys, here it is. Here's the warning, and it's one warning. If I have to come up here again, you guys aren't gonna be here for the game. As much as you just spent a boatload of money for the Islanders-Rangers game, you're gonna go."

I personally broke up fights, many times. Down in the 100s, you were on flat ground. But if you were up in the 300s and you were planning to drag somebody 6-foot-3, 200-something pounds down the stairs, it wasn't easy. If you fell, you didn't fall down one step—you fell until you stopped. Happened all the time. We called them "tumblers."

A lot of our guys had some real tough times with injuries. Your arm was swollen, or you fell on your knee or some other thing. The wives knew. They'd see the Rangers coming up on the calendar—"Better get the ice packs in the freezer."

The biggest fights were at the end of the games, when everyone would leave. We'd be watching hot areas, and then fights would break out in the 300s as they came down or as they got into the lobby. You'd have a whole bunch of Rangers fans, everybody chanting, "Rangers suck," or "Islanders suck" or whatever, and then fights would break out all over the place.

So over the radio, we'd hear it all at once, "We've got a fight at Gate Five! We've got a fight at Gate Fifteen!" Different fights were going on, and we didn't have the manpower to go out and squash every one of them. That was when the cops would get involved.

> *Most of the time, there were no charges pressed. But if there was a girlfriend or a wife, and someone turned around and hit her, now these guys want each other arrested. And if that would happen several times, we'd end up with a whole roomful of people in the security office in Gate Five. We had scenarios for Isles-Rangers where it was standing-room only in there. Then of course, they would start to get frisky in there, so we'd cuff them and put them on the floor.*
>
> *I did personally have a lot of people come up and say, "Thank you," after those games. For the most part, they appreciated what we did.*

The "Simpsons game" was the Rangers' third straight defeat, the beginning of a miserable 1–7–4 stretch that flung their season into oblivion.

Colin Campbell was fired on February 18, 1998, and replaced by sixty-three-year-old former Edmonton Oilers Stanley Cup-winning coach John Muckler. The Rangers missed the playoffs and even finished behind the Islanders in the standings for the first time in five years.

And finishing behind the Isles was nothing easy, especially after the mega-drought the suburbanites endured over the holidays (that is, *all* the holidays—Christmas, Hanukkah, New Years, Martin Luther King Day . . .).

It was a 1–13–2 stretch that would have fans chanting, "WE-SUCK! *Clap-clap!*" by January, would have Isles head coach Rick Bowness following Colin Campbell to the unemployment office by March, and would formally introduce the hockey world to two words that came to dominate the next three years of Islanders history: Mad Mike.

The Milstones

Mad Mike was the other Mike Milbury.

Remember, the calm version of Milbury made a ton of shrewd acquisitions for the Islanders—Kenny Jonsson, Zdeno Chara, Roberto Luongo, Eric Brewer, Robert Reichel, Mariusz Czerkawski, and Jason Blake were all steals for what he paid.

But Milbury had an alter ego. They called him "Mad Mike." Mad Mike was the guy who would trade good young players for no discernible reason.

For Islanders fans, it was like getting dumped right as you're falling in love—five times in a row.

It started with Todd Bertuzzi and Bryan McCabe in February 1998. A year later it was Bryan Berard, then Tommy Salo. And the following summer came the pièce de résistance, Roberto Luongo.

They were young, cheap, and about to become stars. Then they were gone. *Poof!* Just like that. It was impulse. Don't bother looking up what came back in return.

The point is that at the end of the 1990s, the Islanders were a punch line on every level.

New owners Steven Gluckstern and Howard Milstein officially took over operational control of the team on February 28, 1998, and their first move was a wise one. It was announced that the fish stick era would be coming to an end. The "wave jerseys" were leaving for good starting in 1998–99 in favor of the old design, only with navy blue instead of royal. The news broke the hearts of many Rangers fans.

But the group that would come to be known by Islanders fans as "The Milstones" didn't stop at the uniforms.

They made their own puzzling contribution to the rivalry in the form of promotional content that praised the loyalty of their own fan base despite:

". . . foiled attempts to get into the playoffs, management confusion, silly logo changes, an empty place in the heart where the fifth Stanley Cup belongs, long lines to the bathroom, and very rude comments from ignorant Rangers fans made with the kind of language that should not be used in front of children."

It was a red flag. Even Islanders fans found it tacky, or at best extremely corny. Then in the lead-up to the next game against the Rangers, there was this gem . . .

"Islanders fans: the game against the Rangers this Saturday is at two o'clock. Rangers fans: that's when the big hand is on the twelve and the little hand is on the two."

Egad, what a cad!

Islanders fan *n.* [< FANATIC]

loyal, passionate, optimistic, heroic, travels to games in freezing rain and snow, loses sleep over missed shots; goes hoarse yelling advice to coaching staff, even while watching on TV; never, ever gives up hope in the club, despite: foiled attempts to get into the playoffs, management confusion, silly logo changes, an empty place in the heart where the fifth Stanley Cup belongs, long lines to the bathroom, and very rude comments from ignorant Rangers fans in the kind of language that should not be used in front of children...

The late-'90s Islanders' ownership group of Steven Gluckstern and the Milstein Brothers—Howard and Edward—loved antagonizing the Rangers and their fans, as this giveaway pin from their earliest days at the helm demonstrates. *(Jacob Weinstock)*

It was in this environment that the teams reconvened at the Coliseum on that Saturday, April 4, 1998. The game was a mess, and an indelible image of Isles-Rangers nonetheless. Once again, FOX let in all of America.

The Islanders took a 3–0 lead at 12:17 of the third. At that moment, Milbury, who had hopped back behind the bench after canning Rick Bowness, decided to call timeout. It was not appreciated.

"He was trying to embarrass our hockey club," fumed Muckler.

The Rangers were infuriated. Milbury's old friend Ulf Samuelsson skated up and expressed as much.

But Milbury insisted that he only called timeout out of a genuine fear his team might blow the lead, given their recent habits. With 12 minutes to go on March 18 in Ottawa, they managed to turn a 4–0 lead into a 4–4 tie.

Milbury also claimed he mouthed "I'm sorry" to Muckler through the partition.

If he did, it's safe to say the apology was not accepted.

On the ensuing shift, 5-foot-11 P. J. Stock got on his tippy-toes and elbowed 6-foot-9 Zdeno Chara in the face. Then Stock and Darren Langdon chased "Big Z" into the Islanders zone.

Langdon fought Chara for only a few minutes shy of forever. New Islander Trevor Linden fought former Islander Bill Berg, Jeff Beukeboom obliterated Isles defenseman J. J. Daigneault, and Stock attacked Mariusz Czerkawski, who was completely defenseless. The 200-pound Polish playmaker didn't much care for contact *during* the game, let alone after a whistle.

Isles goalie Tommy Salo came to Czerkawski's aid. He swung his blocker at Stock once, an air ball, and the high point of the fight for Salo.

Not two seconds later, Rangers goalie Dan Cloutier was on him.

Salo clung to his attacker's jersey, so Cloutier wisely ducked and slipped out of it. That's when Salo completely gave up, kneeling face-down on the ice as though he were praying.

For the next quarter-minute, Cloutier battered Salo with a dark, bitter look in his eyes. His left fist was cocked for one last good one, but the spunky Quebecois finally laid off. What Salo had become was too pathetic to keep punching.

So Cloutier skated right to the home bench and essentially challenged any or all of the twelve Islanders pointing and chirping at him to step on the ice and fight.

"Things have gotten out of control here on Long Island," proclaimed FOX announcer Kenny Albert.

Beukeboom, fresh out of a three-way tussle with Langdon and Chara, soon joined Cloutier in goading the Islanders bench. On his third pass-by, he flashed them his middle finger.

Referee Denis LaRue gave out 154 penalty minutes and seven ejections at once. After the 3–0 Islanders shutout, Muckler called the late timeout "the worst thing you can do."

"I didn't mean to rub salt in the wounds," contested Milbury. "If Samuelsson doesn't make a big stink of it, it goes away."

"He's not going to take responsibility," Samuelsson replied. "It's not his style. But it backfired. He got five guys beat up."

The Rangers answered, to some degree, eleven days later at the Garden with their only win of the season against the Islanders.

But the final—and best—word on the matter went to Daigneault, who, when asked about the one-sided nature of the brawl, smirked, "They have to justify their payroll with something."

BENCHMARK GAME: THE TIMEOUT

April 4, 1998
Nassau Coliseum

Rangers 0 Islanders 3
(22–35–18) (25–38–10)

Goaltenders were the story of this FOX TV Saturday matinee. Tommy Salo threw a shutout. Dan Cloutier threw a Tommy Salo.

For more, we turn over the mic to Mike. Below is Milbury's side of the story:

First of all you have to remember that my Islanders team was not very good during that period of time.

That meant that if we had an opportunity to win a game, I had to do everything in my power as coach to help the winning process along. In this particular case—even though we had a 3–0 lead—I wanted to be sure that we secured it and, to me, it was the proper time to call a timeout; especially since this particular team had a habit of losing leads.

At the time, I was truly surprised that they interpreted it as an insult. I did not—not in any way—mean to show them up. Their goalie Dan Cloutier beat up on our Tommy Salo, and that was typical of the overreaction up and down the line. If you ask me whether Cloutier overdid it, my answer is that it was just part of all of them overreacting.

If I knew that it would have resulted in all that overreaction, I would not have called the time-out. I wasn't looking for the massive brawl. That surprised me and, all things considered, we could've done without it.

Then again, I never expected that they would make such a fuss about a time-out.

At the end of the time-out, longtime Milbury nemesis Ulf Samuelsson skated over to Milbury and screamed at him. Back when the Isles visited MSG on February 8, 1996, Milbury had been seen spitting at Ulf, which the Blueshirts took as disrespectful, and kind of gross. Decades later, the Sultan of Saliva remembers the incident thusly:

This all happened because Ulf was being a jerk. Nothing new there. That's the way he was as a player.

What I did was spit in his direction, not on him. It was more of a derisive response.

What disappointed me more than anything else was that Ulf went to the media and told the press about it. When I heard that, my reaction was something like, "Here's a guy who'd been a jerk, and over something like this, reacts with an 'Oh my God, look what happened to me!' and finds media guys to tell them about it!"

As it happened, 1997–98 was the first year since the birth of the Isles that both they and the Rangers missed the playoffs. The rivalry was in a weird place. With the "Milstones" behind the wheel, the focus began to shift from moves made on the ice to those made in the board rooms.

The anti-Rangers PR campaign continued. One message read, "Ranger fans . . . We really don't understand how you can tolerate living in our friendly neighborhoods with your sophisticated ways."

It was then that the Rangers decided to cancel their custom of scheduling the Islanders in the preseason. Except for the players who'd get knocked on the noggin in these traditionally brawl-filled scrimmages, the series was largely convenient for both sides, especially the Islanders, who made some money off hosting the Rangers every year. So this decision put a financial hurting on the Nassau-men.

An unnamed NHL official told *Newsday* that the move was in response to certain Islanders' behavior, namely, their refusal to wear white at the Rangers' 1997–98 home opener, the antagonistic marketing campaign late in the year, and Mike Milbury's timeout on April 4.

"Gee, I hadn't even thought of those things," cracked Smith.

Once the 1998–99 regular season got underway, the Garden, with its parent company Cablevision, put another harsh squeeze on the Isles. A series of Islanders games, including the home opener, were blocked out on television to accommodate conflicting Rangers and Devils games as well as New York Knicks and New Jersey Nets basketball games on MSG Network and SportsChannel.

The Isles were deteriorating to minor league status. Fans even chanted, "We want Spano!"

And the Milstone shenanigans continued. On a night the Blueshirts were getting blown out in Buffalo, the Coliseum public address announcer gave the Rangers score *twice*, as opposed to the customary zero times. The following season, the Coliseum scoreboard showed a clip from the movie *Godzilla 2000* in which a fighter jet zeroes in on Manhattan while being commanded to "blow up Madison Square Garden!"

With the NHL's lowest payroll, the 1998–99 Isles collapsed to a record of 24–48–10. The Rangers made some additions to their NHL-leading payroll and went 33–38–11. They had improved but were still not good enough. The best part of their season was slapping around the Islanders.

The Rangers won all five meetings. And while neither team was *deluxe*, at least the games were close and evenly matched:

- On October 22 at the Garden, Mike Richter preserved a 3–2 victory by stopping Claude Lapointe on a penalty shot with just 4:42 remaining, 26 seconds after winger Kevin Stevens scored to give the hosts the lead.

The save improved Richter to 9-for-10 lifetime in penalty shot situations. "I'd be surprised if he *did* score," *kvelled* Rangers captain Brian Leetch.

- On December 2 at the Coliseum, Trevor Linden tackled Ulf Samuelsson and wrestled him to the ice in response to a forearm to Bryan Berard's face with 30 seconds left in another 3–2 Rangers win. "I had to do something," said the Isles captain. "He's a dirty player."

- On January 13, 1999 at the Garden, Rangers fans got their first look at their new favorite Islanders goalie, Felix Potvin, who was acquired in a trade a few days earlier. The delighted home crowd waited not even one minute into the game to scream, "Potvin Sucks!"

The Isles knotted the game with 2:52 to play in regulation, but the Rangers won at 3:08 of overtime on a wonderful backdoor pass by Gretzky to Graves.

- On March 14 at the Coliseum, Graves did it again! He unleashed a left-circle slapper past Tommy Salo for another overtime game-winner.

- On March 29 at the Garden, Wayne Gretzky brought the house down.

With the game tied, 1–1, late in the third, he poked a loose puck past goalie Wade Flaherty to not only win the game for the Rangers, but to move his name above Gordie Howe's on the all-time list of National Hockey League and World Hockey Association goals scored.

It was the final goal of Gretzky's career, number 1,072, one more than Howe's combined output from the NHL and WHA regular season and playoffs.

Simply put, it was the highest goals total ever in major professional hockey.

The crowd stood and cheered "GRETZ-KY! GRETZ-KY!" the entire final 2:07 of the game.

John MacLean clinched the win with an empty-net goal, giving the Blueshirts their first sweep of the Islanders since the expansion year of 1972–73.

It was a history-making night for the visitors, as well, but in a peculiar category, to wit, it was the night coach Bill Stewart had one of the worst brain-cramp, foot-in-mouth, self-sabotaging moments ever on record.

The forty-one-year-old former journeyman defenseman had taken over as Islanders head coach in late January after Milbury stepped aside and was doing a decent job. But about ten straight minutes of Gretzky Fest had "Stewie" stewing. "Have you looked at our lineup?" he asked reporters. "Enough said!"

Obviously, Bill Stewart was not asked back. On May 1, 1999, he was formally succeeded by an Islanders hero, four-time Stanley Cup champion Butch Goring.

Goring had previous coaching experience in the National Hockey League, American Hockey League, and International Hockey League. Leading the Isles was the 49-year-old former Conn Smythe winner's dream job. But who were these Isles he'd be leading?

All the Milstones' attempts at a new building—from buying out the existing lease to a melodramatic "safety" hazard—were going nowhere. So Milbury was asked to lower the payroll even further.

All big-money players—and medium-money players—needed to go, even if that meant trading captain Trevor Linden.

Even if it meant trading Zigmund Palffy.

Even if it meant trading Zigmund Palffy . . . to the Rangers?

Yes, for the right price, even Zigmund Palffy to the Rangers.

Blockbuster Blocked

Oh, Ziggy Palffy.

Fans called him "Ziggy Stardust." The Isles may have chosen to also, if only they could ever afford the royalties.

When it came to the second half of the '90s, Ziggy Palffy was *it* on Long Island. Yeah, he was a perimeter player. But on a 25-win team, what's the difference? The kid was exciting.

Ziggy was tailor-made to be the best player on a losing team. In that way, he and the Isles were perfect for each other. In fact, he was one guy who actually looked good in the fisherman uniform. He had the air, the hair, and the flair, plus the goal totals—43 in '96, 48 in '97, and 45 in '98.

But what he didn't have, come 1998–99, was a contract.

Thus began Ziggy's holdout. The sniper sat home in Slovakia while his agent Paul Kraus and Milbury threw flaming bags of verbal manure at each other. Mike's most widely circulated quotes about Kraus from the negotiation were "Too bad he lives in the city, he's depriving some small village of a pretty good idiot," and "We hope that Ziggy will come to his senses. We have no hope that Paul Kraus will."

In December 1998, Team Palffy released a bombshell of its own, a published report from Slovakia in which Ziggy essentially asked to be traded to the Rangers.

"I want to play hockey, but not for the Islanders anymore," he said. "I want to be traded. I love my teammates, but I don't want to work for these people anymore. They don't want to do anything to help the hockey team."

Ziggy then vowed he would go to "a team that wants to spend money on hockey." The writer asked him his first choice. Palffy replied, "The Rangers."

It was believable, too. Ziggy had just bought a house on Long Island, and word was he did not want to move.

The drama took a recess when the Isles inked Palffy to a five-year deal worth $26 million in December, 1998. "I didn't say I wanted to *be* a New York Ranger," he clarified upon reporting. "I said I wanted to *beat* the New York Rangers."

But come June 1999, it was time to flip Ziggy and his salary for the best offer. Word was the best offer had come from Neil Smith. It started as innuendo, then speculation, then it was rumor, then strong rumor, then it was imminent. Islander fans already suspected doom.

The Isles insisted they would not send their superstar through the tunnel unless the Rangers' bid *far* surpassed all others. The problem was that the Rangers' bid—agreed upon not by the general managers but by both ownership groups in a meeting at Game Six of the New York Knicks-Indiana Pacers NBA Conference Finals, of all places—far surpassed all others.

It was twenty-four-year-old forwards Niklas Sundstrom and Todd Harvey plus a first-round pick in the 1999 draft, $2.5 million in cash, and prospect Pat Leahy for Palffy and Rich Pilon.

Commissioner Gary Bettman was on top of the situation. He told the teams the $2.5 million payment needed to come down to $1 million, or his office would not approve the trade. Then he called the Los Angeles Kings and urged them to join the Ziggy sweepstakes.

But two days after the biggest Knicks game in Islanders-Rangers history, both *Newsday* and the *New York Times* reported that the deal with the Rangers was made. They got all the details right, down to the picks and the cash amount. Someone had leaked the trade.

Then the Kings made an offer. It wasn't quite as good as the Rangers' offer, but it was getting closer.

So Gluckstern and Milstein went back to MSG president Dave Checketts and Cablevision owner Charles Dolan with one last play. They wanted a loan to help build a new arena for the Isles. They wanted Cablesvision to put the team back on TV every game. They wanted the preseason series reinstated.

Ziggy Stardust was being bartered for favors.

Meanwhile, Neil Smith and Mike Milbury were at the annual GM meetings in Buffalo with a continent's worth of hockey media following them around the hotel.

And Smith and Milbury still did not particularly get along.

Finally, after about a ten-minute huddle, the duo stepped toward the big gang of media waiting down the hall.

"There is no trade," said Milbury.

The reporters were shocked.

"It's not just manager to manager," he explained. "It gets kicked up to a different level."

It seemed the "different level" had made its decision. Neither Checketts nor Dolan was going to indulge in Gluckstern and Milstein's funny business. The Isles could keep the most scintillating forward in the tri-state area. The Rangers were out.

"We seemed close to a deal," recalls Milbury. "But our ownership wanted $5 million, and that's when the negotiations fell apart." Of the Milstones' extracurricular demands, Milbury explains, "I wasn't privy to all that went on."

A few days later, Ziggy was finally sent to Los Angeles with Brian Smolinski, Marcel Cousineau, and a fourth-round pick in exchange for Olli Jokinen, Josh Green, Mathieu Biron, and a first-round pick (eighth overall in the 1999 draft).

With the first Islanders-Rangers trade since November 1972 averted, Neil Smith and Mike Milbury were free to bicker again. Smith claimed Todd Harvey had not been part of the deal. Milbury answered, "I must have been talking to a different Neil Smith."

Then Smith accused the Isles of leaking the deal, thus making Harvey upset. "I think Neil's trying to cover his butt," barked Milbury. "I'm all for making his player feel warm and fuzzy, but we're talking about Ziggy Palffy! That wouldn't be so insulting to Todd Harvey, would it?"

If Milbury hadn't already won that argument, it was basically clinched for him when Harvey was traded to the San Jose Sharks for Radek Dvorak three months into the season.

Smith also joked that three players on one of his training camp squads had a higher collective salary than the entire Islanders roster. "I don't know if that's something to be proud of," mused Milbury.

There he had another good point.

Turn of the Century

The 1995 collective bargaining agreement created a system that basically kept players off the market until they were extremely experienced (read "old") and extremely expensive. Aging former stars made up the whole free agent market, and the Rangers were at the front of the buffet line, spending major dough on Pat Verbeek, Ray Ferraro, Luc Robitaille, Ulf Samuelsson, Wayne Gretzky, Mike Keane, Brian Skrudland, and John MacLean.

The results were mixed. For the 1999 offseason, the Blueshirts doubled down, signing six free agents in two weeks.

As was the nature of free agency, all were over thirty and all were past their primes. They were—from most expensive to least expensive—center Tim Taylor, goalie Kirk McLean, defenseman Sylvain Lefebvre, left-wing Valeri Kamensky, defenseman Stephane Quintal, and the Hustle from Russell, a skating, hating, slashing, thrashing, grinning, winning All-Star winger named Theoren W. "Flower" Fleury.

No one knew it at the time, but his personal life was spiraling out of control, and his health hung in precarious balance. New York was the worst place on the continent for him. The Rangers gave him $8 million a year.

Add it all up—or in the case of the Islanders, subtract it all down—and once again the league's by far highest payroll and by far lowest payroll each lived in the Big Apple, or vicinity.

The teams split a contentious quintet of games in 1999–2000:

- On October 11, 1999, at the Coliseum, Zdeno Chara reignited his explosive relationship with Darren Langdon in a 4–2 Rangers win, jumping Langdon and pounding his head into the ice in retaliation for a knee on Kenny Jonsson.

- On November 3, 1999, at the Garden, Chara stole a point from the city boys with a tremendous individual effort, carrying the puck out of the right corner and roofing the tying goal over Mike Richter from along the goal line late in regulation. It was one of the first moments in the future Hall-of-Famer's career that showed maybe he was more than just a set of giant bones.

- On December 23, 1999, at the Coliseum, the Islanders honored the popular Rich Pilon with a video montage before the game. The Rangers had claimed the goateed grinder off waivers from the Isles December 1.

Pilon was second on the Isles' all-time list of penalty minutes with 1,525 in 509 games. One hundred seventy-six of those minutes had come against the Rangers—more per game than against any other team by far—and many of a vicious nature.

Early in the second period of his new team's disappointing 4–2 upset defeat, Pilon took a slashing penalty and skated to the Islanders' penalty box—perhaps unaware that he was wearing a Rangers jersey—and waited. He couldn't understand why the attendant wouldn't open the door. Finally, the guy motioned to the other box. The whole place was laughing.

Later in that period, the league's shortest player, 5-foot-6 Fleury, took down the league's tallest, 6-foot-9 Zdeno Chara, with a two-handed chop.

The diminutive Russell, Manitoba, maniac tested the big Slovakian's patience, chasing Big Z all night and even punching him in the jaw twice behind the play. The next time Fleury came after him, Chara finally swatted him away like a fly. So Theo whacked him in the back of the leg. Chara flopped. Referee Don Koharski called slashing, and Theo went nuts, convinced Big Z had taken a dive. He had to be restrained by both linesmen.

"Just gave him a little love tap," claimed Flower. "The big oak tree fell down with one swipe of the axe."

- On January 15, 2000, at the Coliseum, Islanders agitator Steve Webb started a ten-man ruckus with a hit on star winger Petr Nedved late in a 5–2 Rangers victory that left Nedved livid.

"It was an elbow," barked Nedved. "I think he should get suspended. He'll say he's a tough guy, but he isn't. He should be ashamed of himself."

- On February 13, 2000, at the Garden, the Islanders looked to knock the Blueshirts out of their playoff position.

The Rangers knew the Nassau-men—long since retired from playoff contention—would treat this final meeting like the biggest game of the season and would come at them with everything they had.

At least they should've known.

The Islanders' lineup that evening at MSG was a Who's Who of the NHL, as in, "Really—*who's* who?

Even Zdeno Chara and Kenny Jonsson were out, though they did dress Kenny's brother Jorgen Jonsson, the Jim Belushi of Long Island hockey.

But the Isles got goals from fellows by the name of Jason Krog, Josh Green, and Mathieu Biron before Claude Lapointe sealed the 4–2 shocker into an empty net. Kevin Weekes made 31 saves for his fourth win of the season over the Rangers, split between the Isles and the Vancouver Canucks, where he'd started the campaign.

"You have to respect the opponent!" snapped Rangers coach John Muckler. The next day he put his Blueshirts through a bag skate.

Butch Goring, meanwhile, earned praise for his work with this scrappy bunch of Nassau no-names. Somehow the team matched its exact record from the year before, even after a complete gutting of the roster. Of course, the 1999–2000 Islanders did still miss the playoffs for a sixth straight season. But they had their moments, this Garden upset tops among them.

The game had the effect Islanders fans hoped for. It began a 5–17–4–0 Rangers nosedive that left the team out of the postseason for the third straight year. The most sympathy they were going to get from Islanders fans was, "Hey, welcome to the club."

THE MAVEN REMEMBERS: ZOOMING ALONG WITH THE BIG Z

When it comes to liking post-dynasty Islanders, Zdeno Chara ranks near the top of my list. He came from Slovakia and so did my grandparents, Etel and Simon Friedman. Although he was the biggest player in the league, there was something soft and tender about The Big Z, and we became very friendly.

On November 3, 1999, at Madison Square Garden, I happened to be standing behind the Isles' bench. I watched in disbelief as Zdeno lugged the rubber from the right side deep in the Rangers zone, bulling his way behind the net before doing a U-turn that brought him right in front of the crease, where he roofed the puck past Mike Richter. It was one of the most amazing goals from a super big man I had ever seen.

Neil Smith was fired and replaced by Glen "Slats" Sather, a former Rangers forward who had won five Cups with whom else but the Edmonton Oilers.

Slats slid easily into Smith's old role of verbal sparring with Milbury, who, when asked for his thoughts on Sather's introductory press conference, answered, "I don't give a s—."

Sather got him back a few weeks later at the 2000 NHL Draft in Calgary, where Milbury dealt Roberto Luongo and Olli Jokinen to the Florida Panthers for forwards Mark Parrish and Oleg Kvasha, then used the first overall pick to replace Luongo with goalie Rick DiPietro, thus leaving elite scorers Dany Heatley and Marian Gaborik on the board. "What does he know about goaltenders?" smirked the Blueshirts' new fifty-six-year-old cigar-chewing boss. "Remember, he didn't think Tommy Salo could play, either."

It was a smug remark, since it was Sather who had ripped off Mad Mike in the Salo trade back when he was GM of the Oilers.

"They should mind their own business and worry about their own problems," answered Milbury.

At that point, Mad Mike was like a teenager with no parental supervision, acting out just for attention.

Ownership was again in transition. The Gluckstern-Milstein group finally sold the team to Charles Wang and Sanjay Kumar of Computer Associates International in Islandia, New York—just minutes from the Coliseum.

Wang and Kumar looked to bring an element to the Islanders-Rangers rivalry that it had never known.

They were peacemakers.

Mr. Wang and Mr. Charles Dolan not only smoothed over that pesky pre-season scheduling embargo, but also created a joint program called the "Islanders-Rangers Charity Challenge." It was announced that the winner of the annual crosstown regular-season series would receive $100,000 from the loser for the charity of the winner's choice, plus something called the "Pat LaFontaine Trophy."

At the news conference, Mr. Wang told Mark Messier—there representing the Rangers, with whom he had signed in the offseason—"I'm sure all New York fans are happy to have you back."

Cue about fifty simultaneous head scratches.

The friendly vibes trickled from the owners' suites all the way down to the ice. The 2000–01 season series had zero line brawls. Milbury called one of the games "a lovefest." It was not meant as a compliment.

The Rangers swept a home-and-home in late March to take the LaFontaine Trophy three games to two, and the money went to the MSG Cheering for Children Foundation and the Lustgarten Foundation for Pancreatic Cancer Research.

Despite the mediocre record against the Isles, the 2001 Rangers, who compiled a 33–43–5–1 record, were another expensive disappointment. At 21–51–7–3, the Isles were the worst team in the NHL by a full 3.5 games.

The rivalry needed a shot of caffeine. It was about to get a triple espresso from the teams' most colorful personalities—Theo Fleury and Mike Milbury.

2001–02

The Luongo trade had completely obliterated Milbury's reputation, especially after twenty-two-year-old Oleg Kvasha, the grand prize at the heart of that scheme, came to Long Island and played awkward, unproductive, and too often space-cadet hockey.

Despite it all, Milbury was still the general manager of the Islanders, so he ignored the detractors and pressed forward.

With Mr. Wang willing to spend a little, the Islanders decided to try to become a "now" team. Coming off a 52-point 2000–01 season, it was sheer audacity.

To that miserable roster, Milbury added a rookie head coach and six players. They were Boston Bruins assistant Peter Laviolette, defenseman Adrian Aucoin, star centers Alexei Yashin and Michael Peca, fringe winger Shawn Bates, former Cup-winning goalie Chris Osgood, and his new backup, Garth Snow.

The plan had plenty of doubters.

Laviolette's hiring was panned all over. The thirty-six-year-old former Ranger (he played for the Blueshirts for 12 games in 1988) was thought too young and inexperienced. Even his role with the Bruins was called into question. Meanwhile, Yashin was expensive, both in Mr. Wang's wallet ($87.5 million over ten years) and on the trading block. He was dealt for Bill Muckalt, Zdeno Chara, and the 2001 second overall draft choice to Ottawa.

But after seven straight years without an Islanders playoff appearance, Milbury's offseason was about one thing only: improving the Isles immediately.

And guess what? Just like that—BADA-BING, BADA-BOOM—it worked!

The retooled Islanders strutted into the first Rangers game of the season—November 8 at the Coliseum—with a bewildering record of 11–1–1–1. The Blueshirts showed up at 8–7–1–0 and with plenty of star power in their own right, including Leetch, Richter, Messier, newly acquired former Flyers superstar Eric Lindros, and of course, Mr. Fleury.

Both teams entered on winning streaks for the first time since April 2, 1993. Hockey was suddenly the hottest ticket in New York outside of the Yankees-Diamondbacks World Series.

Before the game, a reporter asked Theo if he considered this matchup with the blazing hot Islanders a measuring stick. "For who?" he replied. "For them?"

Theo had already earned disdain from the Islanders and their fans for his behind-the-play hooking and slashing and other antics.

For example, on Thanksgiving Eve the previous season at the Coliseum, he beat former Blueshirts goalie John Vanbiesbrouck with a power play wrister from the top of the slot with 35 seconds to go in overtime, delighting the Rangers faithful. Then Fleury slid out to center ice across the Islanders logo, a celebration reminiscent of his famous rink-wide dive in the 1989 Campbell Conference Finals.

In two years on Broadway, he'd scored 138 points in 142 games and checked into the league's substance abuse program twice. The first trip was kept private. The second was very public; Theo was suspended by the league down the stretch of the 2000–01 season.

There was a story behind Fleury's problems with drugs and alcohol. He later came forward with the revelation in his 2009 book *Playing With Fire*. When Theo was a teen, a Junior coach named Graham James molested him and other players on an ongoing basis for years.

But very few people knew that back in 2001. To fans of every team but his—including the Isles—he was just a dirty player with dirty drug tests.

So when he came to Nassau for the first time in 2001–02, nothing was off limits. He hit the ice for his first shift. The home fans chanted "CRACK-HEAD-THE-O! *Clap, clap, clap-clap-clap!*"

Which made it sweet, from Theo's perspective, when midway through the first period, he collected the puck in his own end, raced down right wing, and beat Chris Osgood with a wrist shot to tie the game at one.

It got sweeter when Leetch gave the Blueshirts the lead 38 seconds later.

And 27 seconds after that, rugged winger Sandy McCarthy cleaned up linemate Steve McKenna's rebound to make it 3–1 New York Rang—

POP!

Suddenly, big 6-foot-6 ex-Rangers defender Eric Cairns high-sticked 6-foot-3 225-lb. McCarthy in the mouth.

McKenna jumped Cairns and started bruising away. McCarthy and Steve Webb dove in. Charles Wang's friendly Blueshirts-Islanders utopia was coming apart at the seams.

As Cairns was escorted to the penalty box, Fleury started flapping his arms and clucking like a chicken, "Buck-buck-buck-buck-buck-buck . . ."

Theo's message was obvious. "You're a chicken." But his dance had a consequence he probably never anticipated.

"My director said to me, 'You should play the chicken dance,'" remembers longtime Islanders organist Paul Cartier.

Well, give Islanders fans a tune with either a three- or four-syllable ending, and you know which direction they are going to take it.

Cartier played the "Chicken Dance," and the fans replaced the four claps that close every verse of that classic party ditty with a predictable refrain, "The-Ran-gers-suck!"

He would subsequently start to play it at every game, and the crowd would keep shouting off until the team banned the song a decade later.

Meanwhile, McCarthy was gesturing at Cairns, flexing his biceps and pointing at his muscle. It was way more World Wrestling Federation than National Hockey League.

"The reason that Theo did that was because he had seen that Cairns had the chance earlier in the shift to do something and didn't do it," said Sandy after his club's big 6–2 romp.

Calm before the chaos. Isles' defenseman Eric Cairns (33) about to crosscheck
Rangers forward Sandy McCarthy in the mouth, moments after McCarthy has
pushed a rebound past tumbling Nassau goaltender Chris Osgood, to give the
Blueshirts a 3-1 first period lead, November 8, 2001, in Uniondale. *(AP Photo/Ed Betz)*

McCarthy had challenged Cairns to a fight right before the turnover
that led to his goal, and Cairns refused.

Cairns claimed he couldn't fight McCarthy on the play because his
hand was sore.

After the game, Cairns spotted Fleury in the hallway, and yelled,
"You————r!"

"Theo's the kind of guy who does that stuff," said Islanders captain Michael Peca. "I think there's no place for it. It's immature."

"You can't have guys cross-check your players in the face after a goal," barked Rangers coach Ron Low.

Milbury told reporters he was discouraged that Fleury was allowed to walk out of the building "without incident" and said, "It's always good to have the building filled, even if it's with low-IQ Rangers fans."

Those remarks were relayed to Low, who shrugged and said, "Sounds about right."

The next meeting took place on a rollicking Friday night, December 21, in the Garden.

The Nassau-men were still atop the Atlantic Division, but at only 17–9–5–2, just above the 19–13–3–2 City boys.

It was an important game in the Eastern Conference race, but the focus leading up to it was on a third-line defenseman and his supposedly sore hands.

"The guy's had a bad hand for three years now, I guess," said Theo, mocking Cairns. "I'm not sure I would want to fight Sandy, either."

"Maybe he does have sore hands every time we play them," echoed McCarthy. "Maybe it's a coincidence."

No doubt, boxing was on the menu.

After Mats Lindgren gave the visitors the lead just 1:12 in, Eric Cairns stepped onto the ice. McCarthy followed. A buzz went through the arena.

The puck was dropped. The gladiators de-gloved and got right to it.

Cairns dominated early with a flurry of hard right jabs at Sandy's skull. McCarthy gathered himself and swung a few wild uppercuts, but didn't connect. Cairns came back with a couple of haymakers, withstood one heavy right, then sealed the victory with a tackle. The Islanders fans roared.

McCarthy grimaced and shook his head to himself as he sat in the penalty box, as if he wanted another shake at it. "I guess that one's over," he said after the game. "You might as well do it sooner than later. I think we both knew it was going to happen. It was a good fight. He's a tough guy. I never said he wasn't a tough guy."

Well, at least maybe not in those *exact* words.

The game itself, it turned on a frantic sequence late in the first period. With the score tied, 1–1, Radek Dvorak beat Osgood on a shorthanded breakaway, but his slick wrister rang off the crossbar. The suburbanites gathered the rebound, and with the place still humming over Dvorak's near-miss, Michael Peca led an odd-man rush the other way and swished a tricky left-circle shot past Mike Richter.

That zany power play goal held up for the 2–1 Isles win.

"Were we here for honor, or the two points?" Peca pondered. "Probably 50–50.

"The Rangers are a team that think they can intimidate and out-muscle you," he continued. "We weren't going to allow that."

The Blueshirts stumbled into the next meeting—January 22, 2002, at the Coliseum—on a tough 0–7–1–1 stretch that had their rival fans extremely confident, especially a group of about a dozen buddies in section 303, upstairs on the red line, who'd started to put nicknames on the back of their "Rangers Suck" jerseys—that is, a Rangers jersey with the word "SUCK" sewn beneath the traditional diagonal "RANGERS."

On this night, a few of those jerseys said "CRACKHEAD" on the nameplate over Theo Fleury's number 14.

Fleury saw the jerseys. The fans made sure of that by going down to the Rangers' end for warm-ups before the game and showing him. They also wore yellow rubber chicken masks on their heads, a callback to Theo's big clucking routine from November.

The rest of the crowd followed their lead.

CRACK-HEAD-THE-O! *Clap, clap, clap-clap-clap!*

"I'm standing in the hallway," said Fleury, "and some guys started yelling that at me."

Later on, the Coliseum scoreboard operators cut to a live shot of one of the "CRACKHEAD" jerseys for the entire arena to see. Folks chuckled as the fan proudly pointed at the name on his back.

"It's just stupid," remarked Fleury. "Just dumb. Another thing I have to deal with that I created."

It was a wild setup for a wild affair.

The homesters went from down 1–0 to up 4–1 by 8:48 of the first. Mike Richter relieved rookie Dan Blackburn and helped turn things around for the visitors, who crept to within 4–3 by intermission with a late power play tally by Fleury from Leetch and former Islanders whiz kid, Vladimir Malakhov. Needless to say, Theo's celebration was not muted.

Then with the game tied in the middle stages of the third, Islanders defenseman Marko Kiprusoff flubbed a pass attempt at the red line. Fleury rushed him, took the puck, raced in alone on goaltender Garth Snow, and beat him low to the stick side to give the visitors a 5–4 lead.

Again, Flower's reaction was understandably quite animated.

Thanks to Richter and his newly repaired right knee, Theo's breakaway goal stood up as the game-winner in this thrilling 5–4 come-from-behind Rangers win.

The thirty-five-year-old goaltending marvel kept a clean sheet, incredibly, even as the Isles outshot the Rangers, 29–9, over the final two periods.

Richter was named the game's number-one star. In a game when Fleury put up three points while being called "crackhead" the whole night, this was saying something.

As Theo skated off the ice in triumph, he left the crowd with one last gesture—the ol' Southern European forearm jerk. He was fined $1,000 for it.

"I don't mind the booing and all that stuff," explained Theo, "but when you get personal, you're crossing the line, especially when you call me a crackhead. I have never, ever, ever used crack in my life."

The proclamation did not win Fleury any points with the fans in section 303. A few weeks later, they launched an anti-Rangers website called "crackheadtheo.com."

Meanwhile, the goat of the evening, poor Marko Kiprusoff, was sent to the minors by that weekend. Such is the nature of Isles-Rangers.

Mentally exhausting as that classic Coliseum clash was, the schedule commanded they do it again only eight days later, this time at the Garden on January 30, 2002.

Legions of Islanders fans poured off the Long Island Railroad. Their voices were about to get a workout.

Alexei Yashin and Mark Parrish made it 2–0 visitors right off the bat. Later in the first, Yashin scored twice on the same shift. Technically.

In reality, his backhand at 16:11 bounced off the back bar so quickly, the officials initially missed it, and play continued for two minutes. Upon review, the goal was awarded and the clock was reset, at which point Yashin barged through the Rangers zone, slipped the puck between Mark Messier's legs, slithered around the Rangers captain, and beat Richter again for the first hat trick of his Islanders career. It was a complete undressing of a pair of Blueshirts icons. Richter was pulled.

With 1:07 to play in the first, Sandy McCarthy tried to goad Eric Cairns into another fight, but with his team dressing only five defensemen, Cairns abstained.

"I grabbed him before the game and said, 'You can't do that,'" explained Laviolette. "He already won his fight last time. We needed him tonight."

But McCarthy, obviously, had not been in on this meeting. So he started doing the Theo Fleury chicken flap routine in Cairns's face. The stage was set for an explosive second period.

About nine minutes in, Blueshirts defender Tomas Kloucek took a wild run at Michael Peca, setting off a line brawl and a cruiserweight bout between McCarthy and Isles power forward Brad Isbister.

McCarthy dominated "Izzy" and the crowd cheered accordingly, down 4–0 and thirsty for a little blood. The linesmen broke it up. But Izzy followed McCarthy up the boards and gave him a little shove. McCarthy wound up and clocked him on the top of the head. The Garden erupted!

"SAN-DY! SAN-DY!"

"I looked up and he pulled at me," said McCarthy. "So I threw a punch. It was a reaction in self-defense."

That reaction earned McCarthy an immediate ejection.

Two minutes later, the heavyweights took the stage—6-foot-3, 230-pound Dale Purinton for the city, and 6-foot-2, 210-pound Jim Cummins for the suburbs. These guys were really throwing.

Two minutes after that, Mariusz Czerkawski chipped a backhander at Dan Blackburn right after an offsides whistle. It was a terrible, terrible idea.

Rangers defenseman Dave Karpa travelled 50 feet to crosscheck Czerkawski in the head. Kloucek wrestled Yashin to the ice and started beating on him. Once Yashin slipped out of his jersey, he was able to get up and fight back. He even broke Kloucek's nose with a right cross few knew he had in his repertoire. Though, to be fair, it did help that Czerkawski was holding back Kloucek's arms.

"He tried to pull my shirt off," explained Yashin. "I had to fight back."

Meanwhile, Theo Fleury tried to get at Cairns, but linesman Ray Scapinello—fifty-four years old at the time!—body-slammed the Russell Rodent. It was a scene.

"This is fight night at MSG," quipped MSG Network analyst, John Davidson.

Fleury was the last miscreant to be taken to the penalty box. He took full advantage of the attention this afforded him, twirling around the rink while shooting all types of gestures at Cairns. It was like a figure skating routine without the jumps.

"THEEE-O! THEEE-O!" yelled the crowd.

"It just goes to show you what a chicken Cairns really is," Fleury later grumbled. "Sandy challenged him, but he went after me. He jumped me from behind. Typical Cairns. I have no respect for that guy.

"Then you have Snow yelling from the bench, when he couldn't stop a beach ball in a tight game."

Later on, Fleury took Cairns's hockey stick back to the Rangers bench during play and whacked away tirelessly before finally using a skate blade to crack it.

With just 34 seconds to go in the third and the score 6–3, little Isles winger Jason Blake was jumped by Purinton, setting off another wild melee. The fighters were Cairns, Purinton, Karpa, Oleg Kvasha, and Manny Malhotra, and the ejections were . . . nobody cared anymore.

It had been a long night.

When the game finally ended, two full sections worth of fans of both teams came together behind the Rangers net. The brawling, it seemed, was contagious, as this was just two smoke bombs short of a soccer riot. And there was still one match left to play.

BENCHMARK GAME: CHICKEN DANCE

November 8, 2001
Nassau Coliseum

Rangers 6 Islanders 2
(9–7–1–0) (11–2–1–1)

Theoren Fleury's demons have been well documented. But what was it like being the target of Theo's shenanigans back in his playing days?

Eric Cairns knows.

Here is the story of the 2001–02 Battle of New York, as told by the hulking former Ranger, who became a fan-favorite with the Islanders, precisely for his handling of situations like these:

I got challenged by Sandy McCarthy early in that game, but I had stitches in my hand, so I couldn't fight. That just led to everything else.

They came down and scored. I was disappointed. I was frustrated. So I crosschecked him in the face.

We got in a big melee. And everything just kind of went from there. It's all in the rivalry. They were trying to get underneath my skin and show that they scored the goal and they have the upper hand on us. At the time it was frustrating, but looking back on it, it's pretty funny now.

I remember I was doing an interview, and Theo Fleury walked by in the hallway. I don't know if I said, "You————er!" exactly, but I said something. We lost the game. It was fresh. I did say something to him. I can't remember exactly what, but I'm sure it wasn't too nice.

Six weeks later, the Islanders took the railroad to Manhattan for a highly anticipated rematch, which they won, 2–1. This time, both of Cairns's hands were healthy. And on alert.

There was a lot of hype going around the media leading up to that game. All I wanted to do was win. That's all that really mattered to me. But obviously there was something that was going to happen—and needed to happen—between Sandy and myself.

That day, the coaches asked me how I was feeling. I said I want to get out there, get some momentum for our team. If I'm out there against Sandy McCarthy my first shift I want them to leave me out there because I want to go address the situation.

It just so happened that we scored a goal right before that, which is great, and then we got into a fight, and it was a good fight. Both guys did well. And then the one thing I took out of that game was that we won, and that was the most important thing to me.

The next crosstown contest in the Garden was an explosion of Islanders goals in the first period, followed by fisticuffs in the second, to the tune of 12 minor penalties, six majors, two 10-minute misconducts, and two ejections—all in a span of under nine minutes!

Amid all this *mishegas*, Theo Fleury stole Cairns's stick right out of his hands during a shift, took it to the Rangers bench, and broke it.

I just thought it was hilarious. I think we were doing well in that game again. He seemed to be getting pretty frustrated. A lot. So he took my stick, he went to the bench. I saw it on video after. I'm sitting there like, "All right. You can take my stick and break it if you want."

It was very heated that year. It kind of helped me, as far as pushing my game and my emotions past where they had been before. It actually made me into a better hockey player after going through all I went through with the Rangers, pushing the emotion to a higher level. I learned to direct my emotions the right way.

You can be emotional and you can react to things, but make sure that you contain enough and put it in a positive direction. You do that by playing with emotion but also not letting it get the best of you. I think that was important for me to learn with those games against the Rangers.

Fisticuffs aside, the other big story was the visitors, the best Islanders team since the dynasty. They had depth, toughness, goaltending, and terrific coaching. Even downtrodden Oleg Kvasha started making the occasional big play and was soon bestowed with the highest honor available to a player of his limited skill-set—ironic, cult-hero adulation.

Fans began singing the Spanish soccer chant *Olé Olé Olé* with Kvasha's name, "O-lehhhhhg, O-leg-O-leg-O-leg!" The march toward the franchise's first playoff berth in eight years was in cruise control. It was party time. The Rangers, on the other hand, were trying to hang on by the skin of their bruised knuckles.

The clubs needed some time apart, but the rivalry even found its way to the Olympics in Salt Lake City, Utah, where Islanders defenseman Roman Hamrlik of Team Czech Republic leveled Theo Fleury of Team Canada with a vicious cross-check. Theo was completely enraged.

"If I'm on the ice March 25," he warned, "I'm going to run you from behind and break your neck!"

Come March 25, there was Theo on the Nassau Coliseum ice, along with brand-new Rangers Pavel Bure, Tom Poti, Rem Murray, Martin Rucinsky, and Roman Lyashenko.

Sather had loaded up on the trade market in an attempt to get the Rangers into the tournament, which wasn't impossible. They were two games back of eighth place with nine games to play.

"We'd love nothing more than to crush their chances of making the playoffs," said Peca. "With our organization having been the laughing-stock over the last few years, it'd be kind of nice to be looking down on them for a change."

"I'm going to wear ear plugs," joked Fleury, who early on was as vivacious as advertised.

He jabbed Steve Webb in the face 58 seconds in, earning a roughing penalty.

He charged Hamrlik in the Isles' zone and cross-checked him into the net after a whistle, earning an unsportsmanlike conduct.

Then he popped Webb in the eye with a high stick.

Then he scored to tie the game, 1–1, and of course went kicking, punching, and screaming his way out to center ice in lavish celebration.

Then he tackled Webb at the side of the Rangers' goal, prompting the 5-foot-10 basher to threaten Fleury through the partition between the benches.

"Is this guy talking to me?" read Theo's face. He stood up and leaned over the boards to chirp back at Webb, waving his stick menacingly all over the place.

Later, he poked Hamrlik in the very worst possible place he could be poked. Call it "low-sticking."

That was the first period.

At 8:45 of the second, Fleury dumped the puck in at the Islanders blue line. Across the rink, Steve Webb hopped over the boards on a line change and skated a straight line to his target. Webb held his stick in just one hand. Playing the puck was not a priority.

Theo didn't see him. The crowd saw that Theo didn't see him. Webb zeroed in—

"YEEEAAAAAAAHHHHHH!!!!!!"

The home fans bellowed out a dramatic release.

There were eight years of frustration packed into that hit.

Eight years of broomsticks and fish sticks, hat tricks and Starter hats and of course eight years worth of insults.

It was Hextall, Maloney, Muller and Messier, Mad Mike and the Milstones, Campbell, Cloutier, Ulf and Ziggy, Sandy McCarthy and Theo, but now there was Theo rolling around the ice, trying to draw a penalty when none was coming.

Steve Webb flattened Theoren Fleury, and eight years of pent-up energy came spewing out of Nassau Coliseum.

The Rangers went ahead, 2–1, at 5:17 of the third, but everyone— rooters of orange and red alike—knew what was coming.

It *had* to be the Isles on this night; in fact, it almost *had* to be Kvasha, whose attempted pass banked off former Islander Bryan Berard for just his seventh goal of the year with 6:42 to play. 2–2.

Four minutes later, Ollie unleashed a left-circle slap shot that deflected off a Blueshirt skate and in for the go-ahead tally. 3–2.

The centerpiece of the worst trade in Islanders history pumped his fist to the rafters, where songs of "O-Lehhhgg-O-Leg-O-Leg-O-Leg!" would soon fill the air.

"It's obviously better than booing," said the cult hero, a man of few words (at least English ones).

With less than ten seconds to play, Islanders fourth-line center Claude "Lappy" Lapointe won a faceoff in the Rangers end. "Islanders control!" screamed Nassau radio play-by-play announcer Chris King. "THEY'RE GONNA WIN THIS ONE!!!!!!"

"We're Back!" Isles forward Oleg Kvasha (12) pumps a fist upon the first of his two clutch late third-period goals, March 25, 2002, at Nassau Coliseum. Thanks in no small part to this rousing comeback victory, the surprising 2002 Islanders made the playoffs for the first time since 1994, while the Blueshirts missed the postseason for a fifth consecutive year.
(AP Photo/Ed Betz)

Leaving nothing to chance, Lappy slid the puck into the empty net at 19:57. For the fifth consecutive year, the high-priced Manhattan-men weren't going to the playoffs. And for the first time in nine long years, the Nassau-men were going further than they.

BENCHMARK GAME: OLEG THE EXECUTIONER

March 25, 2002
Nassau Coliseum

Rangers 2 Islanders 3
(31–35–4–4) (35–25–7–4)

From the minute Ron Hextall had opened his five-hole in the 1994 playoffs, Metro Area hockey bragging, teasing, and taunting flowed across the river in one direction, west to east, until 2002—and this night in particular—when unlikely Islanders hero Oleg Kvasha scored twice in a late four-minute stretch to erase the Rangers' 2–1 lead, and with it, effectively, their chances in the Eastern Conference.

Thus Kvasha was dubbed "OLEG THE EXECUTIONER" by the back cover of the March 26 *Newsday*.

This game would turn out to be Theoren Fleury's last as a Blueshirt against the Islanders after three years' worth of big goals, outrageous celebrations, and general troublemaking.

When reporters asked NHL associate director of hockey operations Claude Loiselle before the game if Theo's presence and history with the Islanders were the reasons the league disciplinary board was paying such close attention to this game, Loiselle replied, fittingly, "It's not just this guy. It's these teams. It's been going on for 30 years."

Chapter 8

THE THEATER OF HOCKEY

"We've been trying all year to get these guys to concentrate on every game like it's an Islander game."

> —Rangers General Manager Glen Sather

"These games are not easy to win. There are emotions, anger—a lot going on. It's a rivalry."

> —Rangers forward Bobby Holik

"We were walking along and I just hear someone yell, 'Rangers stink!' I've been away for a while, so you sometimes forget about the rivalry. I remember now."

> —Islanders/Rangers defenseman Darius Kasparaitis

"This is a rivalry, regardless of whether it's for the playoffs or not or back-to-back, there's no excuses. This is what our fans look forward to and we look forward to."

> —Islanders goalie Rick DiPietro

"It's all about bragging rights. It's important."

> —Islanders/Rangers defenseman Rich Pilon

Even hastier than the new-look Islanders' transformation to Stanley Cup contention was their relapse to mediocrity.

It happened in one evening—April 26, 2002.

In fact, it happened in a span of about five and a half minutes.

That's how long it took, in playing time, for the two most important Nassau-men—superb defenseman Kenny Jonsson and marvelous captain Michael Peca—to succumb to cheap shots from their playoff captors, the Toronto Maple Leafs, during Game Five of the Eastern Conference quarterfinals.

Jonsson suffered his fourth concussion. Peca endured a busted knee. He was never the same, and neither were the Isles.

The Rangers, on the other hand, were exactly the same, which is to say rebuilding through free agency while searching for a new head coach—seemingly their default off-season status—after bench boss Ron Low was canned.

One free agent not on general manager Glen Sather's agenda was Theoren Fleury. Sather thought Fleury was a bad influence on some of the younger Blueshirts. He signed with the Chicago Blackhawks for what would become his final NHL season.

In only three years on Broadway, Theo cemented his place in the Islanders-Rangers canon with his trash-talking, stick-cracking, crotch-slashing, and chicken dancing. The rivalry could not get any more personal. Or so it was believed.

It was believed, at least, until June 6, 2002, when Sather introduced the 30th head coach in the history of the New York Rangers, and it was Bryan Trottier.

Now *that* was personal.

Trottier's relationship with the club of his youth turned frosty beginning when the Islanders bought out the final two years of his contract in 1990, helping to sink their legendary—albeit debt-ridden—all-time leading scorer into bankruptcy.

After winning two more Stanley Cups with the Pittsburgh Penguins in 1991 and 1992, Trottier returned to the Islanders as an executive assistant, only to quickly depart in dismay over his role.

Over the next eight years he honed his coaching skills as an assistant for Pittsburgh and for the Colorado Avalanche, all while remaining entrenched in a cold war with the Isles over rights to retire his jersey number 19.

Islanders owner Charles Wang extended an olive branch in 2001, and on October 20 of that year, the banner was finally raised. Trottier showed up pro bono. For seven months, all was right in the Coliseum rafters.

But a big fat coaching vacancy lay yawning across the river.

So while Peter Laviolette's troops battled Toronto blow-for-blow in the 2002 playoffs, Trottier and about twenty other head coaching candidates received a nine-page questionnaire from Rangers general manager Glen Sather. Trots blew Sather away with his ninety-page, hand-written reply, which reporters liked to call "the manifesto."

Once his Avalanche were ousted in the seventh game of the Western Conference Finals, news of Trottier's hiring broke. It was like General Douglas MacArthur being sworn in as Emperor of Japan.

For once, Islanders fans and Rangers fans had something to agree over. Neither wanted Bryan Trottier to coach the Blueshirts. Negative fan mail began streaming in to the newspapers.

Sather next set his sights on another former Rangers antagonist—Darius Kasparaitis, who'd used to flip Rangers captain Mark Messier over on a regular basis.

Free agent Kaspar, still a Long Island homeowner, politicked openly to return to the team that traded him to Pittsburgh back in November 1996. On July 2, 2002, he came east, though not as far east as Islanders general manager Mike Milbury had hoped. Sather inked the twenty-nine-year-old Lithuanian lacerator to a six-year deal worth $25 million. He also brought in former Devils center Bobby Holik for $45 million. The Rangers were reloaded yet again.

Kaspar came out hitting, particularly with his mouth. He expressed disappointment in Milbury's tepid courtship, said he'd rather be a Ranger anyway, that the Rangers "overshadow" the Islanders in New York and that he planned to be "a big pain in the butt" against the Isles.

True to his word, Kaspar put pain into a few butts in the first cross-town game of 2002–03—Saturday afternoon, November 23 at the Garden—but unfortunately, his hard checking led to fewer scoring opportunities for his own team than for the opponents.

Darius was on for all three Islanders third-period goals in his squad's 3–1 defeat, dropping his season output to minus-ten in only 23 games! Rangers fans began calling him Darius Kaspar-*minus*.

The Islanders took a decent lead in the standings over their rivals by the reunion, January 21, 2003, in Uniondale. But on that night, the standings were never going to be the story.

The sports media cosmos—be it local, US, or Canadian –could not get over the idea of Bryan Trottier returning to Nassau Coliseum as head coach of the New York Rangers.

"Our fans hate it," said Islanders center Dave "Scatch" Scatchard. "And we love that they hate it."

"I know how much Islander fans hate the Rangers," echoed Kasparaitis. "The Ranger fans boo him; now the Islander fans are going to boo him. I don't think anybody likes him anymore, except us players."

"It's like old hat," scoffed Trottier, predictably downplaying the hoopla. "I've been there as an Avalanche, I've been there as a Penguin . . ."

This was a little different.

Perhaps no one set the scene more vividly than John Buccigross of *ESPN*'s NHL 2NIGHT show, when he promised viewers "a tremendous 'Theater of Hockey' Tuesday night on Long Island."

The curtain rose on Act One in the "Theater" about a half hour earlier than anyone expected, as the players butted heads for not one but two separate melees . . . . during warm-ups.

First, Rangers rough-houser Matthew Barnaby skated over center ice to bump petite Isles winger Jason Blake and shove backup goaltender Garth Snow.

The next thing you knew, line drills for both teams were on temporary hiatus as a quorum jabbed and jousted by the benches. Cooler heads prevailed, but only for about three minutes. Then Blueshirts basher Sandy McCarthy basically invaded the Islanders zone and checked towering Islanders defenseman Eric Cairns, his old nemesis. The teams came together for some more pushing and slashing and "just lipping off," as McCarthy later put it. "You know, 'I'm gonna break your nose,' stuff like that."

Terrific.

Meanwhile, behind the Rangers goal, one of the "crackheadtheo. com" fellows from section 303 held up a big, black cardboard tombstone that read:

R.I.P.
TROTTIER
28 MAY 1974
6 JUNE 2002

Other fans put up signs behind the Rangers bench that said, "TRAITOR." The atmosphere was charged, to say the least.

Coliseum staff egged on the crowd via the first-period Islanders trivia question, which was, "Who holds the club record for most points in a game?

"Choice A: Bryan Trottier . . ." That was all anyone needed to hear.

Fans booed for the duration of the segment through the unveiling of the correct answer, which of course was "A: Bryan Trottier," on December 23, 1978, against the Rangers.

But for Trots, this visit to Nassau went the way of most of his others over the years, meaning his team won easily. 5–0 was the final.

Matthew Barnaby backed up his pre-game war-mongering with two goals, earning the game's first star. The second star was newly-acquired goalie Mike Dunham, with 31 saves. Also of note, Blueshirts top center Eric Lindros vomited on Shawn Bates of the Isles before a faceoff. It was an accident, but symbolic nonetheless.

Islanders fans felt queasy, too. One even paid $28,000 for a full-page ad in *Newsday*, which read "Hey, NY Islanders, Where were you the night we played the Rangers? We, your loyal fans showed up! . . . Where was the energy? . . ."

That is what these games mean to people.

The shellacking was the Rangers' first shutout win over the Islanders since November 23, 1985. It was also the highpoint of Bryan Trottier's career as an NHL head coach. He was fired just a week later, with a record of 21–26–6–1.

Fans of both teams looked to purge the Blueshirts' "Trottier Era" from their brains immediately. That he ever worked a minute in the New

Fans at the Nassau Coliseum, January 21, 2003, let legendary former Islanders center Bryan Trottier know how they feel about his new gig as coach of the New York Rangers. *(AP Photo/Mark Lennihan)*

York Rangers organization was basically forgotten by the teams' third meeting, March 3, 2003, at Madison Square Garden.

Spring was in the air and playoffs were on the table. The Nassau-men clung to sixth place in the Eastern Conference, while the Rangers—surging under interim coach Sather—sat 3.5 games behind eighth.

Things looked promising for the visitors most of the way, but in the end, like so many others, the night belonged to brilliant Blueshirts blue-liner Brian Leetch.

With his club down, 1–0, and just over seven minutes to go in regulation, Leetch puréed the Islanders penalty kill to a pulp, dancing from his own end all the way into the attacking zone, deking around defenseman Mattias Timander, and lifting a backhander over Garth Snow's left shoulder. One day after his 35th birthday, Leetch looked like every bit the guy who won the 1994 Conn Smythe Trophy. 1–1 was the final.

Exactly two weeks later, Leetch scored another clutch power play goal late in the third period against the Nassau-men. This time, it was good enough for a 1–0 St. Patrick's Day win to keep the Rangers' faint pulse pumping.

Mike Dunham had now surrendered only one goal in three whole games against the Islanders since coming over from the Nashville Predators on December 12.

THE MAVEN REMEMBERS: ISLANDERS KILLER, BRIAN LEETCH

If you were a longtime Islanders broadcaster as I was, it was very difficult to root for Brian Leetch. After all, he did too much damage to the Nassau-men.

However, during calmer moments, I deeply appreciated his skill, calm, and ability to look like a latter-day Bobby Orr.

On the other hand, as an interviewer, I found Brian to be both likable and—like many other Rangers such as Mike Richter—eminently affable.

I never expected that I would bond with this Blueshirt. But that unlikely event actually did happen on the afternoon during which I received one of my highest personal honors—the Lester Patrick Trophy for service to hockey in the United States.

At a dinner honoring the Patrick nominees, I shared the dais with the late Rangers PR legend John Halligan, former female hockey star Cammi Granato, and, of course, Brian Leetch.

As it happened, Brian wound up winning a faceoff from me at the affair. After exceeding my five-minute talking time limit with a rather lengthy joke, it was Leetch's turn to speak, and he delivered the perfect squelch. "I told Stan to take two minutes of my speech time," he began. "He took it all."

The Rangers closed the gap on the eighth-place Isles to two games heading into the final week of the regular season. There was one spot left in the Eastern Conference, and only a pair of Big Apple teams left fighting for it.

Which one was headed for the postseason? That would depend mainly on the final Battle of New York, April 1, 2003, at the Coliseum.

The Isles would clinch with a win. Realistically, a tie or an overtime loss was just as good, which meant the Rangers needed to beat them in regulation time in order to have any shot of advancing.

It felt like a playoff game, because in essence it was one, which was why it didn't look out of place when fans were given white rally towels to wave—normally a tradition reserved for the postseason.

During warm-ups, a big banner reading "$76M BUST," a cursory calculation of the Rangers' payroll and performance, was unfurled behind their goal, care of—you guessed it—the guys from section 303. The "Theater of Hockey," Nassau Coliseum, was in its element.

Once red-hot Islanders star Alexei Yashin put his club ahead, 2–0, with a power play goal early in the third, the home crowd could certainly smell the playoff berth, and they made sure to let their guests know about it. But the raucous celebration was a tad premature.

Leetch scored, per usual, to cut the score to 2–1. Then Alexei Kovalev tied the game at 16:01, leaving the Rangers with four minutes to pull off a stunning regulation comeback.

The home-rooters fell quiet, even more so when trusty defenseman Roman Hamrlik was sent off for interference with 1:22 to go.

Anxiety abound. The entire arena stood for the remainder of the third period, too nervous to even chant.

The penalty-killers dug in, gnashed their teeth, churned their legs, and got the job done. The Blueshirts power play did not even muster a shot. The buzzer blew. The crowd erupted. The Isles had secured an enormous point.

Overtime was a party. The fans sang "Na Na Na Na Hey Hey Hey Goodbye" until the final horn made the 2–2 tie official. After seven years of futility, the Nassau-men were headed to the playoffs for the second year in a row, while for the sixth year in a row, the Garden-men were headed anywhere but.

The Season of Frustration

The Long Island festivities were short-lived, though, as the Isles fell to the Ottawa Senators in the first round. A month later, Mike Milbury orchestrated what would become the final grand "Mad Mike-ism" of his Islander career, axing Peter Laviolette and replacing him with Steve Stirling, the fifty-three-year-old coach of the Isles' AHL affiliate, the Bridgeport Sound Tigers.

Stirling never won the trust of the Long Island faithful, even as his 2003–04 Islanders improved to 38–29–11–4.

Meanwhile, the high-priced, aging, uninspired Rangers dropped to 25th overall in the NHL at 27–40–7–8. Season ticket sales began to dip. Those fans who did come back for 2003–04 took to chanting, "Fire Sather!" at home games.

It was ugly, but they had their moments. Six of them actually, as in the six times they took on Stirling's Isles.

There was something funky going on that season—really funky, with *both* teams. Call it the "Season of Frustration" in New York.

The Rangers beat the Islanders a perfect half-dozen times for their third clean sweep in the thirty-two-year history of the rivalry, and second in a span of just six seasons. Goals were 27–13. The Isles led for a total of one minute and 14 seconds the entire series, while the Rangers led for 284:53!

But the rest of the NHL was seldom introduced to these types of Rangers, or to these types of Islanders.

From the initial crosstown-crunking of 2003–04—4–2 on December 4 at the Coliseum—until the end of the season, the Isles went 29–11–9–4 against the NHL's non-Rangers, while the Rangers went 12–31–2–6 against non-Islanders.

It was maddening for both sides.

Had the suburbanites done well against the lowly urbanites, they could have won their first division title since 1988. Instead, they settled for the final playoff spot in the conference and were bounced by the eventual Stanley Cup champion Tampa Bay Lightning in five games. So this was a season-long spoil job. At least Rangers fans could thank their boys for something.

The biggest story of the sweep was Mike Dunham, who won all six games to improve to 8–0–2 against the Islanders as a Rangers goalie and 10–0–2 in his last twelve Islanders games overall, dating back to his days with the Nashville Predators. "Just coincidence," he called it.

Then there was Brian Leetch, who tacked on 3 goals and 6 assists during the series before being traded to the Toronto Maple Leafs on March 3, 2004, closing out his Broadway career with 25 goals and 55 assists in 86 regular season and playoff games against the Islanders, with a plus-24 rating. *Yowza!*

But what the 2003–04 series lacked in competition, it made up for in nastiness, beginning midway through the second period of the first game, when Michael Peca was ejected for a dangerous knee-to-knee blow to promising young center, Jamie Lundmark.

Lundmark missed almost eight weeks with a torn MCL. Peca insisted it was an accident and even went to check on the twenty-two-year-old former ninth overall pick after the incident. Lundmark accepted the apology. Glen Sather did *not*.

"It's intent to injure!" he snapped. "I don't think there's any place in hockey for that kind of stuff."

Sather sent the tape into the league office in hopes of getting Peca suspended. The league chose not to discipline "Captain Crunch."

But Sather was successful in riling up the fanbase, which saw in the hard-hitting Islanders captain and the hot center prospect a modern-day version of Denis Potvin and Ulf Nilsson.

Peca was booed lustily in Madison Square Garden during his team's next few trips into the City. Add that to the frustration of losing to the Rangers repeatedly, and it got to him.

For example, one night in January, Peca bashed Matthew Barnaby, got caught elbowing Tom Poti in the face, then got Petr Nedved with a forearm-elbow combination—all in the first period.

That scrum-infested 4–1 bout was the Rangers' second victory over the Islanders in three nights and fourth on the young season, setting the tone for an angry home-and-home set in late February.

The Rangers jumped ahead, 3–0, early in the Garden-end on goals by Mark Messier, Nedved, and Barnaby, who celebrated by sliding across the ice while twirling his hockey stick like a cowboy lassoing rope. Naturally, Isles winger Arron Asham crosschecked Barnaby in the back, leading to a brouhaha.

Then with four minutes to go in the third and the score 6–2, burly Rangers defenseman Dale Purinton abandoned his right point position to attack unsuspecting Islanders defenseman Eric Cairns in the Islanders crease—retribution for a pair of shots Cairns delivered to the face of Rangers forward Martin Rucinsky. Cairns had no idea what was going on.

Not-so-Pure-inton dropped his mitts and punched Cairns six times in the head. When Cairns eventually escaped, he ran Purinton down at the top of the circle. Big Dale saw him coming. He ducked behind linesman Steve Miller, who in turn took the brunt of Cairns's series of wild right hooks.

"Tell him he's a gutless f———little puke!" Cairns screamed at Rucinsky as he spotted him in the hall after the game, no doubt referring to his hefty assailant.

From there, the night spun out of control.

Two and a half minutes after Dale-fest, Barnaby jumped Dave Scatchard. Scatch declined to fight due to his injured shoulder. So Arron Asham fought Barnaby for the third time in three years. Then Chris Simon popped Scatchard in the face. Little Jason Blake jumped on Simon. So Mark Messier spun Blake around like a child. Therefore twenty-two-year-old goalie Rick DiPietro jabbed forty-three-year-old Messier in the chin. Then Messier literally choked Blake for two minutes.

Long story short, it felt like an Islanders-Rangers game.

Scatchard was so enraged, he forgot about his busted shoulder and wrestled the much bigger Simon to the ice, harness and all.

League disciplinarian Colin Campbell and two of his capos, Kris King and Claude Loiselle, showed up at the Coliseum a week later to warn the Rangers and Islanders that further shenanigans will not be tolerated for the final matchup of the season. Separate meetings were held with Stirling and with brand new Rangers bench boss Tom Renney, the forty-eight-year-old assistant who had taken over as chief the day before, when Glen Sather stepped down.

But Campbell's threat was ineffective with Eric Cairns, who chased Dale Purinton around the rink like Tom chasing Jerry. Purinton wanted no part.

So midway through the first period, Cairns pulled Purinton out of yet another Barnaby-Asham twist up (their fourth of the season against each other and sixth of their young careers), dropped him, and administered five hard punches to the back of the head, earning 17 penalty minutes and an ejection. Purinton turtled. Cairns screamed at him to get up and fight. Big Dale laughed him off.

"I lost a lot of respect for him," said Cairns. "Stand up and be a man. He put his tail between his legs."

"It doesn't matter what people think of me," reasoned Purinton. "We just need points."

The Rangers led by a whopping score of 6–0 by the time the second period was seven minutes old, a fitting exclamation point on their series of dominance.

Proud Rangers-backers chanted "You-Can't-Beat-Us!" *Clap, clap, clap-clap-clap*! To which their orange-and-blue counterparts would calmly reply, "We-Don't-Have-To!"

Some Islanders fans even unfurled a big banner that read, "LET'S GO GOLFING: TEE TIME, 4 APRIL, 8 A.M."

"How many points are they behind us?" begged Arron Asham. "They can beat us six times this year if they want, but I think we're going to be in the playoffs and they're not."

"We're not concerned about the Rangers," said Adrian Aucoin. "I don't think they're going to catch anybody . . . If they think they arrived by beating us, they've got a lot to learn."

The final score was 6–3. For the second time in a row, the number-one star of the game was Jaromir Jagr. The living legend—whom the Isles narrowly missed drafting back in 1990—came to the Blueshirts in a trade on January 23, 2004, and immediately started barbecuing the Islanders, putting up three goals and two assists in the February home-and-home.

BENCHMARK BRAWL: THE SANTA FIGHT

The Rangers' six-game sweep of their neighbors in the 2003–04 season series had everyone on Long Island growing frustrated, even those maintaining to be "jolly."

Before a home win over the Flyers just two days before Christmas, the Isles announced that any fan dressed as Santa Claus could come to the game for free. There is no way a full Santa suit costs less than a hockey ticket, but about 500 St. Nicks showed up at the Coliseum regardless!

After the first period, all Santas were invited onto the ice to parade around and wave to the adoring fans. It was then that a couple of young saboteurs unbuttoned their red sweaters to reveal blue sweaters—as in, Rangers jerseys!

The crowd watched in horror as one young man showed off his Matthew Barnaby jersey, while another flaunted a Pavel Bure cloak.

So what did the other Santas do?

They rushed them.

Security was helpless as the mob of red-suited Islanders fans pummeled the pair of troublemakers, quasi-playfully, along the boards. It was a Santa Brawl.

"All Santas will be escorted from the building," warned the public address announcer. "I repeat, no violence, or all Santas will be escorted from the building."

The two Rangers fans were secured, the mess was cleaned up, and the second period began on time.

"That game when the fans beat up the two Santas," recalls Isles goaltender Rick DiPietro, fondly. "When you step into that rivalry, you can feel it. It's so easy to feed off the crowd."

There was little doubt who had won this battle. It was Long Island's only success against the Blueshirts all season.

For Jagr to shine in Renney's first game as head coach of the Rangers was a fitting portent of things to come, as this tandem would form the backbone of the team moving forward.

Well, along with a young Swedish enigma named Henrik Lundqvist.

2005–06: After the Lockout

The 2004–05 NHL season was aborted due to lockout, and in the process, the owners won their long-desired salary cap, presenting the Rangers with a dilemma (or so it was believed) since their 2003–04 payroll was $90 million, and the new cap was $39 million.

For the Blueshirts of the past few seasons, $39 million barely covered a game's opening shift. Now Sather had to squeeze a full lineup into that figure.

Jagr aside, all big-money players were either bought out or allowed to sign elsewhere. Sather brought in ex-Islander Kevin Weekes to be the starting goaltender and patched together a first line around "Jags" with two affordable veterans—silky Swede Michael Nylander and former Islander Martin Straka.

Straka and Nylander received little offseason buzz, as did other newcomers such as defenseman Michal Rozsival, twenty-three-year-old sniper Petr Prucha, and twenty-three-year-old goaltender Lundqvist.

The result was by far the least star-studded Rangers roster in decades. The pundits were not impressed. Almost all outlets picked the revamped Blueshirts to finish either last or next-to-last in the east, while the Nassau-men, with their additions of Miroslav Satan, Alexei Zhitnik, and former Ranger Mike York, were widely picked near the top.

But 2005–06 was a funny year.

For one thing, Kevin Weekes strained his groin four games into the season, and the seventh-round pick most people hadn't heard of—Lundqvist—had to fill in. Who knew it would be the first step toward legend?

"Hank," or "King Henrik," as he came to be known, within a mere matter of months posted one of the finest rookie seasons in Rangers history, going 30–12–9 with a .922 save percentage and 2.24 goals against average.

And those gaudy numbers hardly even made newly anointed King Henrik the Man of the Year in blue and red.

With the league introducing a new set of rules—or at least an initiative to enforce the old ones—there was no more hooking and no more interference. In other words, no more stopping Jaromir Jagr.

Or Nylander and Straka, for that matter. The sage trio of thirty-three-year-olds led the Rangers in scoring, as Straka posted 76 points, Nylander 79, and Jags an almost-gluttonous 123! Fourth on the team with 55 points was thirty-four-year-old Martin Rucinsky. Florida's fabled "Fountain of Youth," it seemed, had made its way up the coast, and thanks to that, there was magic in Midtown all fall and winter long.

Jagr kept scoring, Lundqvist kept winning, and the crowd kept cheering, so much so that the 2005–06 Rangers invented a new post-victory tradition—the center-ice salute—that remains part of the organization's repertoire and has since been adapted by other teams, too, including the Islanders. The charming, under-the-radar Blueshirts even adopted an official anthem—Jagr's favorite song, "Sweet Caroline" by Neil Diamond, with its triumphant "Oh, Oh, Oh"s.

With Hank dazzling between the pipes and the Jagr line circling opposing defenses until they were dizzy, the Rangers made the playoffs for the first time in almost a decade. Meanwhile, the Isles missed the playoffs for the first time since 2001. Now *they* were the under-achievers.

The teams played eight times in 2005–06, thanks to the "new" NHL's unbalanced schedule. Lundqvist went 3–0–1 with a 1.47 goals against average and a .941 save percentage. His team went 5–2–1. Here are the cliff notes:

- On October 19, 2005, at the Garden, both teams ventured jointly into new territory, with the first shootout in the histories of both franchises.

With the extra point on the line, Jaromir Jagr snapped his own hockey stick in two on an attempted wrister. Miro Satan tallied on the other end, technically ending the Islanders' ten-game winless streak against the Blueshirts.

The number-one star was Rick DiPietro, with 33 brilliant saves during the game.

- The next night, October 20, 2005, at the Coliseum, Jagr kept his sticks together enough to score a hat trick, giving him four goals in two evenings, and even earning compliments from DiPietro.

"You say he scored a hat trick," quipped the outspoken goalie. "I say we *held* him to three."

The Rangers' pregame nap at Long Island's Garden City Hotel had been interrupted when the fire alarm was pulled. It was never discovered by whom, but one could probably guess his or her hockey allegiance.

The ruse appeared to work, at least early on, as the home team went up, 3–0, in the first 147 seconds of the game. The Isles ultimately held on, 5–4, despite Jagr's hatty.

- On October 27, 2005, at the Garden, the Rangers went 11-for-11 on the penalty kill in a 3–1 win!

Jagr was the game's number-one star, with two first-period assists.

- On December 28, 2005, at the Coliseum, the line of Jagr, Nylander, and Straka combined for 12 points.

While the Blueshirts erased an early 2–0 deficit with six unanswered goals, their overjoyed supporters broke out into an impromptu version of "Sweet Caroline," undoubtedly every Islanders fan's least favorite live version of the classic tune.

"OH! OH! OH!"

"There were a lot of Rangers fans here tonight," observed DiPietro.

The game's three stars were Jagr (a goal and 3 assists), Nylander (also a goal and 3 assists) and Straka (2 goals and 2 assists).

By now, New York hockey was as good as flipped. Jagr and his no-name accomplices led the Isles by 5 games for second place in the Atlantic Division after the 6–2 Broadway invasion.

The surge also signaled the end of an era on Long Island.

Two weeks later, the Islanders announced that Steve Stirling would be replaced by his assistant, Brad Shaw, and that Mike Milbury was stepping down as general manager.

- On February 2, 2006, at the Coliseum, the Jagr line continued its assault on every shred of Islanders dignity, with another 7 points in a 5–2 win.

Amazingly, the Blueshirts skaters blocked 25 shots, 2 more than their own goalie, Kevin Weekes, with his 23 saves.

- On March 29, 2006, at the Coliseum, the Rangers franchise record book took a round of edits.

Lundqvist entered tied with Sugar Jim Henry and Johnny Bower for wins by a Rangers rookie goaltender, with 29.

At the same time, Jagr came in tied for the franchise single-season high in goals with Adam Graves, at 52, and in points with Jean Ratelle, at 109.

With the Isles' Mike York in the box for high-sticking just seven minutes in, Jagr slid the puck to rookie Petr Prucha for a one-time strike past DiPietro. It was record-breaking point number 110, and he'd done it on Nassau ice.

The Islanders missed drafting Jaromir Jagr by a whisker. In the end, they were the only Patrick Division team he never played for. In three seasons as a Blueshirt, he tortured the Nassau-men to the tune of 17 goals and 23 assists in 26 games. *(David Perlmutter)*

1:30 later, Jagr set up Straka for point number 111.

5:06 after that, he set up Straka for number 112.

Then, he set up Straka a third time for his fourth assist on the night, and point number 113.

5–1 was the final. Needless to say, Jagr and his linemates owned the Islanders.

The performance earned a few standing ovations from the many city-backers in the crowd. They also chanted "D-P-SUCKS!" a play on the nickname of one Rick "DP" DiPietro, who made only 17 saves.

Lundqvist made 18 saves for his record-setting victory.

"My main goal was just to make the team," said King Henrik.

- On April 6, 2006, at the Garden, late in the second period, the public address announcer called out Jaromir Jagr's 53rd goal of the season, a new Blueshirts record.

The home fans stood and howled.

But Jagr knew he never touched Martin Straka's pass; rather, it deflected in off an Islanders skate. Like a true *mentsh*, he skated over to referee Stephane Auger and broke the news.

"I knew I didn't touch it," he explained. "If I score my 53rd, I don't want it to be that way. I want it to be a good-looking goal. I'm not a cheater."

So Straka was awarded his first of 2 goals on the night, giving him 9 against his former team on the season, good for almost half his eventual total, which was 22.

In eight games against the Isles, Straka had 15 points and was plus-nine, Nylander had 10 points and was plus-eight, and Jagr had 18 points and was plus-10.

The big win put the Rangers 2 games up at the top of the Atlantic Division with only 6 games to play.

And don't worry—Jagr broke the Rangers goals record two nights later in Boston. He finished the season with 54 red lights.

- On April 11, 2006 at the Garden, the Rangers put their two-game lead on the line against an Islanders team hungry to play spoiler.

Or, as DiPietro put it, "I hope we kick the Rangers' a— on Tuesday!"

Coach Tom Renney made sure to bring this quote to his first-place squad's attention.

But DiPietro backed it up, with 36 saves on 38 shots. Miroslav Satan scored twice, as the Isles handed their neighbors loss number 2 of what would become a 5-game skid to end the regular season.

The losing streak basically ruined the Rangers' miracle year, dropping them from first place all the way down to third in the Atlantic Division and sixth in the Eastern Conference.

After a first-round sweep at the hands of the New Jersey Devils, the once unbeatable Rangers had lost 9 consecutive games in regulation by a cumulative 37–13 score, bringing 2005–06 to a disappointing close.

But even so, King Henrik and the Rangers had recaptured the town.

Lundqvist was a sensation. As a mere rookie, he finished fifth overall in goals against average, fourth in save percentage, and was a finalist for the Vezina Trophy, which was won by Miikka Kiprusoff of the Calgary Flames.

Meanwhile, the playoff-less, coach-less, general manager-less Islanders were back in the shadows and would need something radical if they were going to regain relevancy in a hurry. Good thing for them, they had one of the most radical thinkers in pro sports, owner Charles B. Wang.

The Committee

On June 8, 2006, at the Nassau Coliseum Marriott Hotel, Wang unveiled an entire brand new Uniondale regime, a management team that was to work in collaboration, with everyone having a say.

Five proud men stood with Wang on the podium, smiling for pictures, arm-in-arm.

There was executive director of player development, Bryan Trottier—former Islander, turned Ranger, back to Islander.

There was special advisor Pat LaFontaine—former Islander, turned Ranger, back to Islander.

There was general manager Neil Smith—former Islander, turned Ranger, back to Islander.

There was vice president Mike Milbury—Ranger-hater extra-ordinaire.

And there was head coach Ted Nolan, who had not been offered an NHL job in eight years amid rumors that he was a "GM Killer."

Smith was the pick that threw the area into a fit. The former Cup-winning Rangers GM with a reported history of mocking the Islanders publicly and privately was now going to work in a cluster with Milbury?

It lasted 40 days, at which point, on July 18, Smith was fired due to "philosophical differences." Surprisingly, it was actually Milbury more than anyone who pleaded with Wang on Smith's behalf.

Then the Isles got even more creative.

Backup goaltender Garth Snow immediately retired as a player and was hired as Smith's replacement. When reporters asked thirty-seven-year-old "Snowy" minutes later what he thought of hockey players now, he joked, "I think they're all overpaid."

THE MAVEN REMEMBERS: NEIL SMITH COMES—AND GOES—POOF! JUST LIKE THAT

This seemed like a perfect example of turnabout being fair play.

Neil Smith got his first break as a quasi-executive with the Islanders working with Coach Al Arbour and Jimmy Devellano. Eventually, he was catapulted into the general managership of the Rangers and suddenly became an Islanders hater with anti-Isles episodes too numerous to mention.

Neil was a good friend of mine, and I was taken aback by some of his antics, particularly as they related to Al Arbour, who helped give him his start. But if nothing else, Neil was colorful and funny—two of my favorite traits as an interviewer.

After Neil got fired by the Rangers, he had a devil of a time getting another GM job in the NHL. He either had been blacklisted by someone who didn't like him high in the league hierarchy, or simply nobody wanted to take a gamble on such a flamboyant and flippant character.

But then, seemingly out of the blue, Islanders owner Charles Wang produced a new high command that consisted of Hall of Famers Bryan Trottier, Pat LaFontaine, and a new coach in Ted Nolan. Lo and behold, there was Smith, himself, being introduced as general manager.

From my viewpoint, this was a general staff made in heaven—insightful, colorful, energetic, and destined to lift the Islanders to a level of playoff contention.

This thought lasted a grand total of forty days. Matter of fact, I still shake my head in astonishment when I recall how Smith got bounced.

And, guess what, within days I was invited to a luncheon, at which Wang announced that his backup goalie, Garth Snow, was replacing Smith. Stranger things may have happened in the hockey world, but I cannot think of one that topped this madcap merry-go-round.

Oh, by the way, a good ten years later, the backup goalie who was being mocked when named to run the hockey club was still holding forth as boss of the Brooklynites!

Yet the "Summer of Chuck" still wasn't over. On September 12, the Islanders signed Rick DiPietro to a record fifteen-year contract, the first of its kind. People couldn't believe it.

Wang told reporters that the big spoiler win over the Blueshirts back in April helped sell him on the twenty-four-year-old netminder. "Last year he told the Rangers he was going to kick their butts," he said. "And he went out and did it."

But the most incredible part of the wild Summer of 2006—after all the unorthodox and imaginative moves—was the job the front-office-by-committee did in the six weeks it was together.

In fact, many people call Neil Smith the second greatest general manager in Islanders history, next to Bow-Tie Bill Torrey, of course.

Before he was excused, Smith and the group reconfigured the roster by signing underrated thirty-five-year-old center Mike "Silly" Sillinger, gruff thirty-one-year-old defenseman Brendan "Witter" Witt, smart, dependable forward Andy Hilbert, as well as former Rangers Chris Simon and Tom Poti.

Garth Snow then added some finishing touches. From the "If you can't beat 'em, sign 'em department," Mike Dunham came over to fill Snow's old spot as backup goalie. Rugged thirty-six-year-old defenseman Sean Hill penned a cheap one-year contract, as did lanky thirty-one-year-old forward Viktor Kozlov.

The Incredible, Outrageous 2006–07 Season

In terms of the Battle of New York, the Kozlov deal paid immediate dividends. Four of them, to be precise, in the form of a backhander, a rebound, a snapper, and a wrister on December 3, 2006, at the Garden, as Big Vik became the first Isle to score a quartet of goals in a game against the Blueshirts since Bryan Trottier in 1978.

Rangers prized free agent acquisition Brendan Shanahan also recorded a hat trick in his team's 7–4 loss—a wild back-and-forth game, to kick off a wild back-and-forth season.

The teams met two weeks later in the City again, and again ecstatic suburbanites threw hats on the Garden ice. This time the trickster was Jason Blake, who scored his team-leading 17th, 18th, and 19th goals.

DiPietro made 69 saves in the pair of Garden wins. One week later, December 26, he shut out the Blueshirts at the Coliseum, 2–0. "D-P! *Clap-Clap!*" shouted the ecstatic home crowd.

Rangers fans responded "D-P-SUCKS!" But on this night, he certainly did not.

With three straight victories over their rivals to start the season, tipsy Islanders fans even decided to borrow an old Rangers ditty, "You-Can't-Beat-Us!"

It was the Rangers' sixth straight loss. But in this, the craziest roller coaster Isles-Rangers season since 1989–90, it turned out to only be TURNING POINT #1.

Because from there, the Isles went in the tank, losing all 6 games between then and the next Rangers match, January 9, 2007, in the Garden.

Meanwhile, the Rangers entered with a 4-game winning streak. 2006–07 was looking a lot like 2005–06.

Former Ranger Mike York's [16] old team celebrates a goal without him, on December 3, 2006, at Madison Square Garden. *(David Perlmutter)*

Or, this was simply TURNING POINT #2.

DiPietro was marvelous again, as the visitors upended the hot Manhattan-men, 5–3 this time.

"You-Can't-Beat-Us," once an urban-dweller's taunt, was now being directed right back at them in their own arena.

"We're awful against these guys," snapped Rangers coach Tom Renney. "I'm not happy! I'm p————!"

And he stayed so. For the next two months, Renney's boys were 9–9–3, while Nolan's guys went 14–4–6.

It was all DiPietro. The Lefty Laureate started 22 of the 24 games. With the goalie zoned-in, Nolan allowed his troops to push the pace more and more, basically leaving Rico back there alone. It was outrageous, gut-wrenching hockey. In that stretch, the Islanders surrendered, on average, over 31 shots a game. It was ba-na-nas!

Things looked so promising on Long Island, Garth Snow decided to pull the trigger on the biggest deal of NHL deadline day, acquiring Edmonton Oilers captain Ryan Smyth.

Buying at the deadline means you're going for it. Going for it means pressure.

Which brought us to March 5, 2007, the World's Most Famous Arena, and the fifth Islanders-Rangers showdown of the season.

The game was televised nationally on the VERSUS Network. America could not have anticipated what carnage lay ahead.

The Rangers entered in a three-way tie for tenth in the east. The Nassau-men, on the other hand, were living large. From the looks of things, the Blueshirts were a little annoyed by that. They took out their frustration on the Islanders "defense," if one could call it that, and Mr. DiPietro.

Seventeen shots in the first period! Nothing across.

19 more in the second! Nothing.

Finally, 26 seconds into the third, Petr Prucha banged in a rebound off a 3-on-3 rush to tie it up, 1–1. In keeping with the theme of the evening, none of the three Islanders defenders on the play did anything that resembled defending.

The Rangers kept coming, registering 21 more shots in the third period and overtime for a total of 57.

In the process, DiPietro made every type of save there is, and probably invented some new ones. There were stick saves, pad saves, skate saves, and *tuchus* saves. He had saves through traffic and saves in transition, frontward saves, backward saves, and diving saves. There were short-side and far-side saves.

The Rangers shot so much, it's a marvel they had any stick blades intact by the end of the game. And it's a marvel the ice in DiPietro's crease didn't slush all the way through to the base.

"I think when I looked up at the scoreboard and saw 48–24 on the shots," joked Rangers forward Matt Cullen, "it was pretty clear he was having a good night."

DiPietro stopped two of three in the shootout, as well. But his teammates still wouldn't help him. Henrik Lundqvist bested all three Islanders shooters, holding up Cullen's round-two tally as the winner.

While outsiders were enamored by what they had just witnessed, both teams had only one word on their minds. "Thursday."

"We have to atone on Thursday," said Isles defenseman Sean Hill.

"We have to lick our wounds and get ready for Thursday," concurred Ted Nolan.

"We've got to play the same exact way Thursday," crowed Rangers winger Sean Avery.

Ah, Thursday. March 8, 2007.

Few expected the drama to match Monday night's masterpiece in the city. Yet the rematch came out twice as weird.

With under seven minutes to play in a 1–1 game, Rangers forward Ryan Hollweg finished his check on Islanders aggravator Chris Simon, hitting the former Ranger from behind and sending him head-first into the glass. Simon crumbled, popped right back up, noticed Hollweg skating by, and gave him a two-handed slash in the mouth, like a woodsman chopping a tree at shoulder-level.

The axing caught Hollweg off-guard. He went down and stayed down while his teammates ganged up on his attacker. Colton Orr, no prude himself in the world of rough play, leaped over linesman Tim Nowak for his chance to get a shot in. Once a match penalty was assessed, Hollweg got up and went to the bench.

But Simon's brain cramp left his team shorthanded for five minutes in a tie game, starting with only 6:30 to go. The Isles were in deep sewage.

1:17 into the major man-advantage, Michael Nylander schooled Brendan Witt and slid the puck in front to Petr Prucha, who shoveled it along the ice far-side past DiPietro for his second huge third period goal of this classic midweek home-and-home series.

The Rangers led, 2–1. Worse for the homeboys, Simon's major penalty was not set to expire until there was only 1:30 to play in regulation.

But the Isles did not give up.

Needing shorthanded scoring opportunities, their penalty killers began to pinch, at times leaving DiPietro completely deserted. The

Rangers countered, aiming for a two-goal lead. The result was a riveting finale.

DiPietro made an insane blocker save on what appeared to be a Matt Cullen open-netter from along the goal line with 4:22 to go.

About a minute and a half later, the newest Islander, Ryan Smyth, tried to carry the puck from his own corner all the way out of the zone and beyond—a total "no-no" in a normal shorthanded situation, but here an admirable act of desperation. Amazingly, the man they called "Captain Canada" made it over the Rangers blue line, deked around Michal Rozsival on his backhand, and drew a hooking penalty at 17:18. The Isles were back in the game.

Nolan pulled his goalie for an extra attacker. The Rangers killed 49 seconds of a 4-on-6 manpower disadvantage, and were doing well in the 5-on-6, until Tom Poti fed sharp-shooting point-mate Marc-Andre Bergeron for a right-point one-timer. Lundqvist made the save through traffic, but Isles winger Trent Hunter poked the rebound through him . . .

Through the blue paint . . . Up to the goal line . . . Onto the goal line . . .

King Henrik reached behind himself with his right hand—from his knees, contorted as though nearing the conclusion of a brutal game of "Twister"—and paddled the rubber away with his stick.

It was an unbelievable effort on Lundqvist's part. The problem was that the puck was already in.

The crowd went bonkers as arena staff shined the triumphant spotlights. But referee Craig Spada emphatically waved "no-goal." With 20 seconds left in this crucial late-season game, we were off to Toronto for a video review.

The delay lasted as long as the second period, or so it seemed. Scoreboard operators were anything but shy with the replay, showing different angles over and over. Here is what the clips revealed:

Hank's water bottle rested on top of the net, right up against the crossbar. As the puck crossed the goal line, the overhead camera lost it. The rubber disappeared under the bottle. There was no puck on either side of the goal line.

From all other angles, it appeared to bounce over the line, but airborne, and on its side. Toronto couldn't make sense of it.

The Islanders wanted this goal BADLY. The Rangers needed this no-goal to keep their postseason dream alive. With every passing replay, fans roared at one another back and forth.

"HOW IS THAT A GOAL?!?!?!"

"HOW IS THAT NOT A GOAL?!?!?!"

After a chat with Toronto that felt so lengthy, it might have chewed through three international phone cards, the call on the ice stood. No goal.

There was no conclusive direct evidence that the puck had crossed the line. There was conclusive circumstantial evidence, but circumstantial evidence is inadmissible in NHL goal reviews.

"The guys from Toronto need to do their f—ing job," screamed Isles defenseman Brendan Witt. "Obviously it was in."

The following day, NHL vice president Colin Campbell praised the call, referring to the side angle videos as "optical illusions." Needless to say, that did not sit well with Islanders fans, who already disliked Campbell dating back to his days as coach of the Rangers.

Campbell also hit Simon, a repeat offender, with a 25-game suspension. The Nassau County District Attorney's office even considered charging him criminally but eventually backed off.

Simon's smash and King Henrik's remarkable yoga-like save were the difference. The Rangers won, 2–1, leaping into sole possession of eighth place, creeping to within just a game and a half behind the Islanders, and signaling TURNING POINT #3.

Lady Karma, it turned out, was watching hockey that week.

From the moment Simon bashed the chin of Ryan Hollweg, things began breaking great for the Rangers and poorly for the Islanders—from Prucha's goal, to Hunter's no-goal, to five nights later in Montreal, where Rick DiPietro suffered his first concussion on a fluke play at the Islanders' blue line.

In came former Ranger Mike Dunham, who immediately resumed what he'd been doing his entire career—beating the Islanders.

He gave up 18 goals in less than three games, all regulation losses.

Meanwhile, the home-and-home sweep gave the Rangers a swagger they couldn't find all season, catapulting a 9–1–3 stretch that had them up in sixth place, half a game ahead of the Isles.

DiPietro returned in late March and stabilized the situation, going 2–0–1 heading into a nationally televised Islanders-Rangers Sunday matinee at the Coliseum—the first since all the FOX matchups aired back in the 1990s.

He and Lundqvist were both playing for the second afternoon in a row, and once again, both were fabulous, earning first and second star honors with a combined 66 saves.

But DP's day became complicated when Rangers ultra-pest Sean Avery kneed him in his recently concussed noggin—whether intentionally or unintentionally, only Avery knows.

DiPietro stayed in the game and surrendered a Michael Nylander power-play tip-in with 49 seconds to play in overtime, giving the Rangers their fifth straight victory and third straight over the Islanders. The Blueshirts were now in sole possession of sixth place, a game ahead of the Islanders, who were tied for eighth.

And for the Isles, that wasn't even the bad news.

The Rangers' crashing of the Islanders crease had its intended, or unintended, effect. DiPietro experienced post-concussion symptoms. He would have to sit out yet again, and for longer this time.

BENCHMARK GAME: 56

March 5, 2007
Madison Square Garden

Islanders 1 Rangers 2 (Shootout)
(33–23–10) (32–27–7)

It's a hallowed number in New York sports, that old "LVI."

In football, it's Lawrence Taylor's jersey. In baseball, it's Joe DiMaggio's hitting streak. In hockey, it's March 5, 2007.

Here are the thoughts of our 56-save protagonist, Islanders goalie Rick DiPietro, who was so "unconscious" that evening, he swears the whole thing was a blur:

We lost. That is all I remember from that game. We lost in a shootout and Matt Cullen was the one who scored the goal. That is legitimately all I remember.

Outside of the Coliseum, Madison Square Garden was my favorite place to play because of the rivalry and the fans. I came from Boston University, where BU-Boston College was an unbelievable rivalry. The first game I played against the Rangers was probably the best experience of my life. I always said to myself, "Make sure when you go to Madison Square Garden to have your best games." It was a good game, but we ended up losing so it took away from all the saves that I made.

We talk about being "in the zone" on my radio show all the time. Alan Hahn will ask me about different moments and different saves and I will always say, "I don't know if I'm a masochist or a glutton for punishment, but all I can remember are the goals." Outside of the shootout goal and my wife mentioning to me that some of the Rangers fans had a song going on in the stands about the game and how well I was playing—something like that—I don't really remember much. It ended up being disappointing, which is crazy.

This was the first in a quartet of epic, and controversial, March and April Islanders-Rangers games to close out the wild 2006–07 season.

Coach Ted Nolan and the Isles fully believed that Rangers pest Sean Avery purposely kneed DiPietro in the head during a game on March 25, knowing DP had recently suffered a concussion. Here's how Rick sees it:

That's exactly what I remember, being kneed in the head.

It's part of your job as a forward to make goalies as uncomfortable as possible. That's a part of the competition I could appreciate. Unless, of course, you're in a pileup and someone's trying to elbow you in the head.

That was one of the reasons why he was one of the guys who I didn't care for the most. He's one of those guys who recognized that he was good at that, and it was a way for him to contribute, but I had no time for that.

Mike Dunham returned and gave up 8 goals on just 44 shots in two losses. The Islanders dropped to 11th place with no options in net except for Dunham or a thin, short, bald, twenty-eight-year-old career minor leaguer named Wade "Dubie" Dubielewicz. They were cooked.

So Ted Nolan threw in Dubie. What the heck, right? Might as well.

BENCHMARK GAME: HIT AND RUN

March 8, 2007
Nassau Coliseum

Rangers 2 Islanders 1
(33–27–7) (33–24–10)

The turning point of the Rangers' 2006–07 season was a two-hander to the mouth of one of their players. Where else but hockey?

The Rangers went 10–3–3 "post-smack" to close the regular season and 6–4 in the playoffs.

Ex-Blueshirt Chris Simon had a busy night. He scored the Islanders' only goal at 3:33 of the second and was involved in a quarrel early in the first that resulted in matching roughing calls. His partner in that one? Ryan Hollweg.

Perhaps that was what Hollweg was thinking about when he lined Simon up along the boards late in the third.

Simon's smash earned a 25-game docking, his sixth suspension in the NHL. The following year, he received his seventh—30 games—after he stomped on the ankle of Penguins forward Jarkko Ruutu.

The Simon-Hollweg saga culminated in an exhibition game at the Coliseum on September 24, 2007, when Simon bashed the spirited 5-foot-11 Californian from behind, setting off another customary Islanders-Rangers pre-season line brawl, in which Isles goalie Rick DiPietro took down Rangers netminder Al Montoya.

"It seemed like the perfect opportunity to get involved," says Rick.

After the Ruutu incident, Simon was traded to the Minnesota Wild, where he would finish the 2007–08 season, before embarking on a five-year career in Russia's Kontinental Hockey League.

On Tuesday night, April 3, 2007, the streaking Blueshirts trekked to Nassau looking for closure. A Rangers win would clinch a playoff berth. It would also eliminate the Isles with a full week of hockey left.

Asked about his team's chances of sneaking into the postseason, Isles coach Nolan handicapped them at "A million to one."

His math was off. But not by much.

At that moment, actually, according to the Las Vegas line-makers, betting the Islanders to make the playoffs would have paid more than 60-to-1. And that's *after* the sportsbook takes its cut, so figure the true odds were almost 70–1.

The Islanders needed six different results to go their way over the next six days—wins in their own four games, plus two Montreal Canadiens losses.

The steepest hill to climb may have been that first one at Nassau Coliseum on April 3, with the inimitable Henrik Lundqvist at one end, and the anonymous Wade Dubielewicz at the other.

So what happened? Little Dubie stopped 36 of 38 shots in regulation and overtime, including all 17 the visitors threw on net in the first period. The Islanders' season was hanging by that thin thread known as a shootout—third-stringer vs. Vezina finalist.

And the first Ranger Dubie would face was shootout specialist, Michael Nylander. The next two were Hall of Famers, Brendan Shanahan and Jaromir Jagr.

After Miroslav Satan beat the King, it was up to Dubielewicz.

Nylander strolled in slowly. Dubie poke-checked. It worked.

Then came Shanahan. Dubie poke-checked. It worked.

Last was Jagr. This time, Dubie went with . . . poke-check! Game over, 3–2 Islanders.

But would it be TURNING POINT #4?

One down, five to go.

Two nights later, Islanders fans filed into Doolin's Pub on the arena event level to watch the Rangers host the Canadiens, since their own heroes needed help from Big Brother to stay alive.

It was a peculiar position.

When Jagr snapped home a one-timer for a 2–0 lead midway through the second period, a loud "YEAH!" went up in that Nassau Coliseum bar, followed instantly by a contagious shudder—a communal consensus that this didn't feel right. "Whoa, let's not cheer *too* loud," joked one man in Islanders gear. Then it was back into the stands for the second period of the Islanders game.

The Canadiens' 3–1 loss in the Garden went final. Two down, four to go. The Isles rallied for a regulation win over the Leafs. Three down, three to go . . .

That Saturday, the Islanders slipped past the Flyers in Philly—four down, two to go—then watched the Canadiens blow a late 5–3 lead for a wild 6–5 loss in Toronto. Five down, one to go!

That's when things got exciting . . .

As they say in the sports biz, the Islanders controlled their own destiny. Actually, the new guy, Wade Dubielewicz from Kerrobert, Saskatchewan, controlled their destiny.

With Dubie between the pipes and about 14,000 pilgrims in the 18,000-seat Continental Airlines Arena in East Rutherford, New Jersey, screaming "Let's-Go-Isl-an-ders," Ted Nolan's Nassau-men built a 2–0 third period lead over the host Devils on Easter Sunday, April 8, 2007.

Two points would put the Islanders in the playoffs. Anything less would send the Maple Leafs to the postseason.

The heavily pro-Islanders crowd yelled "Dooooob" with every save. But the Doob got lit twice by Devs center John Madden in the final 4:13 of the third period, including a rebound with under one second to go!

Here were the Isles, one breath from the final Eastern Conference playoff spot on Easter Sunday, but it appeared the Devils—and more pertinently, the Maple Leafs—had risen from dead.

If the water bottle review of March 8 felt like an hour to those invested, then the check to see if Madden's backhander indeed beat the clock felt like two hours.

And the scoreless, five-minute overtime felt like three hours. And the Zamboni before the shootout felt like five.

Dubie played the first Devils shooter—Zach Parise—straight up, and Parise made him look like an amateur. Forehand, backhand, and Wade basically fell over.

So for the next Dev, Brian Gionta, Dubielewicz went back to the poke check and picked Gionta's pocket. The Isles led the shootout, 2–1.

The Devils'—and Toronto's—last chance was Sergei Brylin. He should've known what was coming. But he didn't.

POKE CHECK!

Six up, six down. They did it.

New York had one of the most improbable and exciting short-term playoff runs in NHL history, all because of Chris Simon's vicious hack, and Henrik Lundqvist's sprawling save, and his water bottle, and Sean Avery's knee, and the poke checks, and the Rangers' win over Montreal.

"The New York Islanders are headed to the Stanley Cup playoffs, in as dramatic a fashion as you could envision!" yelled MSG Network's Howie Rose.

And it all came because of, in spite of, and with help from, their neighbors of two counties over.

BENCHMARK GAME: DUBIE DUBIE DOO

April 3, 2007
Nassau Coliseum

Rangers 2 Islanders 3 (Shootout)
(39–28–9) (37–30–12)

Legend has it that back when King David felled Goliath with a slingshot in the ninth century BCE, local pundits were calling it a "Dubielewicz vs. Lundqvist, Nylander, Shanahan, and Jagr-level upset."

Or for a more contemporary reference, perhaps this result was more like President Harry S. Truman's 1948 election victory over New York Governor Thomas Dewey, a comeback so unexpected that the *Chicago Tribune* had already printed, "DEWEY DEFEATS TRUMAN" on the following day's front page.

Here playing the role of the *Tribune* would be *MSG Network*'s Rangers play-by-play announcer Sam Rosen, who, at the start of overtime, erroneously declared the Islanders officially eliminated from postseason contention.

One week later, after a wild string of outrageous luck and heroics from "The Doob" put the Nassau-men in the playoffs, *Newsday* printed a letter from a fan in Melville, New York, that read, quoting Mark Twain, "Dear Mr. Sam Rosen: Rumors of our death have been greatly exaggerated. Signed, the New York Islanders."

Here's how Rosen, with a good-natured chuckle, remembers the incident:

As I was gathering my notes to try to figure out everything, for whatever reason, the math was wrong. I thought the Islanders would be eliminated. And unfortunately, I was wrong.

It wasn't done to antagonize anyone, but then it turned into a rallying cry on the part of the fans, so it was one of those things that, in the aftermath, you laugh about, but you don't want to make mistakes. But that's what it was—just an honest mistake.

Another trending story that came out of this game was "spit-gate."

In a rivalry as passionate and crude as this one, it was maybe only a matter of time before the Islanders' Ice Girls became involved.

That depth was finally plunged when a wad of spit allegedly flew off the Rangers bench and onto the skin of one of the members of the Coliseum's famous—and popular—all-female ice crew.

Earlier in the first period, Henrik Lundqvist reportedly slashed a different Ice Girl with his goal-stick, knocking her squeegee into her stomach and bruising her. That incident was witnessed and made it into the referee's game report.

"I know they have an important job to do," said Hank, of the girls, "but so do I."

Henrik did that job, to the tune of 32 saves, but thanks to Dubie, it wasn't enough to put the proverbial nail in the Islanders' coffin.

Dubielewicz came back to the Islanders in 2007–08 and, amazingly, stymied the Rangers in yet another pair of post-overtime parties, bringing his career shootout record to 3–0 against the immortal Henrik Lundqvist, a quirky statistic if ever there was one.

Chapter 9

THE KING, THE KID, AND DUTTON'S DREAM

"It seemed like every regular season game at the Coliseum felt like a playoff game."

—Rangers defenseman Ryan McDonagh

"It's a unique experience. There are very few rivalries in sports that are as intense as this one is."

—Islanders forward Cal Clutterbuck

"To me this is what hockey is all about."

—Islanders coach Jack Capuano

"Circumstances can be thrown out the window. No matter where the teams are in the standings, those games are always fun."

—Islanders forward John Tavares

"The fans are pretty passionate either way. I feel like a lot of people take it pretty personally."

—Islanders forward Cal Clutterbuck

What's more valuable? A top-tier goaltender or a top-tier center? Which is more exciting? Which would you build your team around?

In a town overflowing with major professional sports teams, attention can come at a premium. But one brand that always seems to shoot to the front of the line is that of the "special" player, the "superstar," the rare athlete who transcends his or her team.

As the 2000s morphed into the 20-teens, the New York sports landscape developed a fascination with two such hockey players. On one side of the river, there was goalie Henrik Lundqvist. On the other, there was center John Tavares.

But first, back to 2007.

The Wade Dubielewicz story had been a fantastic one, but it was coming to an end. A week's worth of stirring action and five poke checks earned Dubie a one-year contract for the following season, but the former undrafted free agent out of the University of Denver was never going to take time away from Rick DiPietro.

DiPietro returned for the final four games of the Islanders' first-round playoff series and was predictably terrific, though the team did fall to the first-overall Buffalo Sabres, conquerors of Lundqvist and the Rangers in the second round, as well.

Cleared of any evidence of post-concussion complications, DiPietro was ascending to the top of the goaltending profession. The twenty-five-year-old Massachusetts maestro had been the top pick of the 2000 NHL draft, had finished 2006–07 with a .919 save percentage, and had fourteen years left on his fifteen-year contract.

Who could have foretold that Rick DiPietro's career was coming to an end?

A mere 204 picks down the 2000-draft ladder was Lundqvist, a seventh-round Rangers steal. *He*, it turned out, was just getting started.

With 37 wins, a .917 save percentage, and 2.34 goals-against average, Hank finished tied for third in Vezina Trophy voting for the second consecutive year.

2007–08

So who's better—Lundqvist, the prideful, reserved yet intense, suave Swede, or DiPietro, the loquacious, long-haired all-American boy from Boston University?

Papers and pundits loved posing the question. The fans loved arguing about it. By the 2008 All-Star break, a consensus was emerging. It was DiPietro.

While the Rangers had reloaded in the offseason, inking star free agent forwards Chris Drury and Scott Gomez, the Islanders had *un*loaded, bidding *au revoir* to most of their top players from 2006–07.

DiPietro's play was not affected, however.

He played 44 of his team's 50 games in the first half of 2007–08, stopped 1,132 of 1,242 shots, and had the Islanders seventh in the Eastern Conference—half a game better than the eighth-place Manhattan-men—essentially by himself!

What's more, he bested Lundqvist and the revamped Rangers, 2–1, 3–2, and 2–1 in the first three cross-town matchups of the season.

To no surprise, he was named the East's starting goalie for the 2008 All-Star game in Atlanta. It was not until then and there that a future Ranger, Marian Gaborik—the player the Islanders passed over to draft DP in the first place—would inadvertently solve the Blueshirts' budding DiPietro dilemma.

It started during the annual All-Star skills competition gala's "Elimination Shootout" event. DiPietro made a toe-save on "Gabo" but appeared to be laboring in the aftermath. Next came a brand new competition called the "Breakaway Challenge," which was another shootout, but with judges and style-points. The idea was pizzazz, so any type of shot would be permitted—even a wrap-around.

Gaborik was the first shooter of the first round of the first year of this gimmick. Few knew what to expect. "Mic'd up" for the night, Rick joked (ironically, it would turn out), "He's coming in with speed. I'm gonna have to go take his legs out."

Gabo stopped short at the top of the crease and carried the puck around the net. The goalie—merely a living prop in this "event"—dropped to his belly, went full split, kicked his left skate at Gaborik's stuff attempt, and made the save. Then he raced over to his backup, Tim Thomas of the Boston Bruins, and said, "You go in there. I'm done. I just blew my whole leg out." Everyone heard it. His microphone was still on.

Coffee tables across Long Island were *smacked* by the jaws of fans who must have thought they were in for a night of stress-free, leisurely viewing but were now watching the Isles' season fall apart, live on national TV, with behind-the-scenes audio.

"I just f— my hip up again," Rick told Thomas.

DiPietro stayed in the Islanders lineup despite the "messed up" hip, but he wasn't the same. The team went 11–18–3 in the second half, after which Rico underwent multiple surgeries to repair both his hip and his knee.

With DP and the Islanders spiraling out of the picture, the New York spotlight shined on King Henrik, and boy, did he not disappoint.

Like he would to 28 other teams in hockey, Henrik Lundqvist had a habit of driving the Islanders nuts. *(David Perlmutter)*

Lundqvist went 16–6–5 in the second half of 2007–08 with a .919 save percentage and three shutouts. The Rangers made the second round of the playoffs, where they were eliminated by the stout, Sidney Crosby-led Pittsburgh Penguins. In 2008–09, Hank won 38 games and led the Blueshirts back to the playoffs, where they fell to the Washington Capitals in seven.

Realizing he had a gem on his hands, general manager Glen Sather scurried to build a winner around his goalie. He fired Tom Renney in February 2009, even with the team in playoff contention, and replaced him with former Stanley Cup-winning Tampa Bay Lightning coach John Tortorella. Then in July, he signed the prolific Gaborik to a five-year contract.

Sather's problem was that the Rangers were in NHL "no-man's-land." Neither ascending nor descending, they were stuck in the middle of the Eastern Conference food chain—far from the top, but also far from the bottom, down where the rival Islanders were setting up shop.

Coach Ted Nolan was dismissed after 2007–08 and replaced with longtime Providence Bruins bench boss Scott Gordon. The Islanders went with youth throughout their lineup. They were breaking the roster down to build it back up, and it appeared they were picking a perfect time to do so, because due to front the 2009 amateur draft class was a seventeen-year-old goal-scoring prodigy from Mississauga, Ontario, named John Tavares.

Tank for Tavares

Coach Gordon wanted to play an up-tempo game and thought he had the anchor between the pipes to pull it off. But Rick DiPietro's knees did not behave. The 2008 All-Star was able to play only five games in 2008–09. Quite early in the season, it was clear the Isles were going to be in contention for a top draft pick, maybe even *the* top pick.

On April 14, 2009, the hockey gods smiled on Long Island for the first time since Dubie's magic poke check of 2007. The last-place Islanders won the draft lottery and were awarded the number-one selection of the 2009 draft in Montreal—the same city where they had taken Denis Potvin first in 1973. Good sign?

The legend of John Tavares had years of momentum, beginning when the Ontario Hockey League changed its rules to let him play as a fourteen-year-old, and growing when he broke Wayne Gretzky's OHL record for goals by a sixteen-year-old, with 72.

Now he was eighteen, and ready for the National League. But there were plenty of knocks on his game. Scouts questioned his skating, playmaking, and general off-the-puck play.

With that, the media promulgated a narrative that there were actually two other players worthy of the number-one pick—big Swedish defenseman Viktor Hedman and electric Brampton center Matt Duchene—and that both could possibly turn out better than Tavares!

Isles general manager Garth Snow gave no hints as to whom he was going to take. The fans had a singular opinion and made it clear. They swarmed the Coliseum for the Islanders' Draft Party on June 26, 2009, chanting, "John-Ta-Va-Res!"

Snow said nothing. The clock ticked away toward the Islanders' big pick, and nobody knew who it would be. The tension at the Bell Centre in Montreal was exceeded only by the tension inside the barn on Hempstead Turnpike.

Just 25 minutes before the 7:00 p.m. start time, *Newsday* reported that the Isles were indeed going to draft Duchene. The Coliseum was in an uproar. *How could they!?!*

At about a quarter after, Snow strolled to the podium, thanked the city of Montreal for their hospitality, and acknowledged the 10,000 fans back home at the party. All 10,000 of them were ready to wring his neck if he didn't say the four syllables they came to hear, and say them soon!

"And with the first overall pick," Snow eventually continued, "the New York Islanders select . . ."

He paused. He was toying with them at this point.

"John Tavares."

Finally!

The crowd in Uniondale let out a wild cheer—half relief, half excitement.

Snow and owner Charles Wang handed the kid a blue Islanders jersey and immediately put him to work.

He was the Isles' first-line center from Day One. In fact, he scored a goal on Day One, a power-play backhander at 7:09 of the second period on opening night, October 3, 2009, against the Stanley Cup-champion Penguins. "Kid Rocks," proclaimed the back cover of *Newsday*.

Three weeks later, Tavares beat Lundqvist late in the third period of a 3–1 win at the Coliseum, his first regular season Islanders-Rangers game. It was already evident that blue and red brought out his best.

The Isles totaled three wins over the Rangers in 2009–10, games the City boys surely regretted come the final day of the season, when they lost a shootout in Philadelphia and missed the playoffs by one point.

The Islanders, meanwhile, improved to 34–37–11, thanks almost to Tavares's presence alone.

Kid Genius displayed a level of offensive creativity seldom before seen. He could contort his body into almost any form and employed a menu of head-fakes and eye-fakes that would freeze even top defensemen. Plus his hands were simply sublime. "JT" led the Isles in scoring as an eighteen-year-old rookie, as he would every year to come. The Isles clearly had their plat du jour. But the rest of the squad needed work.

Enter, Jack Capuano

One word best describes the Scott Gordon Era in Uniondale—lackluster. The high command wanted somebody better on all counts and went to the franchise's well in Bridgeport. On November 15, 2010, Jack Capuano went from an unknown Sound Tigers bench boss to new head coach of the New York Islanders.

Unlike Gordon, "Cappy" was more like one of the boys, and his natural amiability won over the local media. As the years would show, the New Englander would accomplish something only one man, Al Arbour, had ever done before, which was to remain the coach of the Islanders for at least three years. Like Arbour, Capuano had plenty of help from his top center.

Tavares was rated plus-five in six Rangers games during his sophomore campaign, 2010–11, while torching Big Brother for eight points. The Blueshirts yielded JT another lofty bundle—nine points—the following season, though that hardly slowed Tortorella's troops down.

With career bests in wins (39), goals-against average (1.97), and save percentage (.930), King Henrik led the 2011–12 Rangers to their first Atlantic Division title since the 1994 Cup-men, capturing the Vezina Trophy along the way. The Blueshirts outclassed their rebuilding neighbors to the east, racking up a 4–1–1 record in the Battle of New York.

Nassau Nomads

As if losses to the Rangers were not bad enough, for the Islanders franchise, there was an even more devastating off-ice defeat, although this one had been almost two decades in the making.

It all had to do with the Islanders' failure to win approval for a new Nassau Coliseum. And it wasn't for lack of trying, either.

The quest began during the managerial stewardship of Bill Torrey, who made it clear to Nassau politicians what was needed.

After Charles Wang became primary owner, he produced an elaborate project that would not only include a new arena, but housing, restaurants, businesses—the works.

The dream became Wang's "white whale," and he chased it through board rooms and courtrooms all over Long Island. The development was to be called "The Lighthouse."

The Lighthouse was a grand plan that would have created an all-purpose hub while ensuring that the Islanders would forever call Nassau home.

In the end it became a battle between Town of Hempstead Supervisor Kate Murray and the club's high command. Murray won out. The ambitious Lighthouse proposal was squashed.

The Isles' lease with the outdated Nassau Coliseum was set to expire at the conclusion of the 2014–15 season. The team needed to either find—or rebuild—a new home, *pronto*. Rumors about possible destinations left frightened Islanders fans sleepless.

In the Spring of 2011, it was announced that a referendum would be held in August that would let Nassau County residents vote for or against public funding for a new arena. Needless to say, Wang and the Isles urged the public to vote "yea," as did the construction unions, but the issue quickly became a "political football," as the plan was slandered and vilified by its opponents. The referendum was decided against the franchise and set in motion the machinery for the club's ultimate emigration from Uniondale to Brooklyn.

Disgusted and dismayed by Long Island's political forces, Wang told Nassau, in the words of the top rock band Phish, who for years delighted crowds in the old barn in Hempstead almost as much as Mike Bossy had, "This has all been wonderful, but now I'm on my way."

Hence, he turned his attention to Barclays Center, a spanking new arena at the downtown intersection of Atlantic and Flatbush Avenues.

Ironically, this was the precise location that the Americans' boss Red Dutton had earmarked for his proposed Amerks home during the 1941–42 season.

In the end, Barclays' leaders made an offer that Wang could not refuse. On October 24, 2012, the Islanders and Barclays Center mutually announced that the team would be moving to Brooklyn for the 2015–16 season and beyond.

Instead of dissolving, the most intense rivalry in hockey was actually about to get *closer*, by a matter of 25 miles! It would be Brooklyn against Manhattan, just as Dutton once hoped it would be.

Shaping Up for Brooklyn

So hockey was on deck for the County of Kings, with just three short years to wait. But what kind of team would it inherit?

The Islanders had not qualified for the playoffs in five seasons. Rick DiPietro had proven unable to overcome his many lower body ailments and was eventually bought out of his lengthy contract. The team's current goaltender, former San Jose Sharks All-Star Evgeni Nabokov, was thirty-seven years old. And though Tavares ascended to the top of the NHL's scoring club in 2011–12, his Isles had finished last in goals for the entire Eastern Conference.

Two-thirds of the way through the lockout-shortened 2013 season, Cappy's crew seemed stuck in the same cesspool of sub-.500 hockey they had been treading for years. Below the surface, however, the energetic squad was preparing to soar.

From March 24 to April 23, 2013, the Islanders lost just 1 of 15 games in regulation! John Tavares's talents were finally set to be showcased in the Stanley Cup playoffs. It was certainly about time.

But at the height of this newfound might, the Isles would run into the defending division champions and, more pertinently, the reigning King Vezina.

The Nassau-men led the Rangers by half a game for seventh in the conference with just two weeks to play. They were about to find out the hard way how Henrik Lundqvist preferred to perform in such moments. On Saturday, April 13, 2013, Hank led the Blueshirts into euphoric Nassau Coliseum for the biggest Islanders-Rangers game in five years.

The ticket market for this one could have made a billionaire blush. If you did not already have one, you were better off watching from home. Either way, you were about to be thoroughly entertained.

Passion, skating, passing, hitting, and nastiness—the game had everything a hockey fan could ask for, except goals.

Four times the veteran King of New York, Lundqvist, denied the young Prince of Hempstead, Tavares, adding four stops of JT's sidekick, Matt Moulson, including a diving glove-save in the second period—one of his best of the year.

Henrik made 28 saves through regulation, while on the other end, "Nabby" nabbed 18. We were off to overtime, deadlocked at doughnuts.

When the Islanders killed off a 4-on-3 Blueshirts power play to begin overtime, it seemed as though it could be their night. But just over three minutes in, new Blueshirts forward Derick Brassard feathered a perfect pass to Dan Girardi streaking down right wing, and the undrafted defenseman beat Evgeni Nabokov top-shelf on the far side to cap this 1–0 Rangers instant classic.

BENCHMARK GAME: THE UNLIKELIEST RANGER OVERTIME HERO

April 13, 2013
Nassau Coliseum

Rangers 1 Islanders 0 (OT)
(21–16–4) (21–16–5)

Outside, it smelled like the playoffs in the muggy, mid-April weekend air. Inside, it *sounded* like the playoffs as Islanders fans and Rangers fans *Ooohed* and *Ahhhed* their way through one period, two periods, *three* periods . . . without a score.

Hence, the most anticipated Islanders-Rangers game in eons carried on, and on, and on—with save, after post, after good save, after crossbar, after great save, after other post!—until a lumbering defenseman in the MSG livery unleashed a thunderous climax.

Dan Girardi was an undrafted blueliner who somehow pushed his way into the NHL and became a Rangers stalwart. Although he was highly regarded for work in his own defensive zone, Girardi was never really considered an offensive threat. This sudden-death winner was just his second goal of the season.

So expertly did Girardi complete the play, that his teammates mobbed him with the enthusiasm usually reserved for the playoffs.

On to the Playoffs

Girardi's goal proved to be the narrow difference between the clubs for the season, as the Rangers finished half a game ahead of the upstart Isles, reserving a first-round matchup with the Washington Capitals while sending their neighbors to Pittsburgh to take on the powerful Pens, who would extinguish the Islanders in six games.

Meanwhile, King Henrik put on a performance for the ages against the Capitals, posting a .947 save percentage for the series, including back-to-back shutouts in Games Six and Seven.

But the Rangers ran into a Boston Bruins club on a mission in round two, as the eventual Eastern Conference champions put Lundqvist and New York to bed in five. Surprisingly, it was the end of the road for Torts.

The John Tortorella epoch in Manhattan was roughly equivalent to a hockey two-ring circus. The first ring featured Torts behind the bench during games and at practice when he was all business. The second ring often was more entertaining, and that featured Tortorella with the media. On some nights, he would abruptly walk out after two questions in a post-game news conference. On another occasion he upbraided a European female reporter over her innocent question. And then there were his battles with the regular media, but particularly the *New York Post*'s Larry Brooks, which ranged from nasty to nastier. Tortorella's antics often enraged the league's high command, and one high league official seriously wondered whether this was "an act."

Act or no act, the Rangers coach was outmatched by New Jersey's Peter DeBoer in the 2012 Eastern Conference Finals, and from that point on, the Tortorella star began falling. He was unceremoniously fired by Glen Sather on May 29, 2013.

2013–14

Upon further review, the Garden's general staff sought a more temperate, thoughtful coach, but one with considerable big-league experience.

Greeting the press at his inaugural media scrum in Radio City Music Hall, the French Canadian Alain Vigneault was the very model of decorum and humor. "Call me AV," he said with the calm and easiness that would come to define his Broadway tenure.

This relaxed tone came in handy early in 2013–2014, when prolonged summer renovations at Madison Square Garden forced the Blueshirts to the road for the first nine games of the season. The trip was less than stellar, and the Rangers limped home at 3–6–0.

But AV kept his cool. His players kept plugging away. They worked hard, improved, and began to put together a marvelous season, keyed by a couple of big "road" wins over local rivals in "the House that Derek Jeter Built."

After slugging it out barbarously for forty-two years exclusively on Seventh Avenue or Hempstead Turnpike, the Islanders and Rangers were ready for a new venue—Yankee Stadium II, in the Bronx.

The dream went all the way back to June of 2006, before the NHL's annual New Year's Day outdoor "Winter Classic" was ever born. Even then, the league, the teams, and the *NBC Network* flirted with met-area stadiums about a Big Apple extravaganza but were never able to get things off the ground.

Some crazy ideas were bruited about, including one that would have Central Park as the site. It took Bettman, Inc. a while to get around to a Gotham-based spectacular, but when the logistics were finally ironed out, it was decided that the Rangers would play two separate stadium games three days apart in 2014, with the Devils playing host on Sunday, January 26, and the Isles entertaining on Wednesday night, January 29.

Part of the *shtick* was that teams playing in this "Stadium Series" were allowed to design—and, more important, sell—new uniforms specifically for the event. The Manhattan-men darkened their blue, switched up their trim pattern, and sewed "N-E-W Y-O-R-K" across the torso instead of "R-A-N-G-E-R-S." The Brooklyn-bound Islanders were more daring. They removed the beloved Long Island silhouette from their logo, leaving only the letters "NY."

As for the action, the Rangers thrashed the Devils, 7–3, then turned their attention to the Isles. On a clear, starry night of seven-degree wind-chill that somehow felt cooler than that, both teams walked across the infield to a huge ovation from 50,027 patrons who apparently loved their hockey more than they loved feeling in their extremities.

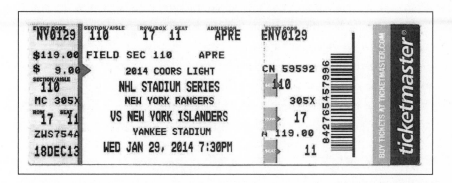

The only thing colder than the weather was the shooting through almost two periods, as Lundqvist and Nabokov were met with little attack. But Brock Nelson broke the proverbial ice for the home team at 18:33 with an even-strength, right-wing one-timer off beautiful passes from Cal Clutterbuck and Matt Donovan.

The Rangers' comeback did not take long to rev up. It began only forty seconds later when forward Benoit Pouliot chipped in a slick Derick Brassard pass from behind the net to send the game to the third tied, 1–1.

Early in the rubber frame, Rangers checking forward Dan Carcillo cashed in a rebound from the low slot to put the senior circuit ahead.

From then on, the Blueshirts hermetically sealed their end, allowing only six Islanders shots in the period, and the first outdoor Battle of New York ended 2–1. Although it was hard to tell at the time, the Rangers' double-dip wins over New Jersey and the Islanders proved to be a portent of things to come, which would be a relentless march to the Stanley Cup Final.

Cup-bound Blueshirts

While the Isles sank to last place, Vigneault's valiants finished second in the new Metropolitan Division and beat Philadelphia in the first round of the playoffs, thanks to another glorious Game Seven effort by the King.

From there, the melodramatic Rangers' script became unreal.

Trailing Crosby and the Penguins three games to one, the Blueshirts suddenly blended a touch of tragedy into unlikely victory. The saga began when news broke that star winger Marty St. Louis's mother died in his native Montreal prior to Game Five. Despite the wrenching news, St. Louis acted in a manner that his mother would have sanctioned and chose to play for his team.

It is debatable how much St. Louis's decision inspired himself and his mates, but there is no disputing the facts. The heretofore fragile Rangers got their act together and vanquished Pittsburgh in three straight games, with Lundqvist—again—standing tall in Game Seven.

They next faced the formidable Montreal Canadiens and their remarkable goaltender Carey Price in the Eastern Conference Finals. But in just the second period of Game One, burly forward Chris Kreider bowled into Carey, injuring Price's leg in the process and leaving him sidelined. Suddenly, the Habs appeared hapless and were over and out in six games. Fittingly, St. Louis roofed a brilliant overtime winner in Game Four. Forward Dominic Moore scored the only goal of the clinching Game Six win, his second game winner of the 2014 playoffs. The Rangers were clicking on all cylinders.

Now things got serious, with the Los Angeles Kings on deck for the Stanley Cup Final. One could say that the five-game series produced Henrik Lundqvist's finest hours. Style-wise, the King was never better, blunting dangerous thrusts over and over again. But his histrionics were not enough.

Nothing said it more than Game Five in L.A., which heart-throb-bingly extended into two sudden-death periods, tied at two. It appeared sharp-shooter Rick Nash would bury the game-winner into a glaringly open net. But, defying all odds, the puck tipped off defenseman Slava Voynov's stick and ricocheted over the goal by an inch.

Barely five minutes later, Kings blueliner Alec Martinez potted a rebound off a three-on-two rush to take the series four games to one, ending the Rangers' crusade for the Cup.

Despite the natural post-series depression, the Rangers flew home secure in the knowledge that—given a few breaks—they could have been the champs.

2014–15

After a painfully slow start in 2014–15, the Rangers got on track around Thanksgiving and began a tireless pursuit of the Isles, who already had a mortgage on first place.

For a time, off-ice events in Uniondale that season overshadowed action aplenty on the ice, as owner Charles Wang sold his majority interest in the hockey club to successful businessmen Jon Ledecky and Scott Malkin. Ledecky's previous hockey experience was as part owner of the Washington Capitals.

Furthermore, it was no kidding around about the fact that this would be the final season of the Islanders calling the old barn on Hempstead Turnpike their home. The theme was "Next Year in Brooklyn."

Fans in Nassau and Suffolk knew that they would be bidding *adieu* to the Coliseum. The team was also well aware of the situation, and they did everything in their power to leave Long Island with a thrill.

Tavares was ably abetted by newcomers Jaroslav Halak in goal as well as Nick Leddy and Johnny Boychuk on defense, not to mention a colorful offense that included what critics called "the best fourth line in the league." That trio included Matt Martin, Casey Cizikas, and Cal Clutterbuck, each one feistier than the other. They could score the odd goal and seemed to think a good evening included hitting every foe in sight at least twice.

On January 27, 2015, the refreshed Islanders spanked the Rangers, 4–1, at the Coliseum for their third blowout of their rivals in as many tries that season. The still-Nassau-men sat alone atop the Metropolitan Division, and crowds were swelling to capacity. Life was good, and getting even better during the fourth Battle of New York, on Presidents Day, February 16 at the barn.

Rangers goalie Cam Talbot, filling in for the injured Henrik Lundqvist, inexplicably handed the puck to John Tavares in the right-wing corner just 11 seconds into the contest, and the Islanders captain one-timed it into the vacated net.

From there, the scoreboard made brief stops at 2–0, 2–1, 3–1, 3–3, then 5–3 Islanders early in the third.

That was when a large group of fans at the top of section 329, also known as the "Blue and Orange Army," began to chant, "You can't beat us!"—a reference to Islanders wins in the first three games of the season series as well as a chant coined by Rangers fans back in 2004, when their Manhattan-men swept the Islanders.

But Alain Vigneault's team was far from dead. In a matter of moments, they knotted this exhilarating game, 5–5, then got a right-circle wrister from defenseman Kevin Klein with 4:32 to play for the 6–5 game-winner, a shot eerily similar to Dan Girardi's killer strike in April 2013.

BENCHMARK GAME: FAREWELL NASSAU

February 16, 2015
Nassau Coliseum

Rangers 6 Islanders 5
(34–16–5) (37–19–1)

The neutral zone looked like the *Autobahn* at three in the morning—no traffic, no speed limit—in this, the penultimate Blueshirts visit to Nassau Coliseum. When shots in a 60-minute game total 43–42, you know you played an entertaining contest.

"Best game I saw all season," recalls one Metropolitan Division scout for a Western Conference team. "By far."

"It was just me and one other scout," he continues. "About midway through we looked at each other and said, 'If you want to sell hockey to people, show them *this*.'"

The incredible comeback, which drew the teams even atop the division, figured to serve as hors d'oeuvres to the eventual entrée that would be the Rangers' final regular season game at Nassau Coliseum—March 10—or to perhaps even the first all-New York playoff series since 1994.

With that in mind, ticket prices for the March 10 game went from "over-the-top" to *"Holy-Cannoli!"* as fans of both teams clamored to get inside. The Rangers led the Metro at 23 games over .500. The Isles sat second at 22 games over.

Islanders finisher Anders Lee—the hockey pride of the University of Notre Dame—put the home team ahead in the first, but a brilliant goal by Rangers rookie Kevin Hayes in the second and a long slapper by Rick Nash early in the third sealed the Isles' fate.

Jaroslav Halak made only 20 saves for the homeboys, while Talbot stopped 29 shots for the win, after which his team cruised to a record of 53–22–7 and the ultra-prestigious Presidents' Trophy as the league's top team.

The pair of shocking crosstown losses seemed to stun the young Islanders, who never fully recovered their "mojo" and slipped to third place. And though they put up the good fight against Washington in the opening round of the playoffs, winning the final game in Nassau Coliseum history in stirring fashion, the Isles fell rather quietly in Game Seven, bringing the Uniondale Era to a sad close.

Over two decades since "1940!" had been laid to rest, Long Islanders now droned on over a different New York hex—and one almost equally remarkable—as their own team had not won a single playoff series in twenty-two years.

It was a much more jubilant story on the Rangers' side, as they beat the Pens in five games in round one. In the next round, Lundqvist conjured Game Seven magic again, icing the Caps, 2–1, on Derek Stepan's overtime goal. The King steered away 35 rubbers, bringing his career Game Seven record to 6–1 with a .966 save percentage.

Heading into the third round, one could hardly blame the Rangers faithful for dreaming about Stanley Cup champagne.

But there were several reasons to remain focused on their next opponent, the Tampa Bay Lightning. The first, the "triplets" line of Tyler Johnson, Nikita Kucherov, and Ondjej Palat. The second, goalie Ben Bishop. And the third, astute coaching by Hofstra University graduate

John Cooper, raised as an Islanders fan, of all things. The Rangers were shut out, 2–0, in the seventh game, ending their run to repeat as Eastern Conference champs.

The Arrival of the Isles in Brooklyn

The New York hockey page was finally ready to be turned to 2015–16, and the long-awaited beginning of the "Subway Series."

It didn't matter whether you were a Rangers fan or an Islanders fan. The fact that the erstwhile Nassau-men were now calling Barclays Center home just didn't sound right.

Major league hockey at the intersection of Flatbush and Atlantic Avenues? *Come on.*

Wasn't this the dream of Mervyn Red Dutton seventy years ago?

Wasn't it 1945 when he told his NHL lodge members that he planned to build a Kings County arena right next to the Long Island Rail Road terminal? It sure was.

The Dutton dream came true, except that the only thing about his beloved Americans in Brooklyn in the fall of 2015 was a magnificent exhibit at the Brooklyn Historical Society (BHS), aptly titled "BROOKLYN AMERICANS."

Opening with fuss and fanfare on the same night that the Isles were playing an exhibition game at Barclays, the BHS exhibit even featured a relative of the immortal Red Dutton himself. That was Mervyn's nephew Bill; and, sure enough, without further ado, cousin Bill let everyone know that his idol, uncle Merv, *did* put that curse on the Rangers.

The more Bill Dutton shmoozed the crowd, the more the standing-room-only audience got the feeling that the contemporary Islanders were simply Dutton's Americans reincarnated.

Better still, presumptive Isles owner John Ledecky delivered more than a few choice words honoring the Americans, then invited everyone in his audience to be his guest at the game just a slapshot away.

Meanwhile, across the river, the Rangers were devising new blueprints to claim King Hank's elusive Cup. The Blueshirts began the campaign 16–3–2 and were playing like the class of the conference.

The first Rangers invasion of Barclays Center took place on December 2, 2015, and the two closest teams in all of hockey—now just 25 minutes by train!—christened the new digs with a gem.

The Islanders' slogan was "Tradition Has a New Home," and twenty minutes before this game, it sure sounded that way, as a near-stampede of fans—pressed up against one another in line to enter—sent "LET'S GO ISLANDERS-LET'S GO RANGERS" chants echoing throughout the building's main rotunda.

Tavares scored the first goal, naturally, and after Viktor Stalberg tied the game, 1–1, Isles forward Kyle Okposo capped the housewarming party with a shootout winner. All who saw it agreed—the first-ever Brooklyn Battle of New York lived up to every ounce of hype.

But the second Islanders-Rangers game of the season was even better, a back-and-forth Barclays track meet on January 14 that the home team won, 3–1.

And the third meeting was even better than *that*, a March 6 Garden thriller that the Nassau—*ahem*—Brooklyn men won, 6–4, on Cal Clutterbuck's dramatic goal at 18:32 of the third, sliding the Isles ahead of the Rangers for second place in the Metro.

By this time, the Blueshirts and Isles appeared destined to meet in the opening round of the playoffs, but the Pittsburgh Penguins had a different idea. Sid Crosby and cronies stormed past both New York teams, sending the Islanders into the conference's other playoff bracket.

But for Capuano and the Islanders, there was still something special to be claimed. No Islanders team had *ever* swept the Rangers in a season series.

Not Potvin's, not LaFontaine's, not Turgeon's or Yashin's. It had never happened.

With 2015–16 winding down, these inaugural Brooklyn skaters had a chance to be the first.

The Isles stormed the city on April 7, 2016, and blew Lundqvist and the Garden men out of the building, chasing Hank after two periods and railing home with their fourth win against the Rangers in four tries.

From a Blueshirts' standpoint, this effort was indicative of matters to come. The club fell to the eventual champion Pens in round one of the playoffs with barely as much as a whimper, while five miles below, the Barclays Center was doing all it could not to explode.

The first playoff game in Brooklyn, a 4–3, come-from-behind overtime win over the Florida Panthers, was nothing but a classic.

One week later, the "House that Dutton (almost) Built" was brought to its knees by Tavares, exactly the man (no longer a kid) who everyone figured should and would introduce the venue to the continental hockey stage.

With the Isles leading the series three games to two, but trailing Game Six, 1–0, with 80 seconds to play, Matt Martin and Nick Leddy frantically turned away a set of Florida attacks that seemed certain to wind up with the puck in the empty Islanders net.

After making a final unlikely save with his skate, Leddy collected the puck and hurried down right wing.

Tavares hopped over the boards on a change.

Leddy curled behind the Panthers' goal and centered.

Former Isles castaway Roberto Luongo made a big stop. Tavares shoveled in the rebound. The place went bonkers! Time was 19:06. It was the biggest goal in Barclays Center history and would remain exactly that . . . for another hour.

With the Brooklyn crowd in a state of mass hysteria, the Isles blitzed the Panthers in overtime to the tune of a 15–8 shots advantage but could not score. In the next extra session, play began to even out, and the Panthers regained their edge.

The Islanders, it was clear, could no longer wear the Floridians down. If they were going to win their first series since 1993, it was going to take a little more magic.

Good thing they had JT. Past the midway point of the fifth period, he took a pass from Kyle Okposo at the top of the right circle and ripped a low wrist shot that *clunked* off Luongo's pad. Two of Florida's top defensemen, Aaron Ekblad and Brian Campbell, hacked and whacked at the Islanders captain, attempting to keep him from capturing his own rebound.

JT knifed through the pairing as sharply as the metaphorical dagger had been stabbing Islanders fans in the heart for decades.

In one legendary motion, he swooped around the cage on his backhand and, from one knee, stuffed twenty-three years of suffering into the back of the Florida Panthers net.

It was over. And it was incredible.

Orange rally towels floated through the air. The party spilled out onto all the neighboring Avenues—be it Flatbush, Atlantic, or Fifth. The bars stayed packed well into Monday morning. And at some point, during all this commotion, something funny happened to the neighborhood and the Barclays Center itself.

Somewhere between the improbable rally of Game Three and the impeccable rally of Game Six, hockey became bigger than politics. At some point during that wild week of JT's brilliance, as drink after drink was poured, served, and devoured, Barclays Center became home.

Back in 1945, Madison Square Garden brass nervously squashed the idea of a rival team in Downtown Brooklyn. When it finally happened, the city embraced it head-on.

In a sense, nothing could be more appropriate than the contemporary version of the Brooklyn-Manhattan hockey rivalry. Writing in *Sports Illustrated*, authors Alex Prewitt and Jeremy Fuchs put it best: "Nearly three-quarters of a century later, Red Dutton's dream of hockey in Brooklyn has materialized, albeit in a slightly different fashion."

Really, the only difference is that instead of the Amerks battling the Blueshirts, it's Brooklynites versus Manhattanites, and this rivalry threatens to go on forever.

ACKNOWLEDGMENTS

Since both of us have been hockey fans since we were knee-high to a grasshopper, this book has been a labor of love. But the beautiful part was that we had a posse of helpers who shared our enthusiasm for this project.

In order to reach our goal of a comprehensive, well-rounded history that also was a "good read," we needed linemates to stickhandle through assorted chores too numerous to mention. These meaningful teammates included the incomparable Rini Krishnan, Patrick McCormack, Leo Scaglione, Alyssa Paolicelli, Sam Stern, James Mauldin, Robert Taub, Glenn Petraitis, Bobby Mills, Richie Rayner, Sarah Holzberg, Paul Lauten, Shannon Hogan, and Dom DeRosa, not to mention photographer David Perlmutter, as well as Olivia Weiner, Jacob Weinstock, Laura Stabbert, Jon Berger, and Noam Hoffman.

In the arena of research, hockey-reference.com, hsp.flyershistory.com, shrpsports.com, and hockeydb.com proved invaluable, as did the Peninsula Public Library database.

Among the hockey personalities who chipped in with anecdotes were Patrick Flatley, Eric Cairns, Don Maloney, Randy Moller, Denis Potvin, Butch Goring, Bill Dutton, Andy Kaplan, Josh Lentin, Paul Cartier, Sam Rosen, Anonymous Security Guard, Anonymous Scout, Rick DiPietro, and especially Kelly Hrudey. Clark Gillies, who appeared on a panel at a Brooklyn hockey soirée, spun many endless tales, some of which appear on these pages.

In the P.R. realm, the ever-reliable Kimber Auerbach, Jesse Eisenberg, John Rosasco, and Ryan Nissan were there when we needed help, as were Rich Nairn and Greg Dillard. Likewise, our colleague at MSG Networks, Alyssa Ross, came through in the clutch.

As hockey teams cannot function without coaches, so it is that authors lean on editors for guidance. In our case, we have been very fortunate to have an editor who not only is peerless on the editorial side, but also happens to be a keen student of the ice game, and who, furthermore, gave us the green light to do this book in the first place. Thank you, Julie Ganz.

Needless to say, fans of both denominations have played a significant part in the rivalry and many have helped us with content and assorted other serendipitous material.

And speaking of good fortune, the much-revered Brooklyn Historical Society opened a first-ever hockey exhibit in September 2015, coinciding with the Islanders' move to Barclays Center. BHS's Marcia Ely not only opened doors for us, but provided valuable interviews for our section on the New York and Brooklyn Americans. Ditto for Steve Cohen, who, in large part, developed the exhibit.